KINGDOM
PROSPERITY

GOD'S PLAN, PROVISION AND PURPOSE FOR YOUR MONEY

Greg Mitchell

Other versions include:

Front and Back Cover Design: Steven Ciaccio

English Version Print Edition ISBN: 979-8-9907176-4-0
English Version Kindle Edition ISBN: 979-8-9907176-5-7

Library of Congress Cataloging-in-Publication Data has been applied for.

Printed in the United States of America

Table of Contents

Dedication

Firstly, I dedicate this book to Pastors Joe Campbell, Mark Aulson, and Tom Payne. Your faithfulness to God in taking offerings and raising money in conferences has blessed thousands of people. You have exhibited breakthrough dimensions of faith in the area of money, and you transmitted that in offerings you have taken in conferences in Prescott and all over the world. You have glorified God in the area of money. You have raised much money over the years for the Kingdom of God, which has been used to bring salvation to the nations. You have inspired people to believe in and obey God in the area of finances, and that has enabled many individuals and churches to experience breakthrough miracles in this area. You have helped people to experience true "Kingdom Prosperity."

Second, I dedicate this book to the incredibly faithful and generous people in the congregation of The Potter's House in Prescott, Arizona. We were birthed in a miracle financial breakthrough that was triggered in a revival preached by evangelist John Metzler in 1970. Since then, the faithful saints in Prescott have given generously for evangelism, church planting and world evangelism, and there has always been abundance due to your faithful, visionary giving. You have literally blessed the world.

Third, I dedicate this book to every person who has given faithfully and generously in conferences in our church in Prescott. You have allowed God to use your money to bless many thousands of people, and you have been a part of reaching many nations of the world through world evangelism. May God help each of you to experience true Kingdom Prosperity.

Fourth, I dedicate this book to my late father, Wayman Mitchell. You broke the curse of poverty off your own life, you gained supernatural financial dominion, you modeled financial integrity and you taught all of us the spiritual power of money. You imparted into Lisa and I the truth that has affected our lives; **If God can get money <u>through</u> you – He can get money <u>to</u> you!** So, we have been able to carry on the same blessing you had in your life.

Foreword

Pastor Greg Mitchell is a gifted pastor, leader, disciple maker, and now author. His first two books, "Healing Power" and "Uprooting Rejection," are the best I have read on those subjects, and there are a lot of books out there. They are written in a way that helps so many people apply those truths to their lives.

As I travel around the world, the subject of discussion is often Pastor Mitchell's books. Pastors are so appreciative of the help, healing, and deliverance they have brought to members of their churches. His books have inspired numerous sermons preached around the world, which continue to be a source of supernatural revelation.

If there is ever an area where God's people need help, it is in the area of finances. That is why I am recommending his latest book, "Kingdom Prosperity." If you can get that area of our lives right, it will release incredible blessings not only for you personally but also in extending the cause of world evangelism. Our churches need to be prospering financially because, as the finances of individual believers go, so goes the advance of the Kingdom of God on earth through the church.

I have learned these principles throughout my ministry. Pastor Wayman Mitchell gave me a scripture at a time when our church needed miracle money, when an opportunity was presented to buy a building; **Proverbs 13:22** *"the wealth of the sinner is stored up for the righteous."* I laid claim to that promise, and God provided the miracle we needed. (That story is told in detail in Chapter 9).

Many believers are worried and anxious about their money and how it relates to their future. God obviously understands wealth. He created it and can channel it into the hands of those whom He can trust. We, as Christians, need to learn how to function according to God's economic system. Once that system is discovered and understood, real, genuine blessing and prosperity can then occur.

God is a God of blessing, and this book, "Kingdom Prosperity," will instruct and inspire you about the possibilities for you and your money. God has a plan, and He knows every need we have. This book will provide you with a roadmap that is not complicated to follow and will guide you toward a greater dimension of blessing in your life. Prayerfully read this book. It will bring to life the many scriptures in the Word of God relating to finances and how to handle, manage, and be a good steward of them.

When revelation is communicated through the written word, it has the power to change and transform your life. The first two books that Pastor Greg Mitchell wrote certainly achieved that for thousands of people, and this book will do the same in one of the most vital areas of your life. All of us want to and need to experience "Kingdom Prosperity." This book will guide you on how to make that a reality in your life.

Pastor Paul Stephens
El Paso, Texas

Preface

Money is not the most important thing in life, but it does affect everything that is important.
Robert Kiyosaki

Money affects your life!
I've had the privilege being in Pastoral ministry the last 40 years and truly believe that money affects your life! I've seen this truth work out in my own life, and the lives of other people.

Money affects your peace and your happiness. It's not supposed to have that effect in the lives of Christians, but based on long experience, I predict there are people reading or listening to this book that lost sleep last night over the issue of money.

Money affects your health: Financial pressures can have a negative effect on your physical health due to worry and anxiety. You will read or hear testimonies in this book of people who lost weight and became sick due to worry and stress while struggling financially.

Money affects your marriage: There are more conflicts over money than intimacy. There are more divorces rooted in financial stress and conflicts than infidelity.

Money affects your salvation: In the Old Testament we read of God's people who became disobedient and wound up worshipping a Canaanite god of money named Mammon. In the New Testament, we read of the Rich Young Ruler who declined to follow Jesus over the issue of money, and Ananias and Saphira who lied to the Holy Spirit and suffered judgment over the issue of money. I have seen too many new converts lost through job offers and pressures, and long-term Christians lose their way trying to bring about security and prosperity through their own efforts.

Money affects your destiny and calling in God: I have seen so many disciples fail to enter into their calling because of wrong financial decisions. I have seen pastors and missionaries leave their ministry over the issue of money.

Money affects your church: For the work of God to be done through a local church, there must be an adequate flow of finances. There are churches struggling to get off the ground because they cannot afford a building to meet in. Other churches are limited because their building is simply inadequate in size, in a bad location, or in very poor condition. There may not be enough room to facilitate the ministries needed to support a growing church. Some churches want to plant new churches or send couples overseas to another nation, but lack of finances are hindering them from being able to do so.

Money affects the Spirit of God: The Book of Acts gives this connection: When the Holy Spirit is moving freely, there is an abundant supply of resources, there is liberality in the hearts of God's people (**Acts 2:43-44**), and most importantly, sinners are being saved and disciples are being raised up to do God's will. Whenever there are Christians, Pastors or churches that do not have a correct understanding of money, the working of the Holy Spirit is hindered. I have seen this to be true all over the world: I have lived and Pastored in three different nations, and I have preached in hundreds of churches all over the world. This is always true.

The effects listed above are often connected in some way or another to <u>poverty</u>, which is defined as *"deficiency or not having enough."*

Therefore, this book is going to look at the issue of **_prosperity_**; Which is defined in the Dictionary as *"A thriving or growing condition – especially as it concerns finances."*

Some questions this book will seek to help you answer:
Is prosperity good?
Is prosperity God's will?
　　If so: What is the path to achieve financial prosperity?
What is the purpose of financial prosperity?
What keeps Christians, Pastors or churches from entering into financial prosperity?

I originally taught much of the material in this book in 2022 as a series of lessons in the Adult Sunday School Class at The Potter's House Christian Fellowship Church in Prescott, Arizona. Since then, I have been blessed to receive thanks, encouraging comments and testimonies from people who have been helped by that teaching. That motivated me to expand it and write it as a book. I pray that God will use this book to help you enter into "Kingdom Prosperity."

Each chapter contains testimonies of people who have experienced deliverance, breakthroughs and blessings to enter into "Kingdom Prosperity." I believe the testimonies will encourage you and stir your faith for your own miracles.

Pastor Greg Mitchell
The Potter's House
Prescott, Arizona

Chapter 1: Is Prosperity God's Will?

To live **with the object of** accumulating wealth is anti–Christian.
Charles Spurgeon

Jim Bakker was one of the early televangelists that focused on the "Prosperity Gospel" with constant fundraising gimmicks and appeals on television. He was convicted of deceptive fundraising and fraud, and in 1988 was sentenced to 45 years in prison. In his book, *"I Was Wrong"* he said, *"I was caught in the trap of success, and I let prosperity deceive me."* In his own words, he says, *"Prison stripped everything from me, but it became the place where I finally met God honestly."*

Does the unhealthy emphasis Jim Bakker placed on prosperity, and his sinful actions concerning money negate the Biblical principle of prosperity?

The Problem With Prosperity

Prosperity is apparently a dirty word. The very word "prosperity" often has negative connotations. "Prosperity Preacher" and "Prosperity Gospel" are at times used as pejoratives by both Christians and unsaved people. (A pejorative means expressing scorn or approval.) The roots of such negative views often are the financial abuses of unscrupulous Preachers through the years. Some Prosperity preachers charge people to receive prayers. Others resort to gimmicks to get people to give: *Send $100 and receive a bottle of water from the Jordan River!* Those promoting the Prosperity Gospel are often known for making every sermon and every teaching be about money.

Others have been exposed for living lavish lifestyles. Some have even been arrested for fraud.

Therefore, the reaction of many Pastors and Christians becomes: *We don't want to be like that!* A common by-product is Pastors who are afraid to preach on money, or Pastors who are afraid to ask for money. I have seen churches advertise and include the words *"no offerings taken."* I have seen Pastors say during an offering, *"We don't want you to think we're after your money."* My question is, *"Then why are you taking an offering at all?"* I spoke to a church consultant one time who told me at his mega-church they tell guests, *"We don't want you to give!"*

I agree in some ways with anti-prosperity people when they decry fraud, manipulation and greed in Prosperity Gospel Preachers. However, it is important that we have a correct perspective. It is foolish to base your beliefs or actions on other people's failures, excesses or sin. I know of many people who are abusive, selfish and manipulative in marriage – but I am not going to stop being married! Why? Because God's word is the foundation of marriage, and the doctrine of marriage. Other people's foolishness, excess, greed or sin does not change God's word. Our beliefs about money must be based on God's word – and the Bible has a lot to say about money

Wrong Teaching About Money

Apart from the abuses of Prosperity preachers, the greatest hinderance to our own prosperity is wrong teaching about money. There are three common false ideas about money you will hear from those who claim prosperity is not good.

False idea #1: Money is evil. This is usually said by someone who claims, *"The Bible says money is the root of all evil."* The full verse actually reads: ***1 Timothy 6:10** For the love of money is a*

root of all kinds of evil, for which some have strayed from the faith in their greediness, and pierced themselves through with many sorrows.

So, the verse doesn't say <u>money</u> is the root of all evil, but the <u>love</u> of money is the root of all kinds of evil. The previous verse explains why we need to know this: *1 Timothy 6:9 But those who desire to be rich fall into temptation and a snare, and into many foolish and harmful lusts which drown men in destruction and perdition.* Other translations say those who want to be rich (NCV), those who crave to be rich (AMP), those who long to be rich (TLB), men who set their hearts on being wealthy (Phillips Modern English Translation). It is speaking of people who make money the main object of their desires and affections. This is the same issue we see repeatedly throughout Scripture—idolatry: when our desire and love for anything begins to take the place of God. An idol is an ultimate thing; it is something you put your trust in, in place of God. Idols begin to determine our choices in life and always lead us away from God. If that is happening in our hearts and lives, then the desire for money has become evil, and will lead us into all kinds of evil.

But for those who insist on saying, "The love of money is evil", we need to ask a simple question: *At what point does money become evil?* Does money become evil at one dollar? One hundred dollars? One thousand dollars? Five thousand dollars? Ten thousand dollars? One hundred thousand dollars? Perhaps we should ask such people a second question: *If money is evil – why do you have any money at all??*

False idea #2: It is spiritual to not have money. Through the years I have met several people (who usually seemed a bit odd) who said they were Christians, and claimed that having no money was somehow spiritual. Then, in the same breath, they would ask <u>me</u> for money! That logic seems contradictory.

Poverty is sometimes presented as a mark of spirituality. Years ago, I attended a church outside our own Fellowship (I read some books written by the Pastor, and I wanted to speak to him). I was wearing a suit, because I was raised to dress up when you go to church as a sign of respect for God. It was not an expensive suit, as I did not have much money back then. But I was the only one wearing a suit in the entire congregation. When the Pastor began preaching, it seemed he was either intimidated or irritated that I was wearing a suit. He started adding comments to the sermon such as, *"Thank God we're not like <u>some people</u> who are all concerned about their clothes, or their things!* Hmmm...I wonder who he is talking about? They believed that if you are really spiritual, you will only dress in old, plain or shabby clothes.

If not having money (which is called poverty) makes you spiritual, then why is poverty always spoken of in the Bible as something vexing or distressing? It is never presented as a blessing, or something spiritual and desirable in itself. ***Proverbs 10:15 NCV*** *Having lots of money protects the rich, but having no money destroys the poor.* In this verse, not having money doesn't make you spiritual, it brings destruction! If you really believe that not having money makes you spiritual, we can pray for you and ask God to take away everything – so you will be <u>really</u> spiritual!

Also, if not having money makes you spiritual, why does God tell us in His word about the financial blessing of His people? ***Genesis 13:2 NCV*** *Abram was very rich in cattle, in silver, and in gold.* Abraham is called *"the friend of God"* in **James 2:23**. **Romans 4** calls him *"the father of the faith."* You can't get much more spiritual than that! But according to anti-prosperity people, he is unspiritual. Job was an extremely wealthy man. Referring to his wealth, in **Job 1:3** he is called *"the greatest man among all the people of the East."* But God Himself gives his opinion of Job:

Job 1:8 Then the Lord said to Satan, "Have you considered My servant Job, that there is none like him on the earth, a blameless and upright man, one who fears God and shuns evil?" David is called by God in *Acts 13:22 "A man after My own heart"* and when he gave a personal offering for the building of the temple it was a huge amount! *1 Chronicles 29:3-5 ³Moreover, because I have set my affection on the house of my God, I have given to the house of my God, over and above all that I have prepared for the holy house, my own special treasure of gold and silver: ⁴three thousand talents of gold, of the gold of Ophir, and seven thousand talents of refined silver, to overlay the walls of the houses; ⁵the gold for things of gold and the silver for things of silver, and for all kinds of work to be done by the hands of craftsmen...* Some scholars place the value of his personal gift at being the modern equivalent of two billion US dollars! So, three giants of the faith and relationship with God were very rich! I don't say that to apply it as *"every believer needs to be extremely rich"* – but rather to refute the idea that poverty somehow makes you spiritual.

False idea #3: It would be rude or presumptuous to ask God for money or material things: Some Christians teach that God is only concerned about spiritual things in our lives. Some even teach that material things are the Devil's realm. But in the Bible, we are encouraged by Jesus Christ Himself to ask God for help – even in material things. *Matthew 7:7-11 ⁷"Ask, and it will be given to you; seek, and you will find; knock, and it will be opened to you. ⁸For everyone who asks receives, and he who seeks finds, and to him who knocks it will be opened. ⁹Or what man is there among you who, if his son asks for bread, will give him a stone? ¹⁰Or if he asks for a fish, will he give him a serpent? ¹¹If you then, being evil, know how to give good gifts to your children, how much more will your Father who is in heaven give good things to those* *who ask Him!* Bread and fish represent material needs such as food – needs that almost always require money to obtain.

In a number of actual instances, God is the one initiating the miracle, because He is concerned about our financial needs. He sent Elijah to a widow facing starvation, to bring a supernatural miracle of provision. **Matthew 15:32** *Now Jesus called His disciples to Himself and said, "I have compassion on the multitude, because they have now continued with Me three days and have nothing to eat. And I do not want to send them away hungry, lest they faint on the way."* He then performed a miracle of provision to feed those who do not have any food.

The Need for Prosperity

The simple fact of life is that people need to prosper. The dictionary definition of the word prosper is *"A thriving or growing condition – especially as concerns finances."* Think about why people (including Christians) need to prosper financially:

People have financial and material needs to survive and function in life: In ancient times Jesus spoke of some basic financial needs in life. **Matthew 6:31** *"Therefore do not worry, saying, 'What shall we eat?' or 'What shall we drink?' or 'What shall we wear?'* He doesn't want us to <u>worry</u> about these things, but He is simply speaking about the common financial needs of life. For people today, some common financial needs could be such things as food, clothing, housing, transport, utilities, medical costs or debt. We simply cannot live without money, or what money can purchase or enable. The reality of life is not only that we have financial needs, but with the rising costs caused by inflation – we need our finances to increase over time to offset those rising costs.

Lack of prosperity causes us problems. Think about some of the problems a lack of money can cause:

Lack of money causes stress: Money is not the most important thing in the world, but when you don't have any, it feels like it is! *Matthew 6:31 "Therefore do not worry, saying, 'What shall we eat?' or 'What shall we drink?' or 'What shall we wear?'* The word <u>worry</u> comes from an old German word **wurgen** which literally means "to struggle" or "to choke." People who don't have enough money lose sleep. People who don't have enough money sometimes become physically sick through stress. Christians who don't have enough money often find it hard to concentrate on God in church, in prayer or when reading their Bible. Intrusive thoughts such as, *"How are we going to pay the bills?"* and *"where can I get some more money?"* can crowd God out.

Lack of money causes marriage conflict: Marriage experts say that couples fight more about money than about sex! Money is often listed as the number one source of marriage conflict. Finances are listed as the leading cause of divorce: Fifty-six percent of all divorces are blamed on financial difficulties! That is four times higher than any other factor, including infidelity! Couples fight because of the stress caused by financial pressures of not having enough. When something is stressing you out, you become irritable and often take it out on the one closest to you; *your spouse!* Couples fight over how money is spent. There is a term called *"financial infidelity."* That means that your spouse cheated on you <u>financially</u>. This could mean that one partner failed to disclose the true amount of debt when they were getting married. Major conflicts can be caused by major purchases made by one spouse without consulting the other. Sometimes these purchases negatively impact their joint financial situation by spending money earmarked for other needs, or by going into debt.

Lack of prosperity limits your ability to help other people: We will discuss this more fully in a later chapter, but one purpose of prosperity – a reason God gives you money is so you can help other people in need. *2 Corinthians 9:8-9 ⁸And God is able to make all grace abound toward you, that you, always having all sufficiency in all things, may have an abundance for every good work. ⁹As it is written: "He has dispersed abroad, He has given to the poor; His righteousness endures forever."* God blesses you – not just for you, but so you can pass the blessing along to others in need. If you are always struggling financially, it limits your ability to help others.

Lack of prosperity affects the work of God: God gives us money so we can be a part of accomplishing His will in the earth. The main vehicle for accomplishing God's will is the church – your local church. Local churches must have money to be able to function and do God's will. But when people are struggling financially it can affect their local church. In the financial crisis of 2008-2009, there were numbers of churches in the Prescott area that had to lay off Pastoral staff or shut down ministries. In the Covid crisis of 2020, there were churches all over America that closed down completely because their finances dried up. There were churches that, in a struggle to survive, found themselves compelled to merge with others.

In 2016, David Platt, the International Mission Board president for the Southern Baptist Convention, announced their plans to cut 600-800 missionaries around the world, because of the inability to financially support that number of missionaries in the field. He said that as it stands now, they are forced to turn people away who desire to serve in the mission field. How tragic!

God's highest mission, world evangelism, being hindered by a lack of finances. That doesn't sound very spiritual to me! God forbid that we should ever not be able to do God's will as a church because of a lack of money!

The God of Prosperity

The basis of this book is to look Biblically at the issue of finances and prosperity. **I say boldly from God's word that it is God's will for you to prosper financially!** This is not my opinion, or denominational belief; it is based on God's word. God wrote in the Bible what He wants to happen in our money! *3 John 2 Beloved, I pray that you may prosper in all things and be in health, just as your soul prospers.* So, let's look at this word. The word Prosper means "a good journey" or that things go well on the journey. In the Parable of the good Samaritan in **Luke 17** a man on his journey was attacked by robbers who took what he had: That was not a good journey, or a prosperous journey; his finances were affected negatively. In Paul's voyage to Rome in **Acts 27** they encountered a storm so severe they had to dump their cargo, the ship's tackle, and they suffered complete shipwreck. That was not a prosperous journey. Their finances did poorly, not well.

There are some Christians or Pastors who claim that the word "prosper" in **3 John 2** is not referring to finances – it is just a common greeting of good wishes. *3 John 2 Beloved, I pray that you may prosper in all things...*isn't <u>money</u> included in "all things? It doesn't say *"except money"* – it says *"all things."* **1 Corinthians 16:2** *Upon the first day of the week let every one of you lay by him in store,* **as God hath prospered him,** *that there be no gatherings when I come.* In this text the word "prosper" clearly is speaking about your money – which can be given to further God's purposes through the church.

The Balance of Prosperity

3 John 2 gives some practical balance to the issue of prosperity. This is why I called the book Kingdom Prosperity; Prosperity must line up with the whole counsel of God.

Balance #1: Money is <u>not</u> the most important thing in life!

3 John 2 adds to the prayer for prosperity *"even as your soul prospers."* This shows us the issue of priority (which means order of importance). Your <u>soul</u> is the most important part of your life – and must come first! *Mark 8:36 For what shall it profit a man, if he shall gain the whole world, and lose his own soul?* Prosperity <u>does</u> have dangers: *What good would it do if you prosper financially, but it causes you to become carnal, disobedient, and fail to do the will of God?* It makes no sense if you allow prosperity to affect your salvation, and you wind up losing your soul!

Balance #2: Prosperity is conditional.

3 John 2 Beloved, *I pray that you may prosper in all things and be in health, <u>just as your soul prospers</u>.*

"Just as" means *"in the same way"*...or *"in line with"* your soul prospering. If your soul (your spiritual life) is not prospering – it will be difficult for you to truly prosper financially. Either you won't be able to prosper, your prosperity won't last, or money will become a curse, rather than a blessing.

Balance #3: God has practical directions for how to prosper.

Critics of prosperity decry it as *"name it and claim it"* – as though all a Christian must do is say the right words of faith or prayer and they will automatically prosper financially. But the Bible is filled with <u>practical directions</u> in how to prosper, or how to receive a financial miracle increase. All of these involve obedience in some way. This book will examine some of the practical steps of obedience and faith that are necessary if we are to prosper.

God Knows What We Need - *Joe Campbell*

We were Pastoring a small Assembly of God church in Marion, Illinois. They were paying us $25.00 a week, and we lived up in the attic of the church. Our kids, Brad and Gail, were about to start school, and we had no money. I was at the altar after church, and I was praying. I said, *"God, I'm desperate. I need finances. My kids are going to go to school. They need shoes, clothes, and book fees."* A businessman in town named Baker: His daughter came up to me while I was praying and said, *"Joe, I apologize. My dad gave me this envelope for you a few weeks ago. I put it in my Bible, and I forgot to give it to you. Here's the envelope."* I got up immediately, went around behind the platform, and when I opened it, there was quite a bit of money in it. God whispered to me, *"I know what you have need of before you even ask."* Praise God! That became a reference point in my faith and spirit.

Interrupted by Provision - *Jonathan and Rachel Heimberg*

When Pastoring in Gallup, New Mexico, I was inspired to purchase a large mobile stage for outreaches in Gallup and around the Reservation. We got a miracle deal on a 54-foot trailer that opened up into a massive stage, and outfitted it with all the equipment needed to do large outdoor outreaches, crusades, and concerts. However, we had to rent a semi-truck each time we wanted to use the trailer. We couldn't find one cheap enough to buy, because they are so expensive.

One night, after reading an article about a multi-million dollar upgrade at some megachurch, I was complaining to Rachel that *"It's just not right that these churches that don't even evangelize have all this money, and we can't even find a truck to pull our trailer..."* and in the middle of the sentence, my phone began to ring. On the phone was a man named Knifewing, someone in the city with whom we had done work before. He asked me if we still had that trailer and if we still needed a truck to pull it with. I told him we did, and he said there's a man in town who has a truck he wants to give you! We organized the legal details, and the man gave the church a beautiful International truck that the church still uses to this day to pull the outreach trailer.

A Miracle Provision - *Andy and Kris Altringer | Salem, Oregon*

In July 2022, I was going through cancer treatment and couldn't preach or go to church for a bit of time, so I would watch services online. During the Prescott Bible Conference in July, we were watching the Wednesday pm service, and Pastor Richard Rubi was taking the offering and used the story of the Widow's Mite. He talked about how we gave everything when we were young, but what about when we're old?

To have our church participate in this conference, we showed the conference video, took up an offering, and submitted it. Later that summer, Pastor Greg Mitchell was taking up an offering at another conference I was watching online, and God reminded me of Pastor Rubi's offering from the July Prescott conference and challenged me to give all the money we had in the church's savings account. At first, I started figuring out ways not to give it all and transfer to cover the next month's bills just to be safe, but God again said, *"All of it."* So, I wrote a check that emptied all of the church's savings and sent it to Prescott (knowing what it costs to support missionaries, the amount wasn't that much) for world evangelism.

Life went on; we never had to worry financially as a church, all the bills still got paid, and finances started going up. In the summer of 2023, a couple came to a Sunday night service because we were one of the few churches in the area that held services on Sunday night. They came again on Wednesday night, and this continued for a few months; they would come on Sunday nights and Wednesdays. Then they started coming to Sunday School, then going to their church service, and then coming back for the PM service. Finally, they started showing up for every service and tithing regularly.

One day, they asked me to come over to their house and said they wanted to buy a building for the church, so we started looking for a building. Still, it wasn't working out, so I told them, *"Let's wait and just come to service, and if it's God's will, something will work out."* About seven months later, they called and said they wanted to show us a building. It was a 9000 sq. ft. Church Building and a 2100 sq ft four-bedroom house on two acres. The building was built in 1950 and needed remodeling. This couple gave the church $1,000,000: $702,000.00 to buy it and $298,000.00 to remodel it. Also, they paid

$80,000.00 to have the parking lot redone with all-new paving. One of the ladies who's been in the church a long time said that an evangelist gave the church a word 20 years ago that the church was going to get a miracle building, and it has come to pass. God is a miracle-working God!

SALEM, OREGON

Chapter 2: Breaking the Curse of Poverty

Poor people are those who only work to try to keep an expensive lifestyle and always want more and more.

Jose Mujica

Poverty is Spiritual

Before we can prosper, it's important to understand the principle of poverty from a Biblical perspective. **The opposite of prosperity is poverty.** By definition, *poverty means deficiency, impoverishment, or not having enough.* The old bumper sticker says, *"I've got too much month at the end of my money!"* Poverty cripples our abilities, leaving us unable to move forward in life or in our financial decisions.

Poverty produces an inward insufficiency: if we are living in poverty, we are unable to pay bills, meet needs, relieve our financial stress, or get ahead financially. Elijah met a mother living in abject poverty in a place called Zarephath. *1 Kings 17:12 So she said, "As the Lord your God lives, I do not have bread, only a handful of flour in a bin, and a little oil in a jar; and see, I am gathering a couple of sticks that I may go in and prepare it for myself and my son, that we may eat it, and die."* Her poverty manifested in an inability to be able to buy food for herself and her son.

2 Kings 4:1 A certain woman of the wives of the sons of the prophets cried out to Elisha, saying, "Your servant my husband is dead, and you know that your servant feared the Lord. And the creditor is coming to take my two sons to be his slaves." Here, poverty manifests as an inability to pay off debt. In ancient times, it was common to fall into debt-slavery. If you borrowed money and couldn't pay it back, they didn't repossess <u>things</u>; they repossessed <u>people</u>! Her husband died, leaving her with debt, and the creditors were going to come and take her sons into slavery to repay it. Her story shows us an important principle: ***Poverty affects children!***

Poverty produces an outward insufficiency: If we are living in poverty, we are unable to bless God and His work, and we are unable to bless other people. ***Mark 6:35-36 NCV*** *35When it was late in the day, his followers came to him and said, "No one lives in this place, and it is already very late. 36Send the people away so they can go to the countryside and towns around here to buy themselves something to eat."* Because the disciples lacked resources and calculated only from a human perspective, they concluded they could not help anyone in need around them.

The Truth about Poverty

The Bible shows us that poverty is <u>supernatural</u>; it is a <u>spiritual</u> force! If you view money and poverty simply as a matter of opportunities, education, or luck, you will never prosper! The Bible uses a word that is connected with finances – the word **curse**. ***Malachi 3:9*** *You are cursed with a curse, For you have robbed Me, Even this whole nation.* In this verse, God is speaking to agricultural people who were struggling financially: Insects were eating their crops, and grapes were falling from the vine before they were ripe enough. They were attributing these problems to natural factors, but God said the actual underlying problem was a <u>curse</u>. The word <u>curse</u> means *"To bind with a spell; To make powerless to resist."* When the Bible uses the word curse, it is always referring to a supernatural, evil dimension. The power of a curse is an **open door**: *A door has been opened in our lives that allows entrance to demonic spiritual powers – and a curse affects our finances!*

The Effects of Poverty

There are two main effects of the curse of poverty:

Poverty effect #1: Poverty produces negative situations that rob our finances. *Malachi 3:11 And I will rebuke the devourer for your sakes, So that he will not destroy the fruit of your ground, Nor shall the vine fail to bear fruit for you in the field, "Says the Lord of hosts;* The negative factors were taking away their crops (which in those days was equivalent to money). But the King James and New King James version personifies the evil effect, causing loss. God calls it 'the devourer.' The means of devouring may have been insects or weather, but the actual underlying cause was supernatural.

Judges 6:3-6 NCV ³Whenever the Israelites planted crops, the Midianites, Amalekites, and other peoples from the east would come and attack them. ⁴They camped in the land and destroyed the crops that the Israelites had planted as far away as Gaza. They left nothing for Israel to eat, and no sheep, cattle, or donkeys. ⁵The Midianites came with their tents and their animals like swarms of locusts to ruin the land. There were so many people and camels they could not be counted. ⁶Israel became very poor because of the Midianites, so they cried out to the Lord. In this instance, there are physical enemies - marauding armies that came each year when it was time to reap the harvest and would steal the crops. This happened six years in a row – seemingly a terrible coincidence. But then God reveals the underlying spiritual reason for these awful coincidences: *Judges 6:10 Also I said to you, "I am the Lord your God; do not fear the gods of the Amorites, in whose land you dwell. "But you have not obeyed My voice."* Disobedience released spiritual factors that produced physical and financial losses. I have seen this story repeated so many times in the lives of Christians. I've had many people tell me, *"Every time we get ahead financially, I lose a job, the car breaks down, someone gets sick, and our finances are eaten up."*

Job 1:14-17 NCV ¹⁴*A messenger came to Job and said, "The oxen were plowing and the donkeys were eating grass nearby,* ¹⁵*when the Sabeans attacked and carried them away. They killed the servants with swords, and I am the only one who escaped to tell you!"*¹⁶*The messenger was still speaking when another messenger arrived and said, "Lightning from God fell from the sky. It burned up the sheep and the servants, and I am the only one who escaped to tell you!"*¹⁷*The second messenger was still speaking when another messenger arrived and said, "The Babylonians sent three groups of attackers that swept down and stole your camels and killed the servants. I am the only one who escaped to tell you!"* This passage is an important one if we are to understand poverty correctly. Job had messengers come one after another with bad financial news: Sabean raiders came and stole your donkeys (five hundred female donkeys alone); lightning struck and burned up your sheep (seven thousand of them); Babylonian attackers came and stole your camels (three thousand of them). A devastating loss; All of his wealth was taken away. If an outsider were looking at these events through natural eyes only, they would assume that Job had a string of negative coincidences or a run of bad luck. But the Book of Job is so fascinating because it offers a spiritual perspective: Satan was involved in these financial losses! *Job 1:12 NCV The Lord said to Satan, "All right, then. Everything Job has is in your power, but you must not touch Job himself." Then Satan left the Lord's presence.*

This teaches us an important lesson about poverty and financial struggles: *there is more going on in your finances than you can see!* There was a supernatural dimension – a spiritual force that harms our finances. While I do not believe that every flat tire is caused by a flat-tire demon (sometimes you simply ran over a nail!), this shows us that we need to be alert to **patterns of poverty**. Patterns of poverty are often repeated events that rob, reduce, or block our financial position.

Here are some common patterns of poverty that are evidence of spiritual assault:
Sickness that costs you money – and keeps you from working and earning money: Many times, I've had people who say, *"Every time I start to get ahead financially, I get sick, or someone in the family gets sick."* The result is a loss of income or unexpected medical costs.

Problems with employment that cost income: I've known people who keep losing jobs in strange ways, that weren't their fault; *my office branch closed, the company went bankrupt, our division was eliminated, etc.* (Please note: Laziness or poor job performance is not the Devil attacking you – that is a self-inflicted wound).

Possessions keep breaking repeatedly, causing financial loss and extra costs: Sometimes people say, *"Every time we start to get ahead financially, something breaks and we are either back to square one, or we go in the hole again."* Like Job, in the passage I quoted before, some people experience strings of financial loss – not just one flat tire. When we were missionaries in South Africa, another missionary had two car crashes and eleven electronic items quit working or blew up within two weeks! Refrigerator, washing machine, computers, amplifiers, etc. Not at the same time, and not due to a power surge. So, this raises an important question: *How many bad things have to happen, or* *how many times do negative things have to occur, before you realize this is not normal?*

Poverty effect #2: Poverty releases spiritual powers that <u>block</u> our financial blessings. *Deuteronomy 28:15, 23 NCV But if you do not obey the Lord your God and carefully follow all his commands and laws I am giving you today, all these curses will come upon you and stay:* **Deuteronomy 28:23** *The sky above will be like bronze, and the ground below will be like iron.* **Deuteronomy 28** describes the curses of disobedience. God says the curse will affect your basket, your kitchen, your crops, your calves, your lambs **(verses 17-18).** All of these were financial provisions, and crops, calves, and lambs were wealth in those days. But **verse 23** says the sky above will be like bronze: This is saying your prayers aren't making a difference. People sometimes lament that *"nothing ever changes,"* and *"I never seem to get ahead."* They may ask, *"Why don't good things ever seem to fall into my lap? Why don't I ever get a good break financially?"* The answer is: **A CURSE!!** The problem isn't coincidence or luck – it is a supernatural problem!

The Entrance of a Curse of Poverty

The Bible speaks of several ways curses enter our lives that affect people financially:

A curse of poverty can enter through a generational curse of sin: Sin doesn't just affect the person who commits it – it affects families: Sin releases negative spiritual forces that are passed down within families. *Deuteronomy 5:9 NCV You must not worship or serve any idol, because I, the Lord your God, am a jealous God. If people sin against me and hate me, I will punish their children, even their grandchildren and great-grandchildren.* One effect of sin is poverty **(Deuteronomy 28:17-18, 38-42).**

This refers to poverty that goes beyond opportunity levels or learned behaviors: *It literally runs in the family!* Researchers speak of generational poverty, defined as: *"a cycle of poverty that persists across two or more generations."* Academics and politicians will blame generational poverty on *"systemic barriers and a lack of resources or education,"* but the Bible says the problem is bigger than that; *It is a <u>curse</u> – it is supernatural!* A door has been opened that causes demonic powers to cause problems for members of a family. When you ask people living in poverty about their families, they often say all or most members of their families also struggle financially. That makes sense if they all grew up in the same place, with the same barriers and educational opportunities, but I've known people who were separated from family at birth for various reasons. When they later meet their relatives, they have repeated the same mistakes and suffered the same effects as their biological family, even if they've had very different environments and opportunities. *The sin and disobedience of your family may have released a curse on you financially!* This doesn't remove your personal responsibility for your finances, but you must understand that education and opportunity alone may not change your financial situation unless you address the underlying spiritual problem of a curse.

A curse of poverty can enter through personal sin and disobedience: It would be nice if we could blame all our current problems on our family or ancestors, but the hard truth is that *many of the financial curses in our lives come from our <u>own</u> decisions!*

We can open doors to curses through sin and disobedience <u>before</u> salvation: All sin can result in judgment eventually, but the Bible speaks of some sins that release a curse (primarily listed in **Deuteronomy 27:14-26**). The most common sins that open the door to curses are witchcraft, idolatry, and perversion.

Salvation forgives our sins, enables us to have a relationship with God, and ultimately allows us to go to heaven. But the effects of cursed sins may still be at work in the lives of believers. This is not a salvation issue! You can be genuinely saved and on your way to heaven yet still experience the effects of a lingering poverty curse from the past. The good news is that God's desire is to break that curse from our lives. *Galatians 3:13 Christ has redeemed us from the curse of the law, having become a curse for us (for it is written, "Cursed is everyone who hangs on a tree").* "Redeemed" means to be bought out of slavery. In ancient times, if you were a slave, someone who loved you could redeem you, which meant *"to pay the purchase price for your freedom."* If someone redeemed you and set you free, the former owner lost all rights and could no longer subject you to the same negative factors you were subjected to before redemption. The answer is to pray and break the curse of poverty off your life.

We can open doors to curses through sin and disobedience <u>after</u> salvation: Unfortunately, believers can choose to disobey God even after they have been saved from sin. Hopefully, you are not returning to witchcraft, idolatry, and perversion after you have been born again, but some believers do disobey God financially. In **Joshua 7**, we read the story of Achan. The Children of Israel attacked the city of Jericho. Jericho was a tithe city (the Sacred Portion): Everything that was in it was set apart for God. They were not to take anything from it. Why? It was simply a way to recognize and demonstrate God's ownership and Lordship; *He is God, and we are not.* But Achan disobeyed God's clear instructions and stole some of the finances of Jericho that had been dedicated to God, and belonged to God. The result of his disobedience and theft was that he and his family were cursed and judged. Sadly, Christians choose to repeat Achan's mistakes when they fail to acknowledge God's ownership and Lordship through the principle of tithing: *Giving the first 10% of* *our income to God.* The result of financial disobedience is a curse: ***Malachi 3:9-10*** *⁹You are cursed with a curse, For you have robbed Me, Even this whole nation. ¹⁰Bring all the tithes into the storehouse, That there may be food in My house, And try Me now in this,* "*Says the Lord of hosts,* "*If I will not open for you the windows of heaven And pour out for you such blessing That there will not be room enough to receive it.* Through the years, I've had people tell me that at some point they stopped tithing, then they told how a financial setback came that equaled the amount of the missing tithe exactly – to the penny!

Some curses of poverty come simply through unrighteous demonic assault: You need to see that the Devil cheats; *He tries to supernaturally assault and rob God's people who don't deserve it! **Job 1:8 NCV** Then the Lord said to Satan,* "*Have you noticed my servant Job? No one else on earth is like him. He is an honest and innocent man, honoring God and staying away from evil.*" God Himself tells us that Job did nothing to deserve a curse, and he did not open the door to a curse – but the Devil attacked his finances anyway! This is in line with his nature – he is a thief! ***John 10:10*** *The thief does not come except to steal, and to kill, and to destroy...* The Devil is the thief! He will sometimes try to rob you – though he has no legal right to do so!

Why does the Devil attack people financially? There can be many reasons:

- He hates you! You belong to God, so he hates you and your relationship with God.
- He uses financial attacks to bring confusion. When things go wrong, people often become confused about themselves (*"maybe I did something wrong"*) or about God (*"He is angry with me and doesn't love me"*).
- He tries to keep you from giving and investing in God's work of redemption.

- He wants you to be so consumed with just trying to make money to make ends meet that you don' t have time to do the will of God.
- He would love you to make wrong decisions out of fear: *Move away from the will of God. Such as taking three jobs to get ahead – but that means you can't come to church.* Elimelech and Naomi disobeyed God during a time of famine by moving to the land of Moab. Their disobedience resulted in poverty for Naomi after the death of her husband.

Some curses of poverty come simply through witchcraft: We pastored for over seven years in South Africa, and I learned a lot about witchcraft. Much of witchcraft involves placing curses on other people to harm them in various ways. Many of the black magic curses placed on people are aimed at their finances! If you have family members involved in witchcraft, or if you are in an area or a culture that is widely involved in witchcraft, you need to be aware of this possibility. If you begin to experience a string of financial losses or setbacks, it may be due to deliberate curses being put on you by others. When I have mentioned this in various places, I have had people make the connection between their financial struggles and witchcraft: When did the financial struggles begin? In many cases, right after they found dead animals, feathers, or witchcraft items at the front door of their house, or their church.

Breaking the Curse of Poverty

The good news for those who are struggling with any form of the curse of poverty: **you don't have to stay cursed!** Jesus paid the price of redemption; freedom from every curse of sin through his death on the cross. *Galatians 3:13-14 ESV Christ redeemed us from the curse of the law by becoming a curse for us,* *for it is written: "Cursed is everyone who is hung on a tree." He redeemed us in order that the blessing given to Abraham might come to the Gentiles through Christ Jesus, so that by faith we might receive the promise of the Spirit.*

Every part of the crucifixion of Jesus carries powerful meaning. He had a crown of thorns forced into His scalp. **Mark 15:17** *And they clothed Him with purple; and they twisted a crown of thorns, put it on His head.* Thorns were the visible symbol of the curse that came when Adam and Eve sinned. Spiritual decisions produced thorns in the ground that Adam had to till to gain food, and the thorns resisted his efforts. This is a picture of the negative spiritual force that resists people in their finances today – producing poverty. But God not only paid for the penalty of sin on the cross (separation from God – and eventual judgment in hell), but He also paid for the power and effects of sin – including the curse of poverty. Jesus took that pain on himself to break the power of that curse! Generational curses, word curses, personal sin and disobedience, even witchcraft may all be true and working against you today; but Jesus broke the curse for us!

Breaking the Curse of Poverty

If you recognize a curse of poverty at work in your life, *how do you break the curse?*
You break the curse of poverty by repentance:
Prayer of repentance: If the curse is due to our own sin and disobedience – we need to confess our own sin and disobedience – and turn away from it! In the Old Testament, when someone became aware of their sin, they needed to bring a goat as a sacrifice, lay their hand on it and confess: *I did this! I know it was wrong – and I repent!* The guilt was symbolically moved from the sinner to the sacrifice. The goat bore the guilt or curse on their

behalf. It doesn't matter whether this was our cursed sin before salvation, or our sin and disobedience after salvation, freedom begins with repentance.

Obedience: It does no good to pray if you remain disobedient. Freedom and blessing come when we change our actions and obey God. *Malachi 3:10 Bring all the tithes into the storehouse, That there may be food in My house, And try Me now in this, "Says the Lord of hosts, "If I will not open for you the windows of heaven And pour out for you such blessing That there will not be room enough to receive it.*

You break the curse of poverty by prayer: Spiritual forces are released when we pray. That prayer may begin with asking God to break family curses. Salvation was paid for on the cross – but it didn't become real until you prayed and asked God to save you. In the same way, Jesus' death on the cross paid for freedom from every curse, but that freedom is activated when you pray to break the curse.

We have already said that poverty can be connected to a supernatural assault. If that is true, it's essential to understand that prayer is not simply a request we make to God – it is a fight! In the Gospels, when Jesus confronted the Devil's work in a person's life, He rebuked the spirit; He gave a command! *Mark 9:25-26 25When Jesus saw that the people came running together, He rebuked the unclean spirit, saying to it, "Deaf and dumb spirit, I command you, come out of him and enter him no more!"26Then the spirit cried out, convulsed him greatly, and came out of him...* This shows us the pattern of prayer we can use to bring freedom. Your prayer may involve rejecting poverty in your spirit as you identify the demonic assault: *This poverty is not God's will – I'm not going to keep living like this!*

The Bible records many stories of battle against the enemies of God's people. One battle story is found in Judges Chapters 6 and 7. For six years the enemy came and attacked each year at harvest time to rob them financially. God's answer was for Gideon and his men to attack the enemy – fight back! The physical battles in the Old Testament show us that we must battle spiritually in prayer.

Pastor Tom Payne told me his personal story of breaking the curse of poverty. For years, he had faithfully participated in tithing, giving offerings and financial pledges, but he was not experiencing the "more than enough" blessing God promises.

Years ago, when he was living in Farmington, New Mexico, he was trying to sell a car. He said every time he got ready to advertise it in the paper to sell, something would break, requiring more money to fix. One day, he said he got sick of it and cried out to God in prayer. He told God, *"It's always been like this, and I'm sick of it."* He passionately prayed and broke every curse in his own life and commanded that spirit to leave. He cried out to God for His promises to be made real in his life!

He said something fundamentally changed at that moment. Not only was he able to sell the car, but he also recognized that a spirit of poverty was broken off his life from that day. He said things were different from that day forward, and his financial experience in life has changed. Once he experienced the blessing of God in his finances, God has enabled him to help many people around the world, and the churches he has pastored since that day have also broken the curse of poverty off their lives and entered into the blessing of God. This has been true both in First World and Third World nations!

Asking for a Miracle - *Kris and Paula Hart*
My story began like so many: a broken home, parents who were filled with guilt due to their bad choices. As a teenager, I manipulated them to get what I wanted. I had an entitlement mentality. I grew into a

young adult on my way to financial disaster. I got my contractor's license and started a drywall business. I was skilled in doing the work, but had no interest in money management, which led to unpaid material bills and tax debts. I made many attempts to rein it in, but I could not. I began to receive threats from bill collectors. Many of my suppliers had me on a cash-only basis. The IRS was sending letters threatening to levy my bank accounts due to my negligence in paying taxes.

In 1988, I genuinely surrendered to Jesus. The only thing that kept me from total mental collapse was my salvation. In early 1990, I made some very serious decisions for God. One of which was tithing, and the other, giving to World Evangelism. We received a letter from the IRS stating we owed $65,000.00, with interest accruing daily. In those statements, we were told that we could not give any contributions to our church and that all monies belonged to the government until the debt was satisfied. Also, I was told by an attorney that the only way to stop the interest was to file for bankruptcy. Then he said to file an "Offer in Compromise" with the IRS, asking them to settle for a lower amount. During that time, my wife and I decided to give to God first. Every week, the letters came threatening to take bank accounts, property, & vehicles. After the reorganization was filed, I kept asking the attorney about the Offer in Compromise. His delay was unacceptable, so I called the IRS. They informed me that, unfortunately, they would not consider an Offer in Compromise while I was in bankruptcy. So, prayerfully, we decided to withdraw from bankruptcy and make an offer to the IRS. The first offer was $5000 for a $65,000 debt. The auditor asked, *"You want us to accept $5000 for a $65,000 debt?"* They said absolutely not, and to try again, so I then offered $6500. We got a call from an IRS agent, and she said, *"You are asking for a miracle to only pay this amount on a $65,000 debt!"* I said, *"Yes, ma'am, that's exactly what I'm expecting."* As we continued to pray and give to our church, still no answer came for weeks. Then one day in the mail, another letter came from the IRS. When I opened the letter, it said we are considering your offer, and an agent will contact you with our decision. That was a miracle moment! Hope was once again the catalyst for more expectancy in prayer. In the days that followed, we received a phone call from an IRS agent. She informed us that the $6,500 offer we submitted has been accepted! Our miracle became a reality in that moment. We knew God helped us only because we honored Him first. God helped me with jobs to gather the money to pay the offer. He then helped me pay off the accounts that I had with suppliers.

God didn't stop there. We were determined to do God's will and pioneer a church. God called us to a remote area on the Navajo reservation. There are no houses to rent there. The only option was to purchase a mobile home and set it up on the reservation, but I had no money to buy one. I went to a man who owns a mobile home business. I told him we planned to start a church. He told me he had a 16' x 80' mobile home that was 7 months old. I told him I had no credit and nothing for a down payment. He wrote something on a piece of paper and handed it to me. It was a zero with a line through it. He said, *"Three days before you came in, God spoke to me and told me to give that mobile home away. God said He would tell me who to give it to when it was time."* Not only did he give us the mobile home, but he also moved it out there with all our possessions inside. Unmerited grace. We serve a God of mercy and grace!

God Does The Miracle - *Adam and Jennifer Porter*

In February of 2014, three smaller churches approached the owner of the building we were renting for our congregation. They told him they wanted to share the space, and that, collectively, they could pay $5,000 more per month than our agreed rent. The landlord called me and said, *"We're raising your rent by $5,000."* I reminded him, *"We still have six months left on our lease."* He replied, *"Well, three churches want to move in and are willing to pay more than you."* I said, *"You can't do that."* He said, *"Then sue me."* I told him, *"We don't have an extra $5,000 to give."* He said, *"Then you have two months to move."*

We were stunned. We began to pray and asked God to help us and open a door. And He did. By a miracle, another building became available almost immediately. But when I spoke with the commercial realtor, he shook his head and said, *"I've been doing this for over 30 years. With all the licensing, inspections, architectural approvals, and city requirements, it will take at least four to six months before you can move in."* I told him, *"Just keep doing what you do, and we'll pray for God to do a miracle."* Our church began to pray. One week later, the realtor called, his voice full of disbelief. He said, *"I've never had this happen before, but we can get you in within a week and a half."* Then he paused and added, *"But you'll need about $20,000 to get the process started."* That Sunday, I brought the need before the church and challenged everyone to give so we could move into the new building. Within four days, $22,000 came in. It was enough to pay all the city fees, architectural costs, government paperwork, and the initial move-in expenses. We moved in immediately. A few months later, we needed additional funds for renovations and further fees. Once again, we prayed. A few days later, I received a phone call from a woman who wasn't even part of our church. She said God stirred her heart to close one of her bank accounts and donate the entire balance to our congregation. She sent us $20,274.80. We stood there in awe, holding the check and cash.

GOD DOES THE MIRACLE

Chapter 3: Changing Poverty Mindsets Part 1

It's awful what happens when people run out of money. They start thinking they're no good.
Barbara Kingsolver

MC Hammer (Stanley Burrell), was one of the most famous music artists of the early 1990s. At the height of his career, Hammer earned over $30 million. Instead of managing his money wisely, he adopted a mistaken mindset would always keep flowing in. He bought a 17-bedroom mansion, luxury cars, racehorses, expensive jewelry, and gave huge amounts of money away without budgeting or long-term planning. When album sales declined, the income stopped — but the spending didn't. By 1996 he filed for bankruptcy, owing over $13 million.

The Mind and Money

Your mind is a powerful factor in your life. How you think will directly affect your life in the area of your finances. *Proverbs 23:7 For as he thinks in his heart, so is he. "Eat and drink!" he says to you, But his heart is not with you.* You are what you think: *What you think about and how you think will ultimately affect every area of life!*

Your mind shapes how you view life when it comes to finances. *Proverbs 21:5 The plans of the diligent lead surely to plenty, But those of everyone who is hasty, surely to poverty.* The word "plans" means "thoughts"; How you view money. Those who wind up in poverty are those who think about taking financial shortcuts or being in a hurry to prosper.

Your mind affects your decisions and actions concerning finances. *Proverbs 28:19 NIV A hard worker has plenty of food, but a person who chases fantasies ends up in poverty.* This scripture says those who wind up in poverty are those who don't think realistically about money. The result is that they make bad decisions chasing after these unrealistic fantasies.

Poverty Mindsets

Poverty is defined as: *A deficiency/impoverishment/not having enough.* But many people have poverty mindsets: They have thinking patterns based on poverty, or in line with poverty. Ruby Payne states in her book "A Framework for Understanding Poverty," *"Poverty is a mindset. People in poverty think differently than those with wealth."*

Poverty Mindset Questions
There are questions that those with poverty mindsets ask:
- **What should I have?** *Is it right to have enough? Is it right to have more than I have now?*
- **What is money for?** *What is the purpose of money? What should we do with our money?*
- **Where does financial success or increase come from?**
- **Can you be financially confident?**

Poverty mindsets answer <u>all</u> these questions incorrectly!
- People with poverty mindsets don't view money correctly.
- People with poverty mindsets don't make correct financial decisions.
- People with poverty mindsets are mentally tormented by money rather than it being a blessing.

Proverbs 10:22 *The blessing of the Lord makes one rich, And He adds no sorrow with it.*

The source of poverty mindsets

Why do people have incorrect mindsets concerning money? Where do these mindsets come from?

Poverty mindset source #1: Past trauma with money. Some people grew up with, or had a period of, financial trauma. They experienced prolonged lack, starvation, homelessness, and constant moving due to financial problems. They often saw their parents in conflict over money. So, their view of money is traumatic! It is emotional. They become protective. They say, *"I never want to feel like that again!"* Families in poverty that have experienced trauma with money tend to teach and reinforce wrong thinking about money in their children. The result of this is that poverty becomes generational: *Poverty is passed down among family members.* This is different than a family curse (a supernatural force): It is inherited wrong thinking patterns. If **Proverbs 23:7** teaches that you are what you think, then past traumas that cause you to think in poverty mindsets produce poverty in you and your family!

Poverty mindset source #2: Wrong teaching about money. Many people who are struggling with poverty got those mindsets from churches or Pastors who taught incorrect things about money. I referred to some of these in Chapter 1.

Money is evil: This idea comes from those who misquote *1 Timothy 6:10 the love of money is the root of all evil...*But they say *'money is the root of all evil.'* If you think money is evil, you will not want to have money!

Being poor is spiritual: *God is somehow more pleased with you if you dress in rags, drive old, beat-up cars, and always struggle financially.*

Having any excess money or having anything nice is selfish and unspiritual: People are taught that they should have barely enough, or else they are being selfish. A spiritual-sounding question is sometimes asked, *"How can you have anything left over when there are people who don't have enough?"*

Poverty has mysterious refining qualities: People are taught that struggling with poverty somehow makes you a better person or a more spiritual Christian. The problem with that idea is that I know kind, good-hearted, spiritual, wealthy people and many, many more poor Christians who have bad attitudes and bad hearts!

Poverty mindset source #3: Emotional insecurity (rejection): When someone has rejected us in the past and we received negative messages about our worth, our sense of value becomes damaged. One result of unhealed rejection is that you view <u>money</u> based on what you think you're <u>worth</u>! Those with rejection issues often feel they don't deserve anything good financially. *Luke 15:19 NLT and I am no longer worthy of being called your son. Please take me on as a hired servant.* The prodigal son didn't feel he deserved the blessings of being a son, so he wanted to live like a servant. People with this mentality feel guilty about being blessed financially. (*I deal with this in more detail in my book Uprooting Rejection*).

Other people with rejection issues go the opposite direction: they use money and possessions to try to <u>establish</u> their worth or <u>prove</u> their worth. *Look at me! I'm valuable because my clothes and bags are from expensive labels! I'm worth more because of what I drive or where I live.*

Destructive Poverty Mindsets

Destructive Poverty Mindset #1: The victim mentality. If someone struggling with poverty asks themselves the questions, *"What part do I play in my prosperity?"* or *"What part do I play in* *my poverty?"* the answer of a poverty spirit is: NOTHING! I AM A VICTIM! This plays out in several ways:

How we view our <u>current</u> situation: *Why are we in the current financial situation we're in?* The answer of a poverty mindset says, *"It's a conspiracy!"* People in poverty tell how evil employers, greedy wealthy people, unjust politicians, and unfair bankers are plotting to make sure they stay poor. *Judges 6:13 "Sir," Gideon replied, "if the Lord is with us, why has all this happened to us? And where are all the miracles our ancestors told us about? Didn't they say, 'The Lord brought us up out of Egypt'? But now the Lord has abandoned us and handed us over to the Midianites."* Gideon blamed God for financial struggles, but he failed to mention the disobedience and bad decisions of his people that opened the door to the enemy, which caused their poverty. People today share the same approach: Those in poverty fail to think about their own lack of budgeting, impulsive buying, bad decisions, poor work ethic, and disobedience to God – but put the blame on anyone but themselves.

How we view our <u>future</u> financial potential: A poverty mentality is pessimistic and unbelieving about one's financial future. Those with a poverty mentality often think, *"There's no use in trying - I'll never succeed." Matthew 25:24-25 NCV* [24]*"Then the servant who had been given one bag of gold came to the master and said, 'Master, I knew that you were a hard man. You harvest things you did not plant. You gather crops where you did not sow any seed.* [25]*So I was afraid and went and hid your money in the ground. Here is your bag of gold.'* A poverty mentality believes that future financial blessings are out of our hands. They may believe that <u>people</u> control their financial future: *I just have to wait for people to give me more.* Or they may believe that <u>God</u> controls their financial future and they interpret God's control to mean, *"It's all up to Him; I don't have to do anything, nor can I do anything to change my financial future."*

Destructive Poverty Mindset #2: An entitlement mentality. Entitlement is defined as *"The feeling or belief that you deserve to be given something."* If those with a poverty mindset ever think about the question *"Where does money come from?"* they will conclude, *"MONEY COMES FROM SOMEONE ELSE!"* They think to themselves, *"If I don't have money, I simply ask someone else for it."* People with a poverty mindset expect other people to give them money – and often get offended when others do not do so. **Joshua 17:14 NIV** *The people of Joseph said to Joshua, "Why have you given us only one allotment and one portion for an inheritance? We are a numerous people and the Lord has blessed us abundantly."* They were irritated that Joshua failed to give them more. Notice that they expected more to be given to them, rather than worked for.

Ruby Payne: A key difference between generational and situational poverty is attitude. In generational poverty, the mindset is generally that society owes one a living. In contrast, situational poverty involves an attitude of pride and rejection of help.

If you fail to take personal responsibility for your finances – you will never prosper!

This brings up a common question I am asked about giving money to those in need. I believe one reason God gives us money is to help other people in need (we will discuss this in further detail later in the book). But having pastored in South Africa among people living in great poverty, I can offer practical wisdom on discerning whether it is wise to give money to certain people. I learned that those who ask you for money easily, as though it is expected, are not actually helped when you give it to them; you are reinforcing their destructive entitlement mentality!

Destructive Poverty Mindset #3: Feeling Guilty for financial blessings. If you don't feel you deserve to be blessed financially, you will feel guilty if financial blessings do come, whether this is a good job, a bonus, or an inheritance.

Those who believe being poor is spiritual: These people become tormented when financial blessings come their way. Blessings produce inner turmoil: *This must mean that I am unspiritual, or evil. God must be displeased with me. He is going to take my blessings away.*

Those who don't feel they are worthy to be blessed because of past rejection: Whenever they get a bit of money, manage to buy something good, or make progress in their job or business, it stirs up inner conflict. Their thoughts turn to, *I shouldn't have this! I don't deserve this!* **Proverbs 10:22** *The blessing of the Lord makes one rich, And He adds no sorrow with it.*

A poverty mentality based on rejection attaches sorrow to blessings.
- *They don't enjoy their blessings.*
- *They may feel compelled to give it away.*
- *They worry that God is going to realize they don't deserve it – and take it away!*

Some wind up sabotaging their blessings. They may do things on the job, in business, or in making poor financial decisions that cause them to lose the good things they have. This lowers their financial status to the level that their rejection makes them feel they truly deserve.

Changing Our Poverty Mindset - *Glen and Maribel Pugliese*
My parents had a hoarding mentality driven by fear of not having enough for the future. They always bought the cheapest in everything,

36

and kept fixing things that needed to be replaced long ago. My mother would patch clothes until they could no longer be patched and then finally buy us something new to wear to school, and even then, it was the bare minimum. All along, they had a significant savings account. As kids, we would never have known they had money, because everything was done on a tight budget. Near the end of my mother's life, she was having a meltdown because she feared they would run out of money, and she would be left with nothing. All along, dad was making almost $8,000 per month in retirement and had a lifetime of savings just sitting in the bank.

I had no idea how much all of this affected my mindset until later in life, and salvation. I thought that living on the bare minimum was somehow pleasing to God. As a result, we struggled immensely and lived under a lot of stress. We always felt like blessings were for everyone else, and we could never find a way out of a bare minimum lifestyle. Deliverance from a poverty mentality was a slow process of God dealing with us, and helping us through His word.

When we bought our first house, there was a turning point. We gained dignity from home ownership, next we upgraded our car. We began to change our thinking, and began to understand that God wanted to bless us. We didn't become materialistic, but we changed our thinking and embraced the idea that God wanted to bless us. We understood that poverty and barely making it financially were not God's will. We felt the dignity of that blessing, then blessings started to come our way.

We realized that if we have more, we can give more. I used to think that giving $100 as an offering was massive because my mindset was so small. My problem was that I couldn't even think in the thousands. I was too limited in my thinking. We have since been blessed to be able to give in the thousands as offerings above our tithes. We are convinced that God wants to bless us and that it is not his will that we live in poverty. We no longer view blessing as compromise, but as being God's will.

I thank God that my children did not move on in life with a poverty mindset. When it was broken in us, they were young enough that they moved forward in life, got married, had children, and are far more blessed at their age than we were at their age. God has done deep work in our lives regarding how we think and how we view blessing. There is such dignity associated with a blessing. All of this puts you in a position to be a blessing to others, which also brings with it great dignity and joy.

Changing Our Future - *Abram and Alyssa Baca*

My wife and I grew up with a poverty mentality. We were raised in Española, New Mexico, and the Santa Clara Pueblo Reservation. I was a disciple at the Potter's House church in Española, New Mexico, under Pastor Tim Miller.

There was a point when Pastor Miller challenged me to get a steady job and step away from construction, which was feast-or-famine. I took a job working the graveyard shift at a casino as a security guard. There was a pay cut from about $28.50 an hour to $11 an hour. My wife and I began to give above and beyond the tithe, and God advanced me in that job to a supervisor making $16 an hour.

During a Bible conference in 2018, during the offering I felt God speak to me to give everything in my wallet. (Around $328) Not much, but it was all we had. That meant we didn't have enough money to get home or eat the rest of the conference. The next morning, we received a call from my father-in-law saying that he had sent us $300. Later, we received a call from my job stating they forgot to pay me for some overtime that I had done, and I had a check for $800 waiting when I got back.

A few months later, the housing director called me into the Tribal Housing Authority. He told me the tribe had offered him a lot of money to stay quiet, but he said that it went against his beliefs. He said he had done an audit of the tribal housing and that they had messed up the contract on my house. So, they took $55,000 off my house. That never happens! We paid $28,000 for a brand new, fully remodeled three-bedroom, 2-bath house with a huge yard.

- I then got a job at the Los Alamos National Laboratories, paying $28 an hour!
- We were also able to settle nearly $43,000 of debt for pennies on the dollar.

By the end of that next year, we were able to be sent out to Pioneer in Great Falls, Montana! I was announced as the first Pueblo Indian Pastor in our fellowship.

These financial miracles have continued in our ministry. God helped us with our church building, where we have only paid $300 a month for 6.5 years! Our building owner finally raised the rent to $375 due to rising electricity prices. We have seen many members of our congregation break through financially from the poverty mentality. I believe this is a testimony of a breakthrough because my wife and I grew up in a poverty mentality in Española, New Mexico, and on the Santa Clara Pueblo Reservation.

Getting My Own Blessing Testimony - *Jeanette Esparza*

Having been part of this fellowship since 2010, I have heard of many examples of how God has provided for people, especially financially. I would hear of these things and marvel and praise God from afar.

Recently, my 13-year-old Toyota Yaris started having issues. I always said I would drive it until the wheels fell off, and little by little it started coming apart. I prayed many times, *"LORD, I don't want a car payment. Please fix my car or help me to find a car that I'm able to afford if I do have to make payments."*

When my car started dying, I noticed my managers at work were acting strangely. They were having more closed-door meetings than usual, and I thought, *"We are slow, maybe they need to lay me off."* The following week, they called me into the office. All the managers were there, and even the owner. I thought, *"LORD, let your will be done; if I get laid off, I trust you."* When I sat down, one of the managers pulled out a small gift bag, put it in front of me, and asked me to open it. Totally confused, I put my hand in the bag and pulled out a set of keys. My manager said, *"We are so grateful to have you on our team. You are a hard worker and a blessing to our company, so we want to bless you with this vehicle."* It was a Honda Pilot SUV! I was in disbelief, and the tears started flowing. At that moment, I remembered the prayers that I had been praying to God. Never in a million years did I ever think that I would be one of those testimonies you hear in our fellowship of being gifted a car. Not only one car but <u>two</u>! They also gave me a truck to give to my son to drive to work!

I had received raises, promotions, and bonuses before the gift of the cars, and since then, there have been even more! This job has been a financial blessing. I give all the praise to God Almighty, He is faithful and true to His word when He says in **Malachi 3:10** *Bring all the tithes into the storehouse that there may be food in my house and try me now in this, says the LORD of Hosts, if I will not open for you the windows of heaven and pour out for you such blessing that there will not be room enough to receive it.*

Chapter 4: Changing Poverty Mindsets Part 2

Money is better than poverty, if only for financial reasons.
Woody Allen

Hetty Green died in 1916 and left an estate valued at USD $100 Million. ($3 billion today!) While she was alive, she ate cold oatmeal because she said it cost too much to heat it. Her son had his leg amputated because she took so long to find a free clinic. She had lots of money, but because she was afraid to spend it, the money didn't do her or her son much good.

In this chapter, we will continue looking at unhealthy poverty mindsets.

Poverty And Fear

Poverty is fear-based thinking: Poverty produces mental torment and mental bondage based on fear. *1 John 4:18 There is no fear in love; but perfect love casts out fear, because **fear involves torment.** But he who fears has not been made perfect in love.*

Poverty involves fear of not having enough: Those who have experienced financial trauma in the past usually hate how it made them feel, and they fear being in that position again. In our current financial situation, we can tend to focus on the <u>negatives</u>: whether that is our <u>past</u> negative experiences or the <u>current</u> negative factors we see. So, poverty causes our decisions about money always to be fear-based. *Ecclesiastes 11:4 NCV Those who wait for perfect weather will never plant seeds; those* who look at every cloud will never harvest crops. The passage employs an agricultural metaphor to show how some people allow fear of risk, or of investing to govern their actions.

Fear also causes people to make foolish, risky decisions with their money. Some spend what little money they have on the lottery or gambling. Fear makes people more susceptible to scammers. Usually, more poor people are scammed than those with wealth, because *they are afraid of future poverty!* **Proverbs 28:19 NIV** *A hard worker has plenty of food, but a person who chases fantasies ends up in poverty.*

Poverty involves fear of failure: We tend to connect money to our <u>worth</u> as human beings, or even as Christians. As a result, people in poverty often resist any efforts to change their financial situation. They can think, *"What's the point in reading books, asking for financial advice, or trying to invest? It probably won't work anyway – then I will be more embarrassed and feel like a failure."* **Matthew 25:24-25 NCV** 24*"Then the servant who had been given one bag of gold came to the master and said, 'Master, I knew that you were a hard man. You harvest things you did not plant. You gather crops where you did not sow any seed.* 25*So I was afraid and went and hid your money in the ground. Here is your bag of gold.'* Fear can make you think that staying at the back of the pack is probably the safest course in life: *If you don't try, you can't fail, so there is no risk of embarrassment or disappointment.* **Poverty convinces you that the most significant win would be not to lose!**

Poverty involves fear of losing finances: *This is a belief that you can "lose it all" despite everything you do.* **Proverbs 10:22** *The blessing of the Lord makes one rich, And He adds no sorrow with it.* Strangely, some people prefer <u>not</u> to be blessed financially. Their thinking is, *"That way you won't be so disappointed when it all goes away!"*

Poverty involves fear of spending: Poverty thinking tells you, *"If you spend money, you will run out and not have enough."*

Here are some ways the fear of spending money manifests:

- Fear of spending money on non-essentials: We say, *"We can live without that."* You could, but sometimes life would be much better if you didn't!
- Constantly searching for the cheapest alternative, even if it's uncomfortable.
- Obsession with getting "deals" and free entry.
- Buying the cheapest alternative, thinking that this will save you money: We think we'll still have some left because we bought it so cheaply. Here is a great saying: **There is no greater delusion than that cheapness is economy.** It's possible we may wind up spending <u>more</u> in the long run – because we've "saved money." If you have to buy the same item five times because it falls apart, or breaks; *you haven't actually saved any money!*
- Losing work because your tools or vehicles break down: Either you spend time chasing repairs, or you are simply unable to get to work.

Poverty involves fear of giving to God: People with poverty mindsets can struggle with the concept of tithing, which is giving God the first 10% of our income. ***Malachi 3:8-10 NCV*** *[8]"Should a person rob God? But you are robbing me. "You ask, 'How have we robbed you?' "You have robbed me in your offerings and the tenth of your crops. [9]So a curse is on you, because the whole nation has robbed me. [10]Bring to the storehouse a full tenth of what you earn so there will be food in my house. Test me in this,"* says the Lord All-Powerful. *"I will open the windows of heaven for you and pour out all the blessings you need.* People with poverty mindsets struggle when God prompts them to give offerings in obedience to Him. Their response when God speaks what He wants them to give is, *"Get behind me, Satan!" "Why would I give money away when I already don't have enough? That doesn't make sense!"*

Poverty involves the fear that opportunities are limited: People with a poverty mindset think that there's only so much money, and only so many opportunities. This limits them from pursuing prosperity and the blessing of God. Their mentality is, *"If I pursue prosperity and blessing, it won't work; because there won't be enough for me."* Some African cultures believe in the idea of **limited good**; *"Life is like a pie, and there's only so many slices available."* If we think this way it produces unhealthy reactions:

- There's probably no point in trying: *Because God will run out of blessing before it gets to me!*
- We can resent those who are blessed: *They just took some of your chances at being blessed!*

Ultimately, the fear of poverty is actually your opinion of GOD: Born-again believers are children of God and therefore are part of God's family; they have a personal relationship with Almighty God! *1 John 3:1 Behold what manner of love the Father has bestowed on us, that we should be called children of God!* When we fear risk, we fear failure, we fear spending, or fear giving: Ultimately, it's because we have a faulty view of God! *Matthew 25:24-25 NCV ²⁴"Then the servant who had been given one bag of gold came to the master and said, 'Master, I knew that you were a hard man. You harvest things you did not plant. You gather crops where you did not sow any seed. ²⁵So I was afraid and went and hid your money in the ground. Here is your bag of gold.'*

Delivered From a Family Curse - *Paul and Kristina Castanon*

My wife and I were saved in 1993. Even though we were faithful in our tithes and pledges, and we gave offerings, we always had financial issues. We couldn't pay our bills on time, couldn't pay off any of vehicles, and couldn't save any money. God did help us in small measures of blessing, but nothing ever lasted. I always felt something wasn't right, but I couldn't put my finger on it.

In 2017, my wife and I were sent to pioneer a church in Guadalupe, Arizona. I learned that I have distant relatives in Guadalupe. One of those relatives was my great-aunt, whom I later learned was a high-ranking curandera (witch doctor). God began to reveal to me that my life was being affected by generational curses of witchcraft, even though I was a Christian. I started praying against longstanding bondages and strongholds through fasting.

God began to move: Six months later, at 47, I was finally able to pay off my first vehicle loan. The curse had been broken! Then in 2019, we needed to buy a handicap van because we have a disabled son in a wheelchair. Our credit score was barely good enough, and all we had for a down payment was $1000. Handicap vans are very expensive. We needed at least $10,000 for a down payment. AMS vans in Phoenix, Arizona, gave us phone numbers of non-profits that might help us out with the down payment. But no one was able to help. The sales lady (Stacey) from AMS vans called me and asked if I had called one particular non-profit. I said yes, but they said they didn't have any funds until 2020. She gave me the executive director's number and said, *"She wants you to call her personally."* I had no idea who this lady was. Still, when I called, she told me that her non-profit just received a donated 2012 Toyota Sienna, a fully loaded handicap van. She wanted to give it to us. It was as if God's blessing was chasing us. On December 30, 2019, we were given this van free of charge. Glory to God!

In 2021, I was announced to be an Evangelist out of the Tempe, Arizona congregation. I wanted my wife and kids to have a reliable van while I was out of town. So, we traded the free handicap van for a brand-new 2021 Honda Odyssey, fully loaded, worth $70,000! In the four years since we bought the new van, we haven't missed a payment, and we haven't been late on any payments! The curse is broken!

DELIVERED FROM A FAMILY CURSE

This testimony is not only about a free van; it's about going from being cursed to blessed. God revealed to me that, because we were willing to obey the call to pioneer, God placed us in the town that held dark secrets of witchcraft that have affected my family and me for four generations. God has broken the longstanding curse of poverty, and we've entered a new dimension of Deuteronomy 28 blessings!

Getting a Breakthrough - *Jamie and Jackie Senn*

Pastor Joe Campbell was preaching at the Midwest Bible Conference and taking an offering. He said someone here has $10,000 you can give tonight. When he said $10,000 it felt like God put his finger in my chest and said, *"This is you."* I was very nervous about it because it was the first time we got ahead in our finances because of a tax return.

At that point, I had been saved for 24 years. God had always taken good care of us, but we never really had much of a savings. We went paycheck to paycheck. Having this money in my account felt like such a wonderful blessing, and I was very nervous to give it, so I aske my wife what she thought. She said, *"We could be raptured tomorrow. Let's just give it."* That is not what I wanted to hear. I wrote the check and handed it in. After I handed it in, I remembered several bills that I was supposed to pay off, and I had completely forgotten about them until

46

after I wrote the check. I was mad and wondered what the heck I was thinking. For the next month, I was very miserable and grumpy.

One afternoon, I was taking a nap, and I had a dream that God spoke to me and said he was going to give me 20 times what I gave. I woke up and realized it was only a dream, but it seemed so real. I owed my dad $20,000, so I called him up the day I had the dream to tell him he would have to wait one more year before I started paying him back. **Miracle number one:** My dad said, *"Don't worry about it."* He had given money to my siblings, and I had never received any money up to that point, so he said it was now a gift.

Miracle number two: The company I worked for provided housing for us. It was a small, cramped trailer. We found it hard to live there with three boys and my wife and me because of the size. The CEO of our company asked anyone was considering leaving the company would share their concerns so they could rectify the situation. I said that my living situation was a too small and wasn't sure how much longer we could live in the trailer. He said, "Find another house, and we will buy it for you." He gave us permission to design our own house the way we wanted and buy it from whoever we wanted. What a blessing! We ordered a custom house exactly as we wanted it. The house and everything that went with it were approximately $150,000, so now we had reached $170,000 in blessings.

There were many other miracles of money that amounted to more than $30,000, which would make it 20 times the amount I gave. The windows of heaven truly opened ever since I gave that money. I cannot believe the financial blessings. I now own rental properties with plenty of money in the bank. I was able to give around $30,000 in tithes and offerings this year alone. We are now pioneering our first church, and even with this, God has blessed our church with plenty of resources and money. The curse has definitely been broken, and God has been so good to us. I thank Jesus for all He has done. And I thank our fellowship for challenging us to believe God!

Guided Into Prosperity - *Alvin and Bethany Malan*

In 2020, I became unemployed and was praying for a new business opportunity while taking on part-time work with Amazon and Uber to get by and stay out of debt. While pioneering a church in San Diego for four years, my wife and I felt that God was calling us to pioneer again elsewhere, so, we made ourselves available in obedience. So, at the 2022 Bible conference in Tempe, Arizona, we answered the call to pioneer a new church in Frisco, Texas. As we handed over our church to a new couple and prepared for the move, we thought the best thing to do was to sell our home in San Diego, purchase a new home in Texas, and find a full-time job there. But God had other plans.

Before we listed the property for sale, we put out a fleece, setting a price in mind that, if God wanted us to sell our home, we would get that number, confirming God's hand in the sale. We listed our house for sale, and the real estate agent who had sold a few homes on our street told us to set the sale price very low to spark a bidding war. We thought that was a great idea.

Right away, we received an offer for the listing price. We knew this was not going to be the price we would sell for; however, our agent unexpectedly said this was the best price we would get and to accept the listed offer because the market changed within a week. We declined the offer, and a few days later, we received another offer, for about $200,000 more than the listed price. But, it was just short of the number we had put before God. So again we declined, believing God would give us clear direction.

At this point, the agent was anxious for us to sell the home so they would get a handsome commission. But one night, a few days later, I had a dream that I would rent the house as a short-term rental. After praying and talking it over with my wife, we decided to delist the home. Instead of taking most of our belongings to Texas, we decided to leave them in the house so that it can be furnished for rentals.

Within 2 weeks, we listed the home as a short-term rental. On the day we listed, we began receiving numerous reservations. Three years later, this has become the primary source of income, blessing my family and me, as well as our new church, which we are pioneering. We now own three properties that we rent short-term, manage 10 others, and do so all remotely from Texas.

We went from not knowing how I would provide or make a living to operating close to a seven-figure business in just 3 years. In obedience, we stepped out into the unknown to start a new church, not knowing exactly how things would work out financially, and God has provided in ways better than we could have imagined possible. The Frisco, TX church has been instrumental in bringing clarity and redemption to the confused and brokenhearted of this city, and we are so profoundly grateful to be in the will of God, wherever He leads.

Chapter 5: Changing Poverty Mindsets Part 3

Anyone who has ever struggled with poverty
knows how extremely expensive it is to be poor.
James Baldwin

Anglicare Australia is the charitable wing of the Anglican church in Australia. In their report Poverty Premium, they documented the high cost of poverty in Australia and found that low-income households routinely pay more for basic essentials because they can't afford to:

- Buy in bulk (which reduces per-unit cost).
- Pay annual bills all at once (so they might miss out on discounts).
- Use more efficient, newer appliances or vehicles (because of upfront cost), meaning they spend more on energy or fuel over time.

Anglicare calls these "penalties" that force low-income people into a poverty premium — paying more for the same things others pay less for.

In this chapter, we will finish looking at unhealthy poverty mindsets.

Accepting Poverty

Christians who are living in poverty accept poverty as being normal and accept it as their portion in life. Let's look at some ways we can accept poverty:

Accepting the lack of abundance: Poverty can be an experience we are going through for a time. But it becomes a <u>spirit</u> meaning "something that supernaturally dominates you" when we <u>accept</u> poverty and financial lack as a normal state of life. How does this manifest?

A poverty mentality lives in denial: *Those living in poverty often comfort themselves with excuses for their poverty.* We may tell ourselves excuses such as:

Everyone has debts: *So why worry about being in debt?* That is actually not true. People who understand money and break the curse of poverty do all they can to get out of debt.

Other people are experiencing the same thing: *We always point to people doing as badly as us, or even worse, to make ourselves feel better about how we're doing.* This is like an alcoholic pointing to another alcoholic who is doing worse to make themselves feel better about their addiction.

That's just the way it is here: We can blame our poverty on the circumstances that surround us. We can point to economic factors, inflation, lack of education or opportunities, or anything else to explain why we are in our current financial situation, and why we can't do anything to change it.

A poverty spirit rejects the idea of abundance:
2 Kings 7:2 TLB The officer assisting the king said to the man of God, "That couldn't happen even if the Lord opened the windows of heaven!" But Elisha replied, "You will see it happen with your own eyes, but you won't be able to eat any of it!" The officer heard Elisha declare that God would totally turn their situation around, and he immediately rejected that as even a remote possibility. He

doesn't even bother to ask how it could possibly happen; he instinctively and immediately rejects the promise of a miracle.

I read a testimony of a man who used to live in poverty. He said, *"Whenever anyone told me I could prosper and enjoy the abundance of all things, I rejected those thoughts the moment they hit my mind, and as a result, I lived in poverty."*

Our rejection of the idea of abundance is often self-protective: We don't like the possibility of failure because that would be embarrassing to us. We think, *"If other people know I am believing for a breakthrough and believing for abundance, and then it doesn't work and I don't get a breakthrough, I would be embarrassed. So it would be safer for my ego to reject the possibility of a financial breakthrough."*

We don't like the possibility of failure because that would be disappointing to us. We hate the feeling of disappointment. In the past, our hopes rose for a while, but then came crashing down when it didn't work out. We hated having our hopes deflated. So, strangely, **some people feel it's safer to stay with poverty!**

In Matthew chapter 9, two blind men asked Jesus to heal their blind eyes. Jesus asked them a question: ***Matthew 9:28 NKJV*** *And when He had come into the house, the blind men came to Him. And Jesus said to them, "Do you believe that I am able to do this?" They said to Him, "Yes, Lord."* Then Jesus told them (and us) a fundamental principle if we want to change our financial situation for the better: ***Matthew 9:29 NKJV*** *Then He touched their eyes, saying, "According to your faith let it be to you."* "According to" means "in line with" or "to the measure of" your faith. In other words, you will live at the level of your faith. I sometimes say, *"You'll have in life what you can live with! You'll have in life what you will settle for!"* This principle is true both positively and negatively. In the Bible, we can see the contrast between those who settle for defeat and those who believe for victory.

Saul and the army were tormented and intimidated by Goliath for 40 days: Nothing changed, and no victory was being won. *1 Samuel 17:11 NKJV When Saul and all Israel heard these words of the Philistine, they were dismayed and greatly afraid.* But when David saw the same situation, he refused to accept that the giant should determine his life. He believed that God was bigger than the giant! *1 Samuel 17:36-37 NKJV 36Your servant has killed both lion and bear; and this uncircumcised Philistine will be like one of them, seeing he has defied the armies of the living God."* *37Moreover David said, "The Lord, who delivered me from the paw of the lion and from the paw of the bear, He will deliver me from the hand of this Philistine." And Saul said to David, "Go, and the Lord be with you!"* Because David chose to believe God, he won a supernatural victory. This principle is true in our lives: we will either accept poverty or believe God for the prosperity He has promised.

Words Of Poverty

Our lives are affected by our words: The Bible teaches us that words <u>create</u> things.

Hebrews 11:3 NKJV By faith we understand that the worlds were <u>framed</u> by the word of God, so that the things which are seen were not made of things which are visible. The word "framed" means 'fitted': The parameters of creation were set by words. What creation became, or the limits of creation were determined by the word of God.

In some ways, <u>our</u> words can determine the limits of our lives (in line with God's word). This spiritual principle can be positive or negative. ***Proverbs 18:21 NKJV*** *Death and life are in the power of the tongue, And those who love it will eat its fruit.* This verse shows us the power and potential of the words we speak:

- You are eating <u>today</u> the fruit of what your past words have produced in your life.
- You will eat<u> tomorrow</u>, or in the future, the fruit of what your words <u>today</u> produce in your life.

The Language of Poverty

People struggling with poverty speak the language of poverty.

People living in poverty create negative spiritual forces by their words: ***They speak poverty!*** Ruby Payne states in her book 'A Framework for Understanding Poverty' – *You have to change your mindsets. You have to change your language, because poverty has a language.*

People living in poverty make statements such as:

- *It never works for me. I can never get ahead. The game is rigged. I'm just unlucky.*
- *I don't have the skills, the education, the opportunities. All my family seems to stay poor.*

Our words have the power to block the blessings God wants to give us. ***Numbers 14:28 NKJV*** *Say to them, 'As I live,' says the Lord, 'just as you have spoken in My hearing, so I will do to you':*
Psalm 78:41 NKJV *Yes, again and again they tempted God, And limited the Holy One of Israel.*

The Law of Attraction: Poverty involves a <u>supernatural</u> dimension! *Why do people in poverty often continue in poverty year after year?* The reason is more than math, more than education, more than opportunities; Poverty is <u>supernatural</u>!

There is a principle in life called the law of attraction. The principle simply stated says, *"like attracts like."* If you have ever played with magnets, you know that a magnet made of metal doesn't attract wood, rubber, or plastic; It attracts <u>metal</u>. *Like attracts like!*

This is true in life in the area of money and poverty because of the power of faith and unbelief. The biblical principle of like attracts like can be summed up as: **Whatever you <u>expect</u>, you attract.** *John 5:6-7 NCV* ⁶*When Jesus saw the man and knew that he had been sick for such a long time, Jesus asked him, "Do you want to be well?"* ⁷*The sick man answered, "Sir, there is no one to help me get into the pool when the water starts moving. While I am coming to the water, someone else always gets in before me."* The man who was sick said, *"I knew it! That always happens to me! Just what I expected."*

The principle of attraction is true in the area of money and poverty. Those who <u>think</u> poverty, <u>expect</u> poverty, and <u>talk</u> poverty trigger negative spiritual forces in their life. These spiritual forces open the door and attract negative forces that affect our money. *Matthew 9:29 NKJV Then touched he their eyes, saying, <u>According to your faith</u> be it unto you.* According to your faith...meaning 'in line with' your faith: *This is both positive and negative*

- If you believe for blessing, help, provision, miracles, and abundance, that's what comes to you!

- If you believe for poverty, reversal, and struggle – that's what comes to you!

This is more than mathematical data; it is a supernatural dimension. For people who are cursed, the door of their life is open due to sin and disobedience. This can be their own sin and disobedience, or that of their ancestors.

This is also because of our unbelief. *Galatians 6:7 NIV Do not be deceived: God cannot be mocked. A man reaps what he sows.* If you sow thoughts, expectations, and words of poverty, THAT'S what you will reap! Someone said, *"No one ever went to the poorhouse who did not attract the poorhouse by a poorhouse mental attitude."*

So, if these things are true: **We need to deal with our mindsets and words!** If we repent of our false mindsets of poverty and the words we have spoken against our prosperity, God is merciful and will help us. Then we can believe God and speak words of faith and provision. This will cause the principle of attraction to be turned around for our benefit and blessing.

Changing The Course of His Life - *Paulus and Selfiela Andrade*
Pastor Chris Plummer tells of a convert in Dili, Timor Leste, whom God delivered from poverty. Paulus was a young convert in Dili, Timor-Leste, when we arrived as missionaries. He was earning no money at all. He was living with some friends from church who were also in deep poverty, drinking water from a well outside, and living on rice that a friend bought for their house each month. He said at the time, *"Sometimes we can get some oil or some salt to have with our rice, then we are excited to eat!"*

A short time later, I taught on budgeting, and Paulus approached me to say God had stirred him to tithe, so he needed to get a job so he could tithe! I later found out that he borrowed $50 USD from another disciple, bought some produce, and made bean soup that he sold. It became a successful small business. He told his landlord his business was blessed because he honored God. The national average income was $150 USD a month. Within less than a year, Paulus was employing 7 workers, paying them about $240 USD a month, and taking home around $ 1000 USD a month!

Paulus is now a pastor.

Transformed in Life and Finances - *Oliver and Brenda Brown*

I was born into complete poverty in Honduras. After coming to the US at age 4, my upbringing was traumatic and filled with abuse. At a young age, I turned to gangs and crime. I was radically saved at age 19 and surrendered my life to Jesus. I immediately got a job at a fast-food restaurant to make honest money. I heard preaching about tithing and giving, and began obeying God with my small salary. As a new believer, I was barely getting by in life, living from paycheck to paycheck. Yet, I was excited to be saved and was faithfully giving. A man offered me a job as a construction laborer. It was the worst job I ever had. But I learned to read blueprints, and by age 25, I got my Contractor's License.

I married and had children, and financially, things were always tight. But we remained faithful to give. As the years went by, I asked God, *"Why is everything tight? Why can't I prosper"?* God showed me that even though I was faithful in giving, I lacked discipline and abilities in my life that kept me in the poverty mindset I grew up in. I had to repent and change my whole thought process. He showed me I had to be a good steward with the little He was giving me to be able to receive more.

I started a construction business, and I was determined to build it on Godly principles. God began to give me favor, and I began to land contracts. I went from 3 employees to about 40 in two months. For the next year and a half, I prospered tremendously. Still, I began to struggle in my walk with God because I became consumed with business and money. I was still faithful in tithing and giving, but I had no idea what I was doing in business or how to handle the money that came with it. Money was becoming a stumbling block.

In 2020, a contractor I was working for failed to pay me a large sum of money. That put me in a horrible situation to the point where I was about to go bankrupt. A contractor I was working for had to pay to finish a house I started because I didn't have the money. It cost him $32,000. But God helped me by giving me some small jobs, and I was able to repay the money within 3 months. It turned out to be a blessing because it showed others that I was willing to do what was right, no matter the cost. The same contractor now uses me for 75% of his jobs. For the past 5 years, I have built over 25 high-end custom homes and become a well-known contractor in the area because of my integrity in business.

Besides the business side of things, I got my heart right and learned how to grow my financial ability. God gave me the understanding that this money does not belong to me; it belongs to Him. With this understanding, I began to take money seriously; money has become spiritual to me. I went from making $75,000 a year to about $2.5 million a year. My purpose and goal are to be a blessing to my Pastor, Church, and Fellowship. God has blessed me so I can bring that river of currency flowing into His Kingdom. I remind myself that this was a work of God and it was given to me with one purpose, to promote the Gospel of Jesus Christ.

Tithing Miracle - *Joe Martin*
I had been around our fellowship for three years. Still, I did not go to church or give my life to GOD until I ended up in the hospital on December 22, 2022, for a ruptured aorta. The doctors could not explain how I survived. It was there in the hospital that a pastor from the fellowship came to pray for me and over me, and it was then that I decided to give my life to GOD. I was released on January 4, 2023, and the following Sunday, I went to my first service. It was there when I first heard about tithing and trusting GOD in your finances. Although reluctant, my wife and I decided to start tithing. In April of 2023, I received a medical bill for $309,281.25, with the first payment of $35,000 due by April 25, 2023. At that point, my wife and I were in disbelief because there was no way we could pay this amount. After every reason we could come up with to not pay, we finally decided to turn to GOD in prayer and trust. The next morning, we called customer service to work out a payment plan we could afford. Upon explaining the situation to the representative, she asked for my

account number. Then she explained to me that my account had a zero balance and that an anonymous donor had paid the full amount! We started to give all thanks and glory to GOD right there in our kitchen. My wife and I are fully involved in our local church, serving God and thanking Him for His goodness!

Chapter 6: Wrong Financial Decisions Part 1

Debts are like children – begotten with pleasure, but brought forth with pain.
Jean–Baptiste Poquelin Moliere

The debt–habit is the twin brother of poverty.
Theodore Munger

In a tragic incident in Gujarat, India, three members of a family reportedly died by suicide due to a heavy burden of debt and pressure from creditors. A suicide note mentioned their financial distress and persistent harassment by moneylenders.

Financial debt has been shown to increase the risk of anxiety, depression, and suicidal thoughts. Stress from financial burdens can also worsen existing mental health conditions. Financial hardship makes suicide more likely because worrying about money can cause extreme levels of stress as well as other types of emotional distress. Experiencing a financial crisis, low socioeconomic status, or the strain of bills you can't pay may also negatively impact a person's self-worth or feelings of helplessness, which can make suicide more likely.

Financial Weeding

If we wish to have good things grow, we must first understand that you can't plant good seed in weed-filled ground. The weeds will prevent the good seed from producing anything good, so we must remove the weeds before we can have a good harvest.

This is true when considering the issue of prosperity: If we are making wrong financial decisions that prevent us from prospering, we must first do some financial weeding to prepare the ground of our lives for prosperity.

In this chapter, we will consider one of the most significant obstacles to prosperity: *Personal debt.*

Decisions and Debt

It's important to understand that poverty is not just having insufficient money: insufficiency is often the result of poor decisions. *(Please note: I am not speaking of those plunged into poverty through a crisis, such as a sickness that creates medical debt, an accident that makes someone unable to work, or the death of a spouse or parent, etc.)* If we want to enter prosperity, we need to look at the roots of wrong financial decisions.

Poverty involves the inability to make right decisions. Often, people living in poverty will make foolish financial decisions.

They will make foolish purchases. *If you are already struggling to pay the rent, it is not a good time to buy new shoes, a purse, a cell phone, a computer, a car, or a boat!* Sometimes, as soon as they are blessed with some money or get slightly ahead financially, they do something financially foolish. People sabotage their own finances in various ways:

They lose their money in scams in an effort to gain big money quickly. If you get an email from someone in Africa needing to put $10 million into your account, and all they need is your account details – DON'T DO IT! It is a scam!

They quit jobs because they are bored or in conflict, without having another job to go to first.
A spirit of poverty works within a person, clouding judgment and making it difficult to make the right decisions. It is a spiritual force that seeks to entrap those not yet in poverty, and

to keep people from making good decisions – so they will stay poor!

Poverty and prosperity are <u>not</u> just about how much money you make. Some people think simplistically, *"If I made more money, I wouldn't be poor."* But the truth is that *you can make a lot of money & still be cursed!* I have several articles about people who make good incomes yet struggle to make ends meet. In one article, a couple who make a combined income of $212,000 a year are now struggling to pay their bills after buying their very large "dream home." In another article, another couple making $20,000 a month ($240,000 a year) say they are still struggling to make ends meet, because as their incomes rose, they spent more. They say the problem is that *"now our bills are larger than when we made less money."* The Federal Reserve Bank of Philadelphia surveyed those who make $100,000 or more a year. More than 1/3 of these earners say, *"they are concerned about making ends meet in the next six months."*

Those who believe in socialism think the answer to poverty is income redistribution. They say, *"If we took money away from the rich and gave it to the poor, there would be no poverty!"* But this is incorrect, because it fails to consider the spiritual dimensions of poverty. There have been many cases where relatively large sums of money were handed out to people living in areas of great poverty. However, it was later discovered that this didn't lift people out of poverty because they didn't change their thinking patterns and poor spending decisions. In a short amount of time, all the money was gone.

Sadly, unless heart attitudes and destructive thinking patterns change, even if you took all the wealth from the rich and handed it to the poor, it wouldn't be long before the poor were poor again and the rich were wealthy again.

Poverty continues in those who don't understand how money works. The Bible says that ignorance brings destruction. *Hosea 4:6 My people are destroyed for lack of knowledge:*

That principle is also true in money. Failing to understand how money works will hurt you! A banker once said:

People who don't understand interest – pay it; People who do understand it – earn it.

Some of the greatest mistakes of poverty concern **debt**. *Definition: Any money owed to anyone for anything.* Debt is **borrowing money to purchase something.** The main reason we are borrowing money is that we don't have it!

Sources of borrowing: People borrow from all kinds of sources.
- Some pay for purchases with credit cards.
- Some take loans from banks.
- Some arrange a vehicle loan through an auto dealer.
- Some resort to high-interest title loans *(using their vehicle as collateral).*
- Some take out payday loans (short-term, high-cost loans that allow lenders to access your bank account for the full amount).
- Some borrow money from friends, family, or employers.
- In extreme cases, some borrow money from loan sharks (criminals).

Reasons for borrowing: People borrow money for a variety of reasons:

Borrowing for life's necessities: Sometimes people borrow (or use a credit card) to pay for essentials they cannot live without. This includes food, transportation, clothing, and medical costs, among other expenses. Borrowing for life's necessities is not God's will: *God wants you to prosper so you can pay for the needs of life! Matthew 6:31-32 31"Therefore do not worry, saying, 'What shall we eat?' or 'What shall we drink?' or 'What shall we* *wear?'* *32For after all these things the Gentiles seek. For your heavenly Father knows that you need all these things.*

Borrowing for things that have no further usefulness: Some of the things we borrow to obtain are only good for that moment. Suppose you borrow to dine out at a restaurant – the good meal is gone the moment you finish eating (however, you may be able to find it later; on your waistline). Borrowing for experiences or for vacations does us no good afterwards – except for memories.

Borrowing for things that have minimal usefulness: People choose to borrow or charge on credit cards to buy lots of Christmas gifts. Parents who do this need to realize they are borrowing to buy things that will break, get lost, or be ignored through boredom – in a matter of days! Long after any joy that came through borrowing for a Christmas experience, the bills will still need to be paid.

Borrowing for things that have a limited life span: Many of the things we choose to buy are designed to not last. We can borrow to buy new clothes that will wear out or go out of fashion quickly. Electronics such as cell phones and computers are soon outdated and discarded. Even vehicles that have greater usefulness will wear out–sometimes before we finish paying for them.

The Cost of Debt

People enjoy buying on credit because credit enables us to live beyond our income or savings. The problem is that many people do not understand the true cost of credit. The definition of credit: *Someone loans you money, but it has to be paid back with interest.* It's estimated that 43% of all American families spend more than they earn every year! Most people think that being able to charge or borrow is very helpful. We can give reasons why we view credit favorably, such as:

It's so convenient: The advertising slogan, originally created by the Franklin National Bank in 1951 to promote the world's first credit card, has made its way into people's normal thinking; *Just charge it!*

It got us out of a financial crisis: *We needed tires, school clothes for the kids, car repairs, but didn't have the money – but we were able to get them anyway.*

We were able to get what we wanted without waiting: *This is the greatest reason people like credit; I wanted it, but didn't have the money, and I didn't want to wait to get it – so I charged it!*

But a most basic understanding of money is: **Debt is not your <u>friend</u> – it is your <u>enemy</u>**! I have to pause here. Anytime I speak about the true costs and dangers of debt, I get people saying, *"But I'm making money through debt, so debt is good!"* I am not speaking of **money-generating debt**: it is possible to buy property on credit and rent it out. (This would be things like a house, duplex, triplex, apartment complex, etc.). In that case, your debt generates income from rentals. Hopefully, the income from the rentals pays the debt, and the asset increases in value over time. If this is done correctly, the income should exceed the payment.

I also must clarify that I am not speaking of an affordable mortgage or home loan. You need to live somewhere, so if you can buy a house and make a payment that is close to what you would pay in rent, I don't think that is bad–that is helpful. But the key to whether it is wise or foolish depends on exercising wisdom (do the math) and practice self-restraint when purchasing a home. Earlier in this chapter, I spoke of a couple who are under financial pressure because they bought their "dream home" and are now struggling financially. Apparently, they spent more for the house than they could afford.

The Curse of Debt

The Bible speaks of debt as a <u>curse</u>: *Something that brings trouble or evil on you.* **Deuteronomy 28:44-45 NCV** 44*Foreigners will lend money to you, but you will not be able to lend to them. They will be like the head, and you will be like the tail.* 45*All these curses will come upon you. They will chase you and catch you and destroy you, because you did not obey the Lord your God and keep the commands and laws he gave you.* The Bible speaks of debt in this verse as being a curse connected to your enemies! The enemy of your soul loves it when Christians go into debt, because he understands how debt affects people's lives negatively. So, let's look at the true cost of debt, and why it becomes a curse:

Debt lesson #1: Debt is expensive! One of the most significant problems with people in debt is that they have never done the math and calculated the true cost of borrowing with interest. Let's give some examples of the mathematics of debt to help us understand its actual cost.

First, look at an example of simple borrowing, which means borrowing without interest: If you borrow $2000 and repay it at a rate of $40 per-month: *It will take 50 months to repay the loan fully. That means it will take 4 years and 2 months to pay it off.*

If you added 20% simple interest (that means a percentage on the <u>total</u> amount): *20% interest would add = $400 in interest. At $40 per month payment, the extra $400 will take an additional 10 months to repay the total amount. So now it will take 5 years total (60 months) to repay $2400.*

If you use credit cards to make purchases: The average credit card rate is 21.39 % APR (Annual Percentage Rate). With credit cards, you repay the principal (the amount borrowed) plus interest (fees charged for loaning you money). But you actually pay <u>compound</u> interest: *That means you pay the cost of the purchase + interest + interest on the interest: It <u>multiplies</u> every month!*

If you charge $2000 @ 20% APR (for instance – to buy a new couch): If you add no other debt – and make the minimum payment of $40 per month; It will take you **9** years to pay off completely. You will pay **$4,336.04** by the end. **Over twice the original cost!**

Let's compare those different scenarios side-by-side:

Initial Amount	Interest Rate	Monthly Payment	Time to Pay Off	Total Paid
$2,000	0 (*Simple Debt*)	$40	4yrs, 2mo	$2,000
$2,000	20% (*Simple Interest*)	$40	5 yrs	$2,400
$2,000	20% (*Comp. Interest*)	$40	9 yrs	$4,336

But debt is a <u>further</u> trap: That couch will wear out long before 31 years, and you will need another one! So you're likely to make a further charge to buy a new couch before the old one is even paid off!

APR (Annual Percentage Rate) depends on your <u>credit score</u>: A credit score is how likely you are to repay; The lower the credit score, the higher the interest rate. So look at how a higher interest rate affects your payments:

If you now charge $2000 @ 25% interest (instead of 20%): If you add no other debt, and make the minimum payment per month; It will take over **40** years to repay. You will now pay

$19,597 by the end. **Almost <u>10</u> times the original cost!** So you see: **Debt is not worth it!!!**

The worst kind of debt is anything like Payday loans: The interest rate is 391% APR – <u>IF</u> you pay it back in 2 weeks! Another terrible option is a Title loan (using your vehicle as collateral): The APR is 300%

Debt lesson #2: Debt doesn't solve your problems: People who get into debt often think, *"I just need a loan – I just need to use a credit card to meet this need. The loan will fix my problem!!*
- But if there is a <u>curse</u> at work: *A loan will never solve your financial problems.*
- If you don't understand how money works: *You will wind up getting into more debt.*
- If it's heart issues or emotional issues that are pushing you into debt: *Then no amount of debt is enough!*

Debt lesson #3: Debt changes your life: Debt is an <u>obligation</u>. *You are legally bound to do something.*
Proverbs 22:7 NCV *The rich rule over the poor, and borrowers are* <u>servants</u> *to lenders. (The word servants is literally* <u>slaves</u>*!)* What will you do with your paycheck this week? *Whatever your debt says!*

Debt demands service: *It controls your decisions!* One man said, *"Many raise their lifestyle by using debt, only to discover that the burden of debt controls their lifestyle."*
Debt limits your choices:
- I would like to have this. I would like to live there - but I can't! Debt determines these choices.
- I would like to give to God in offerings, at conferences, or for world evangelism - but I can't! I have to pay my debts.

- I would like to help people with their financial needs: But I can't! I have to pay my debts.
- I would like to respond to the call to be a Pastor, or go overseas as a missionary: But I can't afford to be in the ministry.

People who are currently pastoring but are in debt have to work so much it winds up hurting the ministry and their calling.

Matthew 22:14 *For many are called, but few are chosen.*

Debt can affect your salvation: Some people are forced to make financial decisions that hurt their salvation. This can come through their jobs: *They may feel they need to take a higher-paying job that makes them miss church. They may have to work overtime to help pay their debt. Some wind up working second or third jobs to try to repay their debts.*

Debt lesson #4: Debt makes you miserable. The Bible shows that money affects our emotions! *2 Kings 4:1 NCV The wife of a man from the company of the prophets cried out to Elisha, "Your servant my husband is dead, and you know that he revered the Lord. But now his creditor is coming to take my two boys as his slaves."*

Debt causes stress. Debt causes lack of sleep. Debt can produce sickness: Stress and worry dump unhealthy chemicals into your blood which can cause sickness. In a 2014 study paper for the National Library of Medicine titled: "The High Price of Debt: Household Financial Debt and Its Impact on Mental and Physical Health" found that high relative debt (debt vs. assets) is correlated with higher perceived stress, more depression, worse self-reported health, and higher diastolic blood pressure. The authors argue that the feeling of being indebted may be especially important for cardiovascular health.

Money affects our relationships: *Money is often the #1 source of conflict in marriage, and the leading cause of divorce!* The stress of finances causes us to be irritable, which causes fights! Parents under the stress from debt can end up taking it out on our children.

Debt lesson #5: Debt blocks the blessing of God. If our debt is based on violating God's wisdom in the Bible or is based on wrong heart issues inside of us: *God is not pleased!* ***Matthew 6:24*** *"No one can serve two masters. Either he will hate the one and love the other, or he will be devoted to the one and despise the other. You cannot serve both God and Money.*

You can't violate spiritual <u>principles</u> and expect spiritual <u>blessings</u>! Many of the parables Jesus told were parables about money. A common theme tells of servants who used their master's money unwisely. In each of the parables, those who used their master's money unwisely either failed to get the blessing the master wanted to give them, or they faced judgment from their master. We need to ensure we fix our <u>heart</u> issues so we can experience God's blessing of prosperity.

Becoming Good Stewards - *Robert and Imelda Diaz*

Here is our testimony about how God transformed our finances when we chose to become good stewards and obey Him when He challenged us to get out of debt, even when our situation seemed overwhelming.

My wife and I were married in March of 2006. Just a few months into our marriage, we realized that we were over $20,000 in debt. I worked a dead-end, low-paying job, and my wife worked for the Government. The weight of this burden created more tension in our marriage. When we married, my wife had a four-year-old girl and was trying to figure out how to be a father and a new husband, and now we were in debt. I told my wife openly that I had no intention of ever paying that debt since most of it was hers, even some from her previous marriage. We really felt trapped and hopeless.

But one Sunday morning, everything changed. During song service, as we sang and lifted our hands to God, God spoke to me clearly. He said, *"You are going to deal with that debt!"* At the time, I wasn't sure if God was dealing with me because I was being a jerk with my wife, or because God didn't like debt. I knew we needed to make a change.

I began to take control of our finances. We created a budget and stopped overspending. My wife and I discussed the importance of spending only on necessities, and she reluctantly agreed to a $20-a-week budget, even though she had a better job than I did. (I'm still embarrassed about the budget I imposed on her till this very day). Things didn't get better; they got worse! Shortly after that, my wife found out she was pregnant, and shortly after, she began feeling sick and had to quit her job. I told her not to worry; I would figure things out. That's when God began to move.

Two things happened almost simultaneously. First, doors began to open for additional income and increased financial resources, something that hadn't been possible before. Second, I reached out to our debtors, and, surprisingly, they were willing to dramatically reduce the total amount owed. By the time my son was born in May 2007, we were completely debt-free. I had also been promoted into a new role that allowed me to earn four times the income my wife and I had made previously combined, and now she could be a stay-at-home mom with our newborn son.

Freedom Changes Marriage - *Doug and Anita Ponder*

I have been in and out of debt for more than 30 years, mostly in. When my wife and I were married, we were debt-free for about a month, and then for the next nine years, we were in debt and would argue about money almost every day! This debt put a major strain on our marriage, so we knew we needed to do something. We struggled to develop and apply a budget. At this point, we were $30,000 in debt, from credit card use, fluctuating income, and just poor management.

Pastor Chris Plummer did a series on financial management. We had the Plummer's over, and they helped to put the budget in place. Pastor prayed for us and broke curses. (We felt something break). We used two quotes from Pastor Plummer to inspire us and keep us on track: "Live in prosperity rather than poverty," and "Be diligent to know the state of your flocks."

God began to give me miracle work, and, at Pastor Plummer's suggestion, we went to a creditor and offered them a payout. We offered less than half of what we owed, and they accepted it. Within 9 months, we had paid off $30,000 in debt. Then, in the next 9 months, we saved $30,000! We used that as a deposit to buy a house!

Some of the benefits of getting out of debt:
- No more arguments about money.
- No more arguments about money!!!
- Ministry opportunities opened up.
- Favor with pastors, people in church, and favor at work.
- New and deeper relationships
- I became a bible study leader, built foundations and then was sent out to preach. All this happened very quickly, but all after getting out of debt.
- People that we normally had limited relations at church became good friends.
- We entered new financial possibilities.
- We began living in prosperity.
- We received a portion of an inheritance. That money went straight onto our home loan.

Unexpected Provision - *Jack and Niccolene Mefford*

In May of 2025, it became clear that I would be leaving my job in June. My boss had been fired a few months earlier, and my position was being eliminated. Although I interviewed for a newly created position in the same organization, I did not get it. My wife and I, along with our five kids, had been out pioneering for seven years at this point. It was a time of financial difficulty. When we left our mother church to pioneer, I had taken a pay cut, and over the past seven years, we had been in the black only rarely each month. We had managed to stay afloat through various means, but it was always a struggle and lingering anxiety. By spring of 2025, we had about $35,000 in credit card debt and a maxed-out home equity loan (second mortgage) of $100,000. I began looking for jobs, but by July, I still hadn't found anything despite completing multiple applications and interviews.

During these months, I spoke frequently with my pastor. During one discussion, among other issues, he felt we needed to pursue a financial breakthrough. He said we needed to command the release of financial provision and referenced a sermon by Pastor Greg Mitchell that he had recently watched online. We prayed together over the phone and claimed God's provision for our family, church, and calling. That Sunday night, our family watched Pastor Greg's sermon on financial breakthrough and prayed.

The following week, we met with a real estate agent about selling our house and possibly relocating back to our mother church. An hour after that meeting, my wife received an email to create a "payment portal." We had no idea what it was referring to. After looking into it, we were shocked to discover that the pharmaceutical company my wife's father had started years ago was being acquired by drug giant Eli Lilly for $1 billion, and that they were paying dividends to all shareholders. My wife's father had passed away nine years earlier, and as part of her inheritance, she had received some of this stock. Until the acquisition, it was worth nothing, and we had practically forgotten we even had it. Two weeks after that email, we received almost $700,000 in dividends from her father's stock, more than enough to pay off all our debts and give me time to continue my job search and find God's direction in this new season of our lives. By September, I was employed full-time, and we are continuing to pastor our pioneer church.

Our Faithful God - *Brandon and Elizabeth Kwesiga*

I got saved at the Potter's House in Wandsworth, England. My upbringing was rough. Crime was normal. I grew up in the kind of South London neighborhood where you bury friends because of postcode wars. By the time I gave my life to Christ, I was a typical young man from my area, stuck in a dead-end job and making choices that were only leading to prison or a coffin.

When I got saved, it took me a while to start giving faithfully. Tithing was a personal battle. But once I surrendered in that area, my finances turned into a stream of miracles. The first one came fast. I was a junior sales consultant, the lowest role in a bathroom company, but they promoted me to branch manager, bypassing multiple positions without me even applying. And because of a computer glitch, I was paid the highest salary for that position, the same as people with 10+ years of experience.

At the same time, I was praying about marriage. Out of nowhere, the bank sent me a repayment of about £2,000. I used that money to buy the engagement ring and cover some wedding costs. After 18 months of marriage, we answered the call to pioneer our first church.

Right then, I was made redundant. I prayed, and felt God tell me not to apply for a job and that He would provide. It made no sense, but I obeyed. Two months went by. Savings were disappearing. I was nervous but still believing. Then the bank contacted me again and said they owed me the amount I would have earned if I had still been employed.

Not long after, I was called in for an interview and offered a job with a company car. Later, I discovered that my former manager knew I would be made redundant and had contacted all her business connections, telling them about me. I had no idea.

During that job, my wife and I were pioneering, and now, with three children, we needed more income. I prayed again. Shortly after, the Managing Director of an IT company, a complete unbeliever, had a vivid dream after meeting me. He said he saw me leading his company and saw a blessing on my life. He offered me double my salary and the job on the spot with no interview.

The next job doubled my salary again. Then I became a leader in the largest company in Europe in my industry. My wife and I were also running a couple of businesses, but they were draining time and pulling us away from ministry. She challenged me to prioritize the kingdom over the comfort those businesses were giving us. We shut them down.

At the end of last year, the market turned, and I lost my job. The same conviction came into my heart again: do not apply for a job and trust God. This time it was harder. I was in my mid-to-late 30s, with four children and heavy financial responsibilities. But I obeyed. The exact month my savings were about to run out, I was offered a Managing Director role overseeing multiple businesses, with the freedom to keep my church first, and a high six-figure salary.

I was saved at 20 years old in Wandsworth, as a single father in debt. Since then, I have pioneered two churches, served my mother church as an assistant pastor, become one of the most recognized figures in my industry, and now lead my second church. By the choices I made pre-salvation, I should be dead or in prison. But God has been faithful every step of the way.

Chapter 7: Wrong Financial Decisions Part 2

Acquiring debt is enjoyable, but retiring it is not.
Ogden Nash

Debt is normal. Be weird.
Dave Ramsey

A man who was over USD $70,000 in debt cried out to God for a miracle and for the wisdom to know how to get out of debt. God did help him get out of debt through several miracles, but I like what he says about the change it has made in his life. He said, *"My trip from financial desperation to God's provision taught me lessons beyond just managing money. The three-year wilderness path from drowning in debt to financial freedom changed our bank accounts and our relationship with God."*

The Roots of Debt

It's essential to understand the <u>root</u> of debt. You must be able to answer this question for yourself: ***How did you get into debt?*** If you don't understand <u>how</u> or <u>why</u> you got into debt, any fix will be temporary! *I read of a couple who were in Credit Card debt USD $40,000. They were able to pay it off, but they are now paying off their second round of $40,000 debt!*

Our problem is <u>not</u> how much money we have or make. **The cure for debt is <u>not</u> more money!** There is an old saying: *More money in, more money out.* You must understand a simple danger of making more money: the more you make, the more debt you qualify for! This is true because credit is based on your income level. So if you earn more income, instead of having two credit cards with a total limit of $2,000, you will now qualify to have 15 credit cards with a combined limit of $40,000! When people start making more money, they are deceived into thinking they can afford a lot more things, and more expensive ones. What's the first thing people do when they land a good-paying job? They buy things! They borrow to buy things! They buy things on credit cards! Debt has roots: that means it is a product of things at work within people.

Root of debt #1: Financial ignorance. (This is what we discussed in the last chapter.) If we don't understand how interest works, we can easily slide into debt. Credit cards use compound interest—so what you owe doesn't just grow, it multiplies.

Root of debt #2: Magical thinking. Some people apparently must believe in a debt fairy with a magic wand, because they think vaguely, *"Somehow we will pay off our debt!"* But they don't actually have a plan to accomplish that goal. *Proverbs 28:19 NIV A hard worker has plenty of food, but a person who chases fantasies ends up in poverty.* I knew a family that was expecting an inheritance, so they went into debt. They said, *"It's ok, we'll pay it off when we get the inheritance from Grandpa!"* But later, someone else in the family got Grandpa to change the will, so they got nothing – but they still had the debt! Anyone who doesn't have an actual plan or strategy to get out of debt usually keeps adding debt. *Galatians 6:7 NLT Don't be misled—you cannot mock the justice of God. You will always harvest what you plant.*

The Heart of Debt

The Bible teaches that debt is a heart issue. It's not just a math issue. It's not just an income or a cost issue. The choices and actions of our lives flow from the <u>heart</u>. ***Proverbs 4:23 NLT*** *Guard your heart above all else, for it determines the course of your life.* This means that whatever is in our hearts determines how we view things and determines our decisions. We must understand that debt is not the problem; it is a <u>symptom</u> of the real problem in our heart. Let's look at some heart issues that affect debt.

The heart of pride: The Bible tells us that our constant battle, and the enemy of believers, is the world. When the Bible speaks of "the world," it is defined as "Society organized without God." The world has to do with the values & priorities of unsaved people: *What is important or valuable to unbelievers.*

1 John 2:15-16 NLT *15Do not love this world nor the things it offers you, for when you love the world, you do not have the love of the Father in you. 16For the world offers only a craving for physical pleasure, a craving for everything we see, and pride in our achievements and possessions. These are not from the Father, but are from this world.* We are constantly exposed to the world's values through advertising and the media. They bring us a constant barrage of images and messages. The continual message of the world is that your worth and your value are dependent on money and possessions: *What we have, what we wear, what we drive, and where we live all determine our worth.* We are told what is cool, what's acceptable, and what's fashionable. The point of advertising is to tell us what we simply must have. Their goal is to stir up a desire inside us so that we eventually conclude, "*I* <u>*need*</u> *that!*"

Because of worldly messages, people buy things, believing they are purchasing worth, status, approval or love. This is why people are obsessed with famous brands. They don't simply want a clothing item that fits well, or a purse or bag that is functional; they want a famous brand clearly emblazoned on it because they want other people to <u>see</u> that they have worth as a human being! The old saying speaks of this tendency:

We buy things we don't need, with money we don't have, to impress people we don't like.

Pastor Adam Porter used to work at a Louis Vuitton store on the island of Guam. He tells of Japanese tourists who used to come and buy many Louis Vuitton items, and how some would start weeping when they realized there was no more room on their credit cards to buy anything else. They weren't buying a purse or wallet; *they were buying self-worth!*

People whom others have rejected in the past are given the message that they have no value or are worth less. Rejected people are especially susceptible to the mistaken tendency of trying to buy inner worth. So, they are tempted to use money as <u>medicine</u>: *Buying things to try to heal a negative emotion inside.* Rejected people sometimes buy things to try and produce a feeling of value. They mistakenly think valuable clothes, shoes, bags, jewelry, or vehicles somehow make them valuable as human beings. The need for inner worth and value is such a desperate need in people that they will overspend and go into <u>debt</u> to try to buy worth and value. **Luke 12:15 NIV** *Then he said to them, "Watch out! Be on your guard against all kinds of greed; a man's life does not consist in the abundance of his possessions."*

The Heart of Greed

The Bible uses the word <u>covetousness</u>, which is often translated as "greed." **Colossians 3:5** *Therefore put to death your members which are on the earth: fornication, uncleanness, passion, evil desire, and covetousness, which is idolatry.* The word covetousness in the original language means: *The desire for more, or literally the <u>lust</u> for more.* The mark of lust and greed is <u>impatience</u>: *We are in a <u>hurry</u> to get more/to get good things.* **Proverbs 28:22 NCV**

Selfish people are in a hurry to get rich and do not realize they soon will be poor. Debt is evidence that we are unwilling to delay gratification until the right time. Wisdom says that if you want something, save up until you can pay for it with cash. That way, there is no ongoing burden. Here are some wise sayings about debt and greed:

> *Debt is funding our <u>greeds</u> now – instead of our <u>needs.</u>*
> *Greed captures the monkey. Debt is evidence of human greed – and it traps just as surely.*
> *The world leads people to believe they are owed or have a right to a lifestyle that is beyond what they can afford.*

If you are a Christian, you must understand that debt is displeasing to God because it is idolatry: *We are worshipping a false god.* **Colossians 3:5** *Therefore put to death your members which are on the earth: fornication, uncleanness, passion, evil desire, and covetousness, <u>which is idolatry</u>.*

Healing Debt

No doubt, people are reading or listening to this book who are in debt right now. You have started to understand the true cost of debt, the reasons you got into debt, and that debt is displeasing to God. So you may be asking, *"How can I get out of debt?"*

Step #1: Getting free from debt begins with repentance. Repentance means you change your mind about debt and see it like God sees it. To God, debt is <u>not</u> an acceptable way to live! Our repentance may involve some specific things we are repenting of, and some things we are deciding to turn away from. We may need to repent of our poor stewardship. We have not planned or managed the money God has given us well. We may need to repent of whatever heart attitudes have fueled our bad financial decisions. Some need to repent of their magical thinking. Others need to repent of pride. Some need to repent of their greed and impatience. I will help you to pray that God will help you get out of debt, but if you don't repent first, prayer won't help fix your debt problem. Even giving offerings won't fix your debt problem without repentance.

Step #2: Stop adding debt! There is a wise old saying we can apply to the problem of debt: *If you find you're in the hole; STOP DIGGING!* This includes <u>all</u> forms of debt, whether credit card debt, bank loans, or loans from friends, family, or employers. If you stop adding debt, it doesn't fix the problem of existing debt, but it keeps the problem from getting worse. That will enable you to start to pay off debt. For many people, I highly recommend plastic surgery (not from a doctor)! If credit cards are what got you into trouble, cut them up and get rid of them! If you want to keep an emergency card, some debt counselors recommend keeping it in the freezer, frozen in a block of ice. The idea is to make it <u>difficult</u> to use – only in an emergency.

Step #3: Begin to pay back the accumulated debt. Snowball the payments, meaning you pay your smallest, highest-interest debt <u>first</u>. This creates a snowball effect: Once that one card is paid off, apply all the money that was going to pay it to another debt. Why pay the smallest one first? Because you will feel the reward and sense of accomplishment. It makes you feel like you are making progress.

Step #4: Believe God for miracles to help you pay off debt. You need to understand that God is willing to help people in debt who want to get out of debt. There are several examples in the Bible of God helping people pay their debts through His miraculous help. In **2 Kings chapter 4**, we read of the widow of a prophet. He died and left her in debt. Why were they in debt? Why didn't her husband plan better? The Bible doesn't tell us. But when she went to Elisha and asked God for help because her sons were going to be taken as debt-slaves, God did a miracle by multiplying the small amount of oil she had in the house so she could sell it and pay the debt off. *2 Kings 4:7 Then she came and told the man of God. And he said, "Go, sell the oil and pay your debt; and you and your sons live on the rest."*

In **Matthew chapter 17,** we see that apparently neither Peter nor Jesus had yet paid the temple tax. Jesus instructs him to take a step of obedience so God can do a financial miracle. **Matthew 17:27 NCV** *But we don't want to upset these tax collectors. So go to the lake and fish. After you catch the first fish, open its mouth and you will find a coin. Take that coin and give it to the tax collectors for you and me."*

Getting out of debt will change your life! You will be able to sleep at night. It will help your marriage. It will bless your family. You will not miss church due to work. You will be able to get involved. You will be able to do the will of God. If all that is true, surely your Father in heaven would love to do a miracle to help you get out of debt.

Deliverance Came Faster Than We Thought
Reuben and Danielle Ricciardi
About a year after being married, I knew I needed help with our finances. If we wanted to do God's will, we needed to get out of debt. We had multiple debts, mostly credit cards or personal loans, totaling approximately $27,000. We met with Pastor Chris and Skye Plummer to sit down and work out a budget. By the end of the calculations, we figured it would take 7 years to be debt-free at the maximum rate of debt repayment we could afford. We prayed and believed God for a financial breakthrough.

We determined we would keep to a strict budget but would not stop tithing or giving where we could. We also budgeted to give in pledges, as well as a freewill offering every week. At that time, I shared our plans with a work colleague. He told me he had about the same amount of debt and was desperate to get out of debt. He told me he was also making budgets and planning.

But God supernaturally blessed us with finances. I got extra side jobs as a Plumber, and supernatural favor with employers. My wife was given an opportunity to work for a short season, and eleven months later, we were just two payments away from being debt-free! At that time, I told my work colleague that I was just two more payments away from paying off the $27,000 debt. He was stunned. I asked him where he was with his own debts, and he told me he was in the same position as before. None of his debt had been paid off, even though he said he was trying.

God supernaturally wiped out our debts in 11 short months, and the next year we went on to serve as Outreach Directors in the Church, and then we were sent out to pastor!

God Speaks His Will - *Pat and Mariah Brick*

My name is Pat Brick. I was an alcoholic from the streets in Brixton, UK. I was sent to Norwich for community service when I was 17. My wife Vicky and I got saved in 1992, when I was 24. The day I got saved, I was delivered from being an alcoholic. I never drank alcohol again. But I was a gambler. I was 15,000 pounds in debt when I got saved. We had the very first Bible Conference in the UK in 1993. During the conference, I gambled badly and lost all the conference hotel money, our rent money; I lost everything. I repented at the conference on Friday night in November 1993. I never went back to gambling, but I still had the debts. A 15,000-pound debt today would be like 40,000 pounds or around $60,000 US dollars. I was still paying this debt till May 1998. They were taking money out of my wages. I was still 14,000 pounds in debt at that time.

God spoke to me to give an offering taken for the church in Sierra Leone. Then, 5 weeks before the May conference, God said, *"Trust me, and step out in faith."* Now, you're not supposed to give while in debt. But I gave over 1000 pounds. When I gave the money to God, then paid the rent and all my bills, then I had 100 pounds left for shopping. We had a newborn son and an 8-year-old daughter at the time. I would put 90 pounds of cash in the offering and keep only 10 pounds for shopping. My Pastor questioned me about the money I was giving. He asked me not to do this. But I told him God spoke to me and said, *"I will pay all your debts off by conference."*

So, I went shopping with the 10 pounds we had left. I brought 60 cans of baked beans (a very cheap brand) and 25 loaves of cheap bread, which you can freeze in the freezer for long life. So basically, we were going to live off beans and toast for the next 2 months. My wife began to cry and asked, *"What have you done?"* I told her, *"I want to be free from this debt."* She said, *"OK. I trust you."* We prayed over the shopping list my wife had written. I wanted to show her my faith that God is a provider.

Then, 1 hour after we prayed, a lady turned up at the door with 30 bags of food! I didn't tell anyone what I had done or how much I had given, as I didn't want people to feel sorry for us. The woman with this food said, *"God told me to bless you and your family with food."* The food was better brands than we would normally buy!

Then my wife noticed we had no nappies (diapers in the USA). I told her we can pray right now for nappies. She was not happy with me. She prayed reluctantly, *"Lord I pray for nappies."* There was a knock at the door. A man dropped off a highchair we lent him a few years ago. He handed us 10 pounds, but I said, *"Sorry, we don't take money."* When he left, my wife was so upset with me! She said, *"That was the nappy money!"* I said, *"No, we need God to provide nappies!"* 10 minutes later, the man came back and handed my wife two bags of nappies. He said God told him to buy us nappies out of that money.

Before the next UK conference, a relative died and left us 20,000 pounds in their will. It was quite a surprise, as he told me specifically that he was not leaving us anything in his will, as he did not agree with me being a Christian. I was able to bring him to Christ 3 months before he died. Somehow, he changed his mind about the will. We didn't know about the will until a solicitor called to tell us he had left us money in it. The 20,000 pounds were wonderful! We gave 20% as tithes and offerings off the top, and then I paid off the debts!

Should I have given while I was in debt? Maybe not, but my crazy faith released a miracle from God. I encourage you, as the scripture says, **Luke 6:38** *Give, and it will be given to you.*

84

God Tells the Truth - *Ed and Socorro Kidwell*

When we were in the Tempe, Arizona, congregation, we were in a lot of debt. We wanted to become Pastors, but our debt was making that impossible. We were challenged to honor God in tithing and giving offerings. At times, we chose to tithe instead of buying groceries. God gave us some miracles of provision in groceries and food.

During a time of fasting and prayer at the beginning of the year, God spoke to me and said, *"You will be out of debt this year."* I was afraid to tell my wife what God said. God spoke to me again as I was driving home from prayer, *"Tell your wife!"* I finally told her. She just sat in silence. In August that year, I went to the landlord of the apartments where I was living to see if there were any apartments for sale. I figured that if I'm in debt, I might as well try to buy an apartment because I'll be here for a while. My credit was terrible, and I had already been denied for a pre-approval request. My unsaved landlord discovered that he had one of the last "Non-Qualifying Assumable" loans on the planet. He said, *"If you'll pay the transfer fees of $250, the townhouse is yours."*

Immediately, we had $14,000 in equity! We sold the apartment within a month and paid off all our debts before the end of the year. Thus, the promise God made me on New Year's Eve came true! The next conference we were sent out to pastor a church.

God Knows our Need - *Mike and Valerie Gomez*

In 1996, we were hit by a financial crisis, in part because my past life was catching up with me. I was hit with a financial judgment against me, and it came at the worst possible time. At my job, they were laying people off, and I was next on the list due to lack of seniority. Also, our only car completely broke down, and I had to find rides to work. When the judgment came, it took nearly all of my paycheck, leaving me with less than 15% of my wage. This was devastating for our young family.

At that time, I was the song leader in our church, and we had a revival with Dennis Wright. I had borrowed a car and picked someone up for church. That night, brother Wright said, *"There are two people here that need a financial miracle, a man and a woman."* I knew I was the man and started walking forward. To my surprise, the man that I picked up for church was also walking forward. I was thinking to myself that he had better sit down, because I was the one in need! As we approached the front, Dennis Wright looked at the other man and told him he would pray for him, then looked at me and said that I was the one God wanted him to pray for. He then gave me a word that said God was going to do a miracle in one year (I was thinking to myself, I need a miracle <u>now</u>), but I received the word and went back to my seat. Later that week, Evangelist Wright challenged the entire church to double tithe for three months. When my wife and I heard that, we silently looked at each other and agreed without saying a word. After double tithing, we were left with no money, but during that time, all of our needs were met; groceries were given to us, and somehow our rent got paid. I was able to get an adjustment on the court judgment, which allowed me to make reasonable payments. I got a new job, (which I didn't qualify for) at twice my previous salary. I was able to buy a used car well below market value. I believe God gave me favor in the judgment against me, wisdom to navigate the difficulties, and blessed me with a better job because of taking on the challenge to double tithe.

Chapter 8: Holy Budgeting

If we command our wealth, we shall be rich and free. If our wealth
commands us, we are poor indeed.
Edmund Burke

A good roadmap will get you to your destination.
Floyd Talbot

Dave Ramsey has helped thousands of people get out of debt.
But getting out of debt begins with establishing a budget, and
the results of budgeting go beyond money. One woman tells the
impact that establishing a budget together had on her marriage.
She says, *"Doing the budget together and being on the same page
made such a difference in our marriage. I feel like we are so much
more unified on what our goals are and what our plan is. It's such
a freedom to know where we are and that we can move forward—
together. Our marriage is better off now."*

In this chapter, we will continue to look at wrong financial
decisions that prevent us from prospering financially. Apart from
debt, failing to plan our finances in advance causes the greatest
problems in most people's lives. We will learn in this chapter
that a financial plan is called a <u>budget</u>, **and budgeting is Holy to
God!**

Planning to Fail

Our financial future is determined by decisions made beforehand.
If you want a better financial future, you must establish a plan. A
plan means you make organized decisions <u>in advance</u>, based on
the end result you want or need. *Luke 14:28 NIV "Suppose one of
you wants to build a tower. Will he not first sit down and estimate
the cost to see if he has enough money to complete it?"* In this

passage, Jesus shows some simple aspects of planning: *How much does the thing I want cost? Do I currently have enough money to obtain it?* **So how do we begin planning?**

Planning involves thinking: *You cannot succeed financially unless you <u>think</u>!* **Luke 14:31 NCV** *"If a king is going to fight another king, first he will sit down and plan. He will decide if he and his ten thousand soldiers can defeat the other king who has twenty thousand soldiers.* This is an ancient battle story, but some elements that apply to finances. The king begins thinking about what is coming towards him. Based on what's coming towards him, he made a plan to meet it. If we apply that to our finances, we need to think about what is coming toward us financially: *There are <u>expenses</u> coming toward us! So **plan** for them!* We must plan in advance to be prepared for the expenses that are coming toward us.

The biggest mistake people make in finances is lack of planning. Most people are <u>responders</u> rather than planners. We <u>respond</u> to advertising, we respond to family and friends, we respond to our emotions rather than plan our spending.

Women buy items responsively: *Shoes, purses, clothes, and jewelry.*

Men buy items responsively: *Guns, cars, electronics, sports equipment, and boats.*

If we buy responsively, we wind up spending money we don't have or spending more than we can afford. You can't spend more than you earn: *Your spending must be determined by your income!* There's an old saying I heard my father say hundreds of times:

> *If your outgo exceeds your income, then your upkeep will be your downfall.*

The Bible is clear: The result of a lack of wisdom and a lack of planning will always be poverty, or financial lack. **Proverbs**

6:6-11 NCV *⁶Go watch the ants, you lazy person. Watch what they do and be wise. ⁷Ants have no commander, no leader or ruler, ⁸but they store up food in the summer and gather their supplies at harvest. ⁹How long will you lie there, you lazy person? When will you get up from sleeping? ¹⁰You sleep a little; you take a nap. You fold your hands and lie down to rest. ¹¹So you will be as poor as if you had been robbed; you will have as little as if you had been held up.* The lessons God shows us in these verses: The ant is wise because of its planning ahead. The ant's plan is to store up food for the coming winter. Poverty comes when we don't plan in advance. *(So don't let an ant be smarter than you!)* **If you don't have a financial plan, then you are planning to fail.**

Planning is important to God because <u>God</u> is a planner! God planned the universe, which operates by plans. The plans of nature are actually <u>laws</u>. A law is something that is always true. The world operates on laws such as sowing and reaping, seedtime and harvest – and God planned all these laws. **Genesis 8:22** *"While the earth remains, Seedtime and harvest, Cold and heat, Winter and summer, And day and night Shall not cease."* If God is a God of planning, and if we want God's favor, we also must plan in finances.

Having a Plan

A financial plan is called a **budget**, or a **spending plan**: *A budget, or spending plan, is simply a written plan for your money. (Whether written on paper or electronically)* A budget controls the flow of our money or allocating it. Allocating means setting aside a portion of our money for a specific purpose. The oldest and simplest systems were the jar or envelope system of budgeting: *You put money aside in jars or envelopes marked for each cost or need you will have in your finances.* Each jar or envelope would be marked: *Rent, fuel, utilities, etc.*

A budget is telling your money where to go instead of wondering where it went.

There are two aspects of budgeting:

Determine in advance where you need the money to go. This goes back to what we said in a previous chapter: You cannot succeed financially without thinking! You have to think about what your expenses are and how much money is required to meet those needs.

Decide in advance how you will allocate your money to where it must go. Someone said, "A budget is a traffic policeman *telling your money where to go; It is not a tracking device to tell you where it went!*"

Budgeting is biblical, so that means God will bless it supernaturally! *Genesis 41:33-36 NCV* ³³"*So let the king choose a man who is very wise and understanding and set him over the land of Egypt.* ³⁴*And let the king also appoint officers over the land, who should take one-fifth of all the food that is grown during the seven good years.* ³⁵*They should gather all the food that is produced during the good years that are coming, and under the king's authority they should store the grain in the cities and guard it.* ³⁶*That food should be saved to use during the seven years of hunger that will come on the land of Egypt. Then the people in Egypt will not die during the seven years of hunger.*" Here we see the wisdom of Joseph in planning. He knew how many years of plenty were coming (seven years), and he knew how many years of famine would follow that (seven years). Knowing what was coming, he made a plan in advance to set food aside for the time of famine. Joseph's plan was to budget the surplus grain in the years of plenty to ensure they had enough food to survive the years of famine. Joseph budgeted the food supply! The result was God's supernatural favor. *Genesis 41:37-38* ³⁷*This seemed like a very good idea to the king, and all his officers agreed.* ³⁸*And the king* asked them, *"Can we find a better man than Joseph to take this job? God's spirit is truly in him!"* The result of his holy budgeting was that God helped him. The nation of Egypt was saved, his family was saved, and far greater than that, the purposes of God were preserved.

Making a Budget

For those who have never established a budget in the past, let's look at the practical steps involved in making a budget.

Step #1: Track your expenses for a month. Simply keep track and write down everything you spend for 30 days. This is not a budget; it simply tells you where your money went and, therefore, gives you an idea of where you are at financially. When I was a young seventeen-year-old disciple, I had a roommate who made more than five times as much money per week as I did, yet he always complained that he had no money. I was incredulous! You have five times as much money every week than I do? (*At that time, I couldn't imagine what it would be like to make that much money!*) So, I asked him, "*What do you mean you have no money?*" (this was just a few days after he got paid). "*Where did your money go?*" He said, "*I have no idea.*" That was why he had no money! When you track your money for a month, you will see areas of spending that are unnecessary or wasteful. You will see where your spending habits need to change. When people begin budgeting for the first time, it often keeps them from making unwise purchases and throwing money away. ***Proverbs 24:3*** *Through wisdom a house is built; and by understanding it is established:*

Step #2: Determine your income. This should be fairly simple, but many people have fluctuating incomes: *They don't make exactly the same amount every week, due to fluctuating hours, overtime, bonuses, expenses, etc.* So, the answer to varying income amounts is **averaging**. If you add your 4 weeks of salary or income together to get a total, then divide the amount by four. For example, if your salary is $1000 per week, you add four weeks of salary together: $ 1000 + $1000 + $1000 + $1000 = $4000. Or multiply $1000 x 4 = $4000. To get the average weekly income, you divide the total by the time or frequency: $4000 ÷ 4 = $1000. That is easy, because all the weekly amounts are the same. But if you made different amounts, it still works the same. $1000 + $700 + $1400 + $1300 = $4400 total income. Then divide by 4: $4400 ÷ 4 = $1100 average weekly salary.

If you are self-employed or a sub-contractor: *Your income is after expenses (tools, materials, etc.)*

Make sure you write down all forms of income: *Salary, interest, dividends, etc.*

Step #3: Determine your expenses.

Determine the amount of the expense: In other words, take one expense and work out how often it comes. For instance, the rent is $1600, once per month.

Determine the interval of the expense (how often it comes): *Weekly, monthly, every 3 months, every 6 months, etc.* Average the bill according to the length of the budget: *Weekly or monthly.* If the rent is $1600 per month, you divide $1600 by 4. $1600 ÷ 4 = $400. *That means you must set aside $400 per week in order to pay the rent of $1600 per month.*

Find out which expenses are non-negotiable: *That means the amount cannot be changed or lowered.* If you are a Christian, the tithe (10% of your income) cannot be lowered. Taxes cannot be lowered. A set-amount bill cannot be lowered. *(such as rent, utilities, etc.)*

Determine which expenses are negotiable: *That means the amount can be adjusted.* If you are buying food: Can you buy steak, or ground beef? *(that is determined by your income)* Eating out at restaurants: Do you choose an expensive restaurant, or eat fast food?

Add up your total expenses and subtract them from your income: That figure tells you where you're at.

- If you have extra or surplus money after paying all your expenses, you can choose to save it, invest it, spend it, or give it away.
- If you spend more than you take in: *You are in trouble financially!* Something must change: That usually is your negotiable purchases.

The difficult possibility: *Downsizing.* That means cutting expenses by getting rid of unnecessary expenses, or getting a cheaper car, less expensive housing, etc.

Remember scheduled disasters: Every car needs maintenance regularly. This is not a surprise; you know you have to service the car every 5,000 miles or so. Your children will need shoes, clothes, and school supplies regularly. To budget for these, determine the amount needed and the length of time until it's needed. Then divide the amount by the time, and you must be setting aside that amount weekly or monthly to be able to pay it when it comes.

No budget is ever successful unless it includes savings: If you have no savings, the first time an emergency arises, the budget will already become ineffective. *A budget without savings is a budget waiting to blow up!* The absolute starting point you want to aim for in setting aside savings for emergencies is **one month's salary.** As God begins to bless you, you'll wind up with a lot more savings than that, but this is a start. Most financial experts say you should aim to have 3 to 6 months' worth of living expenses and an emergency fund. That way, if you lose your job temporarily, or the washing machine breaks down, you have a margin of safety that keeps you from needing to go into debt to survive.

God blesses planning and budgeting. *Proverbs 10:4 NIV Lazy hands make a man poor, but diligent hands bring wealth.* Budgeting is more than simple math; it causes God to get involved in your life in a supernatural dimension of blessing. A budget makes you like God, who is a planner. A budget is a revelation of your current character: It shows that you can restrain your unhealthy tendencies. A budget helps develop character over time. You will change as you learn to restrain your fleshly tendencies: You will change if you begin to budget your finances. Through the years, I have had many people who start to budget speak of the change it brings in their spiritual life, their marriage, and their personal happiness. I urge you to begin budgeting today.

To help those first starting to budget, I will recommend some tools to help you.

Website

https://gatewaypeople.com/resources/stewardship   This website by Gateway Church has a number of helpful tools. You don't need to belong to their church in order to take advantage of the tools on this site.

Budget Apps:

For those who prefer to do things electronically, there are a number of helpful budget apps you can download that will help you budget. These are extremely helpful for anyone who struggles with math!

Free Apps:	**Apps that cost money:**
Empower Personal Dashbord	Every Dollar (Dave Ramsey)
Nerdwallet	YNAB (You Need a Budget)
Rocket Money	Wallet by BudgetBakers
Goodbudget	Rocket Money
Fudget	Monarch
Every Dollar	Quicken Simplifi

You will need to do some research and find which one will work best for you.

Overwhelmed by Miracles - *James & Liz Wilson*

We owed $97,000 on our first mortgage to one bank, and I was falling behind on that mortgage. We also owed another bank $23,000 on a second mortgage and $21,000 on a credit card. I had been skipping payments on one bill to be able to pay the other. I was getting phone calls, emails, and threatening letters in the mail. Our mortgage had already been turned over to a collection agency, and it was becoming desperate. I also had an $11,000 medical bill that I was trying to pay monthly. On top of all those, we also owed a combined $5,000 on smaller, higher-interest Credit Cards and small personal loans. I was trying to 'strategically' skip payments on each one every other month so as not to also get them sent to a collection agency. We were in debt a total of $157,000 ($60,000 unsecured), and I wasn't making very good money. We were in serious trouble. It was horribly oppressive, and we were sinking. My debt was creating more debt. My wife and I were getting sick, losing sleep, anxious, depressed, and we finally got sick and tired of it.

We had both started earnestly praying for God to help us get out of debt. We knew it was our fault, and I was very transparent with my Pastor Jonathan Heimberg about our financial crisis. Things were so tight: One week, I told my Pastor that I had to pay a $2.00 tithe in pennies! But I paid it!

But this was a start, and my miracles were coming. Here's what happened: First, I felt God telling us it was time to sell the house. The problem was that New Mexico was still reeling from the national housing market downturn that started in 2008-2011, and we were still feeling the effects in 2012. The realtor we were listing with plainly told us that, *"Now is absolutely NOT the time to sell. It is an aggressive buyer's market. Our houses have not been selling, please wait."* But we really felt we needed to list it. So, we did, and we listed it for $10,000 more than she recommended. In less than 2 weeks, our house sold for exactly what we were asking, and we closed in less than 4 weeks. That one sale paid off our first mortgage, our second mortgage, and our $5,000 miscellaneous credit cards and loans.

We knew something supernatural was taking place. We paid tithes on the very small profit of that sale, and we added a small but significant (to us) offering in gratitude on top of the tithe. That very same week, the county called my wife and said they paid her $11,000 medical bill! She asked, *"Why? What happened, and why our bill?"* The lady from the county said, *"Every year, if we have extra money in the county budget, it goes to our indigent fund."* She said we were selected, and our hospital bill was paid in full out of that fund! Wow!

That extra $10,000 on the listing price in the sale of our home was going to matter more than I realized. Remember: I still owed the bank $21,000 on my credit card, and we only had $10,000 left after everything else was paid. This credit card bill was daunting to us. The interest alone was about 21%. Ugh. This was the really aggressive one. They were hounding me daily. I was trying to negotiate the $21,000 debt with the bank so I wouldn't still owe $11,000 after paying them the remaining $10,000 from the sale of the house.

So, I called the bank and said, *"We have $10,000 left from the sale of my home. If we send you the $10,000, would you be willing to write off the remaining debt on this credit card? Otherwise, we'll keep the $10,000 and start paying you the minimum going forward."* (Every month after I paid the minimum, only $7.00 was going toward the principal.) It was going to be a very long process to get that credit card paid off. The bank didn't accept immediately; instead, they told me to formally apply for hardship assistance while they reviewed my offer. While waiting to hear back from the bank, we had that $10,000 set aside in cash specifically for the settlement offer. But our real emergency savings were only $1,000 cash that I kept in the dresser drawer. Our final miracle was right around the corner, but I didn't know it yet. One day, I was talking with a friend, and he told me about his debt, how he was falling behind, and had no food, etc. Right then, I felt like God told me to give the brother $100 because he was in desperate need. (More than us it seemed). I went home and told my wife, and she cried, but we gave it to him.

The very next day, the Credit Card Bank sent an email stating that they forgave the remaining $11,000 debt! Praise God! Our debt was GONE! At the same time, I got offered a dream job as a director with an incredible salary, and now my housing was included on top of my salary as an added bonus! To this day, we are still so overwhelmed by those miracles. Our God is so, so good!

Debt Freedom - *Brett and Tina Knitter*

For the first 15 years of my salvation, I was always struggling with finances, never having enough money to pay bills on time. I was always wondering why; I was tithing and giving offerings, yet still no real breakthrough living week to week.

One day Pastor Chris Plummer began teaching an adult bible hour series on finances. How to budget, what a budget even looks like. From that moment, I realized we needed a budget. We were around $22,000 in debt. I asked Pastor Plummer if he could help us with a budget. In that meeting, Pastor Plummer led us in a prayer of repentance for being bad stewards of what God had given us and for being people-pleasers, because we always liked to entertain and bless others, yet we did so with money that really wasn't ours to spend.

I cut up my credit card, cancelled subscriptions, and realized we were renting a house we couldn't afford, so we decided to look for a cheaper rental. After that prayer, we believed God had forgiven us and trusted that He would help us. I got a pay raise. Our old neighbor bought the house next door to her. She rang us and asked us to move in, saying we didn't have to pay a bond (deposit) or pay any rent in advance. The rent was for a better and cheaper house than the one we were living in.

I started to get more work, which helped pay off our debts faster. We found jewelry in the new house we moved into. The owner told us to keep it. We wanted to be blameless, so we took it to the police. Three months later, they said it was legally ours with papers to prove it. We then sold that jewelry for $3,600, which went straight to paying our debt. I worked for a company where I fixed appliances, and through that, I started a side business by making fire pits out of old washing machines, making 100% profit, selling more than one a day for $60 each.

After 18 months, we were debt-free! I was able to take my family on our first holiday together. We were even given $1,000 for our holiday. Being debt-free has blessed my marriage; we no longer argue over finances. My wife was no longer stressed about how to make ends meet. I became a children's church leader and a Bible study leader, and we followed up on new converts. Being debt-free made doing all those things stress-free; it liberated us. We were then able to have new converts and others over every Sunday without guilt, only pure joy.

My wife Tina and I are now missionaries in New Zealand!

Learning to Trust God - *Adrianne Tegegne*

My first financial miracle came immediately. I went to a new convert's class, couldn't afford a Bible. I borrowed a study Bible someone had brought so that I could read my scriptures, and that night I prayed and told God, *"I would really like that Bible."* A few nights later, I heard a rustling sound, and someone dropped a brand new one off on my porch! I hadn't even told anyone.

My second one came a year after salvation. I was attending church in Yuma, Arizona, and the Pastor preached a sermon on giving. I had gotten into a lot of debt before getting saved. I had been in a relationship where he stole 2 of my credit cards and used them primarily for cash advances (higher interest rate to pay back). I had one credit card with a $1,500 limit maxed out and another with a $5,000 limit maxed out, so I owed $6,500. I could barely make my payments. When the Pastor preached about giving offerings above the tithe, I felt God was telling me to pay offerings also. I was so scared at the time, and I remember shaking as I put my check in the offering. That night, a coworker called me and asked if I would like to start carpooling to save on gas, but she'd pick me up and take me to work every shift and pay for the gas. I was so relieved, I said yes! The next day, another coworker told me they were going to start having lunch cookouts every day for all the staff. But, since I was in college, I wouldn't have to contribute. She then gave me a box of brand-new nursing scrubs (uniforms) that she had purchased and didn't like. God immediately fed me, clothed me, and took care of my gas!

With that giving, I would write out my bills every paycheck, and I really couldn't afford all of them. The numbers wouldn't add up. But I didn't stop paying my offering, and every single time a bill and those credit card debts were due, I had enough money. I had signed a five-year contract with the debt collectors to not pay interest if I made my payments on time. I made every single payment, and I even paid off my debts 2.5 years early. It was such a miracle to get out of that debt.

We also had a large financial miracle happen to us while we were still living in Tennessee but driving to Prescott for a conference in July 2022. I had gotten my bachelor's in nursing in Tennessee when we first got married. Still, I had had multiple issues with the school administration that had prevented me from taking my last class for over a year. By the time I had graduated in 2018, I had set aside my career to raise my kids. We were working to pay off college debt when the government launched a program called the Borrower's Defense Application, which said that if you had administrative issues with specific colleges, you could apply for the government to forgive and pay off your college tuition. I had gone to one of the schools they mentioned. Ayele and I fasted and prayed for my application to be accepted, but the government kept delaying the program. Every time we fasted and prayed, we would bring up this prayer request. During that week of the Conference, I received a letter from the government stating that they had accepted my request and paid off my loans. I had borrowed $12,447, and with interest, it was closer to $15,000. The government paid off my loan and then gave back all of the money that we had already paid in payments, so I was able to also finish paying off my associate's degree loans. Many people I know were denied in this program, and many lawsuits were filed against the government for denying their applications. Ours went through, and we received the money immediately after receiving the letter. We directly correlated that to our continued giving, praying, and fasting, and asking God to answer this prayer.

Stewardship Rewarded - *Nigel and Carol Brown*

In the Waltham Forest, UK, Church that I Pastor, I try to be a good steward. However, there was a time earlier in 2025 when the church's finances seemed to be increasingly hard to manage. Too much was going on and in too many places! Larger staff, larger needs, more people making decisions, etc. I called a meeting with our church accountant and one of our council members (who runs a very successful accounting company) to see if we could do better. We went through the accounts item by item. Within a week (we hadn't even had time to implement some changes we had identified), the church received the highest ever one-person donation out of the blue. £150,000. I believe God responded to our desire to be better stewards. I don't believe the timing was accidental.

Even Backsliders Help Provide - *Sylvester and Liz Pegues III*

My wife and I were sent to the Oklahoma City, Oklahoma area to pioneer a church. God miraculously opened a door for us to rent a building. At first, the building and the location were decent, but over the next couple of years, the neighborhood became rougher and rougher. On top of that, finances became a challenge as we tried to keep everything moving in the right direction.

We began to feel strongly that God wanted us to move, but the financial reality made that difficult. Most of the available locations were more expensive than what we were already paying, though there were options out there.

During that time, I attended a pioneer rally where we were challenged to give. I gave an offering on behalf of our church—a sacrificial offering—knowing that we really needed to start saving for a new location. At the rally, I also had the opportunity to ask one of our fellowship leaders during a question-and-answer session whether it was wiser to stay where we were or to move, considering the increasing danger of the area and the financial strain. We were encouraged to trust God, seek counsel from my pastor, and start looking for a new building.

Three days after giving that sacrificial offering for World Evangelism, I received a call from a backslider who said God had put it on his heart to meet with me and give to the church. When we met, he handed me a check for $10,000. It was more than enough for us to leave our current building and move into a better location. God is faithful!

Unseen Provision - *Ron and Kerry Chisholm*

My wife and I took over the pastorate of the church in Midland, West Australia, in 2013. A couple of months after taking over, we started some work on the front windows of the church to renew the window advertising with very large window stickers. When we removed the sticker, we discovered the glass window had cracked from one corner to the other and needed to be replaced. I filed an insurance claim, but the insurance company said the damage was not due to malicious damage but to natural movement, caused by the windowpane not being seated correctly during installation. They would not cover natural movement, and so we have no claim. The cost to replace the glass was over $2400, which, at the time, was a large sum for a small church.

We prayed, *"God, we need your help. We believe you can help us."* Two days later, one of the ladies in the church was cleaning, and she saw an envelope pushed to the back of the letter box. The letter box is mounted on its side, so the envelope being pushed back was hard to see. She brought the envelope to me. When I opened it, there was $4000 cash inside. That was enough to replace the window and have the other side roller door repaired as well. God is good, and clearly it was God taking care of the needs of His church as He does, because he met the need, and then some!

Chapter 9: The Source of Supply

God will never cease to help us until we cease to need.
C.H. Spurgeon

Linda, who ministers to drug-addicted women in California, faced a severe financial crisis when her husband became disabled and their income dropped too almost nothing. Linda and her disabled husband felt led to give her last $5 as a step of faith. Soon after, they unexpectedly received $5,000 in the mail. Later, a woman Linda prayed for at church became part of a family that began generously supporting them, even giving a $20,000 gift. Linda believes God used her small act of obedience to open the door to ongoing provision for her ministry and household. This was a clear sign that God was the source of her provision.

We began the book by looking at negatives: The things that can stop us from entering into prosperity. Now we will start looking at the positives: The things that will help us enter into prosperity. It's important that we understand the foundations of prosperity correctly. God's kingdom is built on order and progression. *Mark 4:26-29* *26He also said, "This is what the kingdom of God is like. A man scatters seed on the ground. 27Night and day, whether he sleeps or gets up, the seed sprouts and grows, though he does not know how. 28All by itself the soil produces grain —first the stalk, then the head, then the full kernel in the head. 29As soon as the grain is ripe, he puts the sickle to it, because the harvest has come."* This passage explains how things grow in God's Kingdom: In order! The order seen here is seed first, then the stalk, then the head, and finally the grain. If you want a harvest, you can't start with the grain; you start with the seed.

When you desire to prosper financially, you don't start with prayers, or a formula of confession, or the provision: You start with God! We need to understand the source of supply if we want to prosper, and *the source of supply is God!* This book isn't a book of formulas or positive confessions; it is a book about God. When you know who God is, you can move into God's miracle supply.

The Nature of the Supplier

Financial supply and prosperity are based on the character of God. Character is what you are on the inside, or what comes naturally to you. You don't have to beg a liar to lie: *It's in there!* You don't have to beg a thief to steal: *It's in there!* You don't have to beg a pervert to be perverse: *It's in there!* And you don't have to beg a faithful person to be faithful: *It's in there!* People will always wind up doing what comes naturally to them. This is especially true concerning the character of God. The Bible speaks a lot about the name of God. *1 Chronicles 16:10 NIV Glory in his holy name; let the hearts of those who seek the Lord rejoice.* In the Bible, a name equals character, or what stands behind it. If you are receiving a check from someone, the name on the check makes all the difference! Who would you prefer getting a check from, Bubba Jones, or Elon Musk? A whole lot more money stands behind the name of Elon Musk!

Psalm 9:10 NIV Those who know your name will trust in you, for you, Lord, have never forsaken those who seek you.

The Names of God: The Bible speaks about the different names of God. God reveals Himself by many different names, and each name reveals **who God is, what His character is like**, and **what He will do**. The Bible lists over **900** different names or titles of God. God is so big! He can do so much! One name or description of God is not enough. In each situation we face in life, the specific name God reveals Himself to us is tailor-made according to our need. If you're in a battle in life, you don't need to know that God is righteous; you need to know that He is the Lord of Hosts, which means the God of angel armies! That name is relevant to your need.

God's Names of Provision: God reveals His character in provision by three distinct names that we should understand. If you know who God is concerning provision, you will be able to believe Him for the provision His name promises us.

Provision Name #1: El-Elyon (Most High God). *Genesis 14:19 KJV And he blessed him, and said, Blessed be Abram of the most high God, possessor of heaven and earth:* In English, our text says God's name is **Most High God**. But in the original Hebrew, it says El-Elyon. In Hebrew Elyon means <u>highest</u>, and El means <u>God</u>. So, His name is <u>the Highest God</u>. But after saying God's name, Melchizedek then tells what that name means for Abram (and for us!). *God <u>possesses</u> everything, because He <u>created</u> everything!* If that is who God is in His power and character, the practical application is provision: ***Then we can trust the God who owns everything to give us finances.*** Abram immediately responded to this revelation of God in a practical way when the king of Sodom offers to let him have all the money. *Genesis 14:22-23 NIV* ²²*But Abram said to the king of Sodom, "I have raised my hand to the Lord, God Most High, Creator of heaven and earth, and have taken an oath* ²³*that I will accept nothing belonging to you, not even a thread or the thong of a sandal, so that you will never be able to say, 'I made Abram rich.'* Abram says you (or any other human being) are not the source of my financial supply. My source of supply is the God who made everything and possesses everything.

Provision Name #2: El-Shaddai (Almighty God). *Genesis 17:1 NCV When Abram was ninety-nine years old, the Lord appeared to him and said, "I am God Almighty. Obey me and do what is right.* In English, the name of God is "Almighty God." But in the original Hebrew, it says El- Shaddai. El means <u>God</u>, and Shaddai comes from the root of a Hebrew word which means "the breast." This is a word picture of a mother who supplies the nourishment needs of a baby through breastfeeding. In other words, *"God will meet your needs."* But some scholars say more accurately it says, "Many breasted." I don't mean to be crude, but for babies – two are enough! But God is **more than you need**! Our God is **more than enough**!

Our faith in God's provision is often situational: That means we think God's ability to provide depends on the situation. In other words, if the need is small, if the economy is good, and if inflation isn't high, then God can provide! But God wants us to understand that it doesn't matter the size of the need, or any other factor. *God is more than enough!*

Provision Name #3: Jehovah-Jireh (God will Provide). *Genesis 22:14 KJV And Abraham called the name of that place Jehovah-jireh: as it is said to this day, In the mount of the Lord it shall be seen.* The King James Version gives the name of God in Hebrew: Jehovah-Jireh. Jehovah means "the Covenant God," or "the self-existent God." Jireh means "will provide" and the root of the word means "to see." Abraham needed a sacrifice (instead of his son.) This is when God enters his need: *Genesis 22:13 NCV Then Abraham looked up and saw a male sheep caught in a bush by its horns. So Abraham went and took the sheep and killed it. He offered it as a whole burnt offering to God, and his son was saved.* Abraham's response after seeing God's provision is found in the next verse: *Genesis 22:14 KJV And Abraham called the name of that place Jehovah-jireh: as it is said to this day, In the mount of* *the Lord it shall be seen.* He said, "the Lord <u>sees</u> what I need and <u>provides</u> what I need!"

Those two aspects of God's character in provision encourage every Christian who is facing a financial need:

     1. **God already sees what you need!** He sees your bills, your debt, your job, your housing situation, your vehicle, the building needs of your church; God sees every need!

     2. **God is already working to provide your needs**! Right now, God is already working and arranging things in housing, job openings, landlords and anyone else who can be used by God to meet your need.

Applying Provision

The point of God revealing these names to us is to spark faith in our hearts. He wants our confidence to be in God. *2 Timothy 1:12 NIV That is why I am suffering as I am. Yet I am not ashamed, because I know whom I have believed, and am convinced that he is able to guard what I have entrusted to him for that day.* Paul doesn't say, "I know some interesting facts and doctrines about God," he said, *"I know <u>Whom</u> I have believed!"* A person – Almighty God! Faith has a foundation, and that foundation is the character of God. So, when we are facing financial needs or a crisis of supply, we look to God, who is a provider. **Provision is not what God <u>does</u> – provision is who God <u>is</u>!**

The Love of the Supplier

Some people are at a disadvantage when they are in financial need because they have the wrong concepts of who God is. Perhaps in the past, they had parents who could not supply or did not want to supply their needs. Maybe, they said to you, *"I don't want to spoil you by helping you,"* or, *"I grew up with nothing, so you too can do without."* The problem is that even after being saved, they still see God this way: *God doesn't really care about my needs. God wants me to suffer for some mysterious reason. I can't bother God about my problems when He is so busy running the universe!* God's supply of our material needs is based on His love for His children. The Bible says that when we are born again, we are the children of God! *1 John 3:1 NIV How great is the love the Father has lavished on us, that we should be called children of God! And that is what we are!* In a healthy home, being a child means you are favored. You are viewed in a special light. God wants to help His children, and more than wanting to help - God loves to help His children!

Matthew 7:11 NLT *So if you sinful people know how to give good gifts to your children, how much more will your heavenly Father give good gifts to those who ask him.*

John 21:5-6 *⁵Then Jesus said to them, "Children, have you any food?" They answered Him, "No." ⁶And He said to them, "Cast the net on the right side of the boat, and you will find some." So they cast, and now they were not able to draw it in because of the multitude of fish.*

Romans 8:32 *He who did not spare His own Son, but delivered Him up for us all, how shall He not with Him also freely give us all things?*

When our daughter Emily was born, we were so overjoyed that we loved to buy her nice things. My wife would come home with a gift for Emily, and she would be excited that she found something good to give her. I would be traveling somewhere in the world, and I would find a pretty dress to bring home to my beautiful girl. Emily didn't have to beg or pressure us to give her good gifts; *we loved giving to her!* That is an inadequate illustration of God's love for you. As Jesus said in **Matthew 7:11** *how much more will your heavenly Father give good gifts to those who ask him.* If you understand how much you are loved by God, it's natural to trust him for supply, to ask Him for supply, to ask Him for more!

Joshua 15:18-19 NIV *18One day when she came to Othniel, she urged him to ask her father for a field. When she got off her donkey, Caleb asked her, "What can I do for you?" 19She replied, "Do me a special favor. Since you have given me land in the Negev, give me also springs of water." So Caleb gave her the upper and lower springs.* Othniel married Caleb's daughter. They were given land for their own inheritance. But Achsah understood that her father loved her and wanted to bless her. So she boldly asks for more! Land isn't enough, give us water as well. She judged her father's love correctly, because Caleb gave her <u>more</u>!

The Source of Our Supply

When seeking God's prosperity, we can make mistakes about who is the <u>source</u> of our supply. **Our Source** means, *"who do we look to, where do we place our trust in, to supply our needs?"* Many people are looking to the wrong source. They think, *"My job is my source. My boss is my source. My parents are my source. The economy is my source. The president is my source."* But none of those are our true source of supply. If you look to the wrong source you can come to wrong conclusions.

We can lose faith or get depressed based on those unreliable sources when things go wrong.

When the stock market crashes, people commit suicide: *They mistakenly think that <u>stocks</u> are their source!* They can fail to believe God as their source based on their circumstances, because they are looking at the wrong source: *I can't believe for supply with an employer like mine. I can't believe for supply with this president, or these politicians in charge. I can't believe for supply in this economy, or these circumstances.*

We can wind up honoring the wrong source because we think our life is dependent on them.

Christians think: *I have to miss church so my employer doesn't get upset!*

Christians let ungodly people tell them what to do in life, or with their money: *I don't want to upset them, or they won't help me with my financial needs.*

The Bible is clear that <u>God</u> is our source of supply! ***Genesis 14:19 KJV** And he blessed him, and said, Blessed be Abram of the most high God, possessor of heaven and earth:*

God is Most High: That means He is above everything; He is not affected by anything happening on the earth. He owns everything because He created it all. That also means that He can create more, if necessary. ***Genesis 14:22-23 NLT** 22Abram replied to the king of Sodom, "I solemnly swear to the Lord, God Most High, Creator of heaven and earth, 23that I will not take so much as a single thread or sandal thong from what belongs to you. Otherwise you might say, 'I am the one who made Abram rich.'*

It seems like Abram was given an incredible opportunity by an ungodly King: ***Genesis 14:21 NLT** The king of Sodom said to Abram, "Give back my people who were captured. But you may keep for yourself all the goods you have recovered."* He is making an incredible financial offer: You can keep all the money and possessions from two entire cities! You will be set for life! You will be rich! This is always the lie of the enemy: if you look to people and the world's methods, you will do well financially.

But Abram responds correctly, because God had shown him His name and character through Melchizedek. He refused because he recognized that people are not my source! Circumstances are not my source! He said, I can release finances, because the owner of it all will help me! ***Genesis 14:20 NLT** 20And blessed be God Most High, who has defeated your enemies* *for you." Then Abram gave Melchizedek a tenth of all the goods he had recovered.*

Acknowledging our Source: God wants us to recognize and acknowledge Him as the source of our supply. There are some questions that every person has to answer for themselves concerning the source of their supply:

Who is your source in life? Who are you placing your confidence in to meet your needs? How you answer those questions will determine your financial future.

God Provides Through Strangers - *Joe Campbell*

We were pioneering in Marion, Illinois, and after morning prayer, I stopped at a restaurant to get a cup of coffee. I was sitting there drinking a cup of coffee. A family was sitting across from me: A father, a mother, and two teenage boys. I could see they were talking, then they would look at me, talk some more, and look at me again. I was thinking, *"God, I don't want any problems this morning. I just want to go home. Connie loves me!"* I had been street preaching at the high school outside when the kids would get out of school. I thought, *"That's probably what it is. These kids are telling their parents, that's the guy that's out there preaching all the time."* I just didn't want any problems that morning.

Sure enough, the father came walking toward me, and I thought, *"Oh, no."* I just kept my head down. He said, *"Sir?"* and I said, *"Yes?"* He said, *"My family and I are Christians. We're on vacation, on the way to New Orleans, and God spoke to my wife, my kids, and me to give you this."* He reached into his pocket and pulled out a big wad of money - large bills. He laid it on the table and walked out. God said to me, *"I can do that anytime I want."* That is biblical. God said in **Luke 6:38 KJV** *Give, and it shall be given unto you; good measure, pressed down, and shaken together, and running over, shall men give into your bosom.* That became a reference point.

God Speaks to the Unwilling - *Mark and Michelle Aulson*

In 1995, we returned from the Philippines after 9 years as missionaries. We came back to our home church in Prescott, Arizona. The plan was for me to serve as an evangelist out of the Prescott congregation. We needed to find a house to rent. My Pastor, Wayman Mitchell, warned us that rent had increased dramatically and that we probably wouldn't be able to afford a home in Prescott (which has more mountains), but would likely need to rent in Prescott Valley (which is flatter). I told my wife, Michelle, what our Pastor said, but she said she would pray that God would help us. She was praying God would give us a house in the mountains with mature landscaping so she could enjoy the view.

I found a house up in the mountains in the Prescott area. Michelle liked the house when she saw it, just what she had prayed for. When I called the owner, he asked what I did for a living. I told him I was an evangelist. He said, *"I once rented to a Christian, and they didn't pay the rent."* I assured him we were not like that. He asked what my income was, and I told him it was difficult to say, as I depended on the love offerings given when I preached in various churches. He was not impressed. Then he asked how many children we have. When I told him we had three kids, two of whom were teenagers, he was very unimpressed. He said, *"The last time I rented to someone with teenagers, they skipped school, smoked marijuana, and destroyed my house!"* I said I was sorry to hear that, but my kids aren't like that. He said, *"I'm going to think about it. I have some other people who have called and are interested, so I'm going to make my decision. If I choose you, I'll call you, **don't** call me!"*

We desperately needed a house, so the next day I called him four times. He wouldn't come to the phone because he was working on his truck. On the final call, I was talking to his daughter, so I pleaded with her, *"I'm sorry to be disturbing him, but I have to know his decision. We're staying in a motel, and I have to find some place to live."* He came to the phone and was not happy to be disturbed. As I was talking with him, Michelle walked into the motel room. I was seized with inspiration, so I said, *"Sir, my wife wants to talk to you!"* I handed her the phone and she told him, *"Sir, your house is exactly what I have prayed to my Heavenly Father about, it has mature landscaping and I love that the kitchen window is toward the east so when I get up and make coffee in morning I have light and then when I make dinner it is on the cooler side of the house."* Then she gave the phone back to me. The man paused, then blurted out, *"If I let you have the place, do you promise to take good care of it? That house will be my retirement home in 5 years."* I said, *"Sir, if you allow us to live there, I will take care of your house as if I owned it myself!"* He paused, then said, *"**I don't know why I'm going to do this**, but I'm going to go ahead and let you have the house at a rent of $750.00."* That is precisely the amount I needed it to be. He made arrangements to get us the keys to move in and to meet us at the house.

The following Monday, I invited him to lunch, and he accepted. As we sat down, the man looked intently at me and said, *"Preacher, I want you to know something. I had already decided that **you were <u>not</u> going to get the house**, as I had another couple who both had professional jobs and no kids. But when your wife said that she had prayed to her Heavenly Father, I heard a voice inside of me that said, "**You better rent to them, or you're going to hell!**"*

I was stunned, but in great amazement, at the goodness of God toward our family. We lived very happily in that place for the year that I was an evangelist.

A Building Miracle - *Paul and Renee Stephens, El Paso, Texas*

In the early 2000s, we were looking to get out of renting our church building. We wanted to buy an existing building or build a new one. At the time, Ernie Lopez was managing a Levi's Factory in El Paso. Levi was closing all US manufacturing, and his factory was closing down in November 2002. Ernie gave a tour of the building and machinery to an individual who was manufacturing military uniforms. He ended up buying the entire building and all the equipment and hiring Ernie as his chief operating officer.

The Levi's building proved too small for the increase in uniform orders they were receiving from the US Government. So, the building lay empty, and Ernie began pressing his boss to sell the building to the Church. I met him a few times, and he never agreed to sell it. So, the church council and I decided to move on.

The following week, Ernie's boss called him into his office and told him to tell *'The Preacher'* to make him an offer on the Levi's Building. Ernie came to my office, and we wrote out an offer. I never inquired about what the building was worth or what he expected to get out of it. I was guided by what we could afford. (At the time, the building was appraised at $2.7 million). I offered $1.2 million, no money down (I needed the money we had saved for remodeling), no payments for 6 months, and the mortgage could be no more than $10 thousand a month, 4% interest, and he carries the note. I called my real estate lawyer, and he said, *"Don't do it. Come to my office, and we'll make a more reasonable offer."* I said, "We're going with this offer." I just felt good about it. Ernie took it to his boss's office. Ernie said he looked at it for about 30 seconds and said, *"OK!"* So, we got the building; no banks, no loans, no credit checks. it. So, when we moved in, we had $1.5 million in equity. The building is now worth $8-$10 million.

The back story of this miracle: When Richard Rubi bought their Church building back in the 1990s, he had two older Jewish men who financed him and helped him get into the building. They financed it for 2 years, and by then Richard got a bank loan. He had a service where he thanked these men before the Church for their help. When Richard told me that, I began to pray, *"God, give me someone who will help us, and I will honor them before the church."'* That prayer was specifically answered through Ernie's boss. When we had our grand opening service in December of 2004, I invited him to the service and presented him with a plaque expressing our gratitude, and he said a few words to our Church.

My encouragement for others is, *"God has building miracles! Obey God, do right, have faith, and God can provide!"*

A BUILDING MIRACLE

Helping With A Miracle and Receiving a Miracle
Albert and Narcie Berkeley

In 2014, Albert and Narcie Berkeley were involved in a terrible car accident. They were backslidden at the time. As a result of the accident, they came back to church in McAllen, Texas, and repented. In 2016, Roman Gutierrez took the first offering for the construction of a new building.

Albert and Narcie had just received the settlement payout from their accident. They felt moved to give $300,000. Pastor Roman Gutierrez had just given a substantial offering at the Tucson Bible Conference from money they had saved to build the new building. When God stirred him to give, he felt God tell him, *"If you give what I tell you, I will move supernaturally for you in your building."* Just a few weeks after he obeyed and gave, the Berkeleys received their settlement and gave the $300,000.

In 2018, Narcie got pregnant and had a baby, Aaliah, prematurely at only 25 weeks. The baby weighed 1 lb. 5 oz. and she wound up having 17 blood transfusions. Pastor Roman went and prayed for her, and the baby survived. As of 2025, Aaliah is 7 years old. The Berkeleys told Pastor Roman that they felt their obedience to God and their giving to the building pledge saved their baby!

In 2020, Albert and Narcie were sent out to a Pastor in the Bronx, New York City, New York.

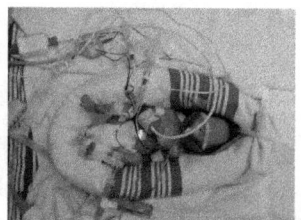

HELPING WITH A MIRACLE AND RECEIVING A MIRACLE

Chapter 10: The God of Abundance

The more we live rooted in God's faithfulness, the more we experience God's present abundance.
Jodi Harris

When you glimpse God's abundance, created for you, you will never be the same again.
Benson Andrew Idahosa

God's work done in God's way will never lack God's supply.
Hudson Taylor

A waitress at a restaurant in West Virginia received a life-changing tip. Manhattan Deming was serving an older couple at Davinci's Restaurant, and they began asking her about herself. She shared some of the struggles she had been experiencing, such as her car and her phone, which has no service. She is unable to contact anyone unless she is on Wi-Fi. This makes it hard for her to check on her three-year-old daughter when she is at work. When they paid the $148.41 bill, they added an extra $2000 as a tip. Deming said, "When he handed me back the receipt, I said, *'What? What is this? What does this say?'*, and he said, *"It says $2000."* I broke down crying. I couldn't hold it in. That's a once in a lifetime thing. The rest of the day I felt different, like, what just happened here? I never anticipated that." Her life was changed by an abundant gift!

We are looking at the issue of **prosperity**. The dictionary definition of prosperity is: *A thriving or growing condition, especially as concerns finances.* It will be difficult to believe for 'thriving or growing' finances, unless we understand the abundance of God. The Bible tells us that God is a God of abundance!

The God of Abundance

Those who are in need can be mistaken about God's ability to supply. We often look at the wrong things, and that ends up discouraging our faith. ***John 6:8-9 NLT*** *⁸Then Andrew, Simon Peter's brother, spoke up. ⁹"There's a young boy here with five barley loaves and two fish. But what good is that with this huge crowd?"*

Andrew started so well: In response to the need to feed the multitude, he went and found a possible answer in a boy willing to give his bread and fish. But then he began looking at the small amount of food compared to the huge number of people. When he looked at the wrong thing, he came to the wrong conclusion; it's impossible! He said, *"But what good is that with this huge crowd?"*

This is what we do when faced with our financial needs. We need a miracle, but we start looking at our circumstances: our small income, lack of education, large bills, high inflation, a difficult economy, high interest rates, and high costs in our area. When we do this, our faith gets discouraged, and we come to the same conclusion Andrew did: It's impossible! We can't look at the wrong thing and come to the right conclusion. When Andrew looked at the small amount of food and the size of the crowd, he told Jesus Christ, who is God in the flesh; *Supply is impossible!*

When faced with our need, we should be looking at God. Financial supply and prosperity are based on the character of God and the power of God. It is absolutely crucial to see that **God is the God of <u>abundance</u>!** God is not the God of less than enough. He is not the God of barely enough. He is not the God of 'only if things are easy will there be enough.' **God is more than enough!**

God's nature and power are abundant! Abundant means *'available in large quantities, more than enough.'* Everything God is, and everything God does, is abundant! *1 Timothy 1:14 And the grace of our Lord was exceedingly <u>abundant</u>, with faith and love which are in Christ Jesus.*

The word abundant here means "to abound exceedingly, or to be super-supplied, more than is needed." Abundance is the very essence of God's character and power. *Genesis 17:1 NCV When Abram was ninety-nine years old, the Lord appeared to him and said, "I am God Almighty. Obey me and do what is right.* I spoke in a previous chapter how that God revealed his name to Abraham as El-Shaddai, Almighty God. The root of Shaddai is "the breast," and some translators say it means "many-breasted." God is telling His people He <u>is</u> more than enough. He <u>has</u> more than you will ever need. *Genesis 14:19 KJV And he blessed him, and said, Blessed be Abram of the most high God, possessor of heaven and earth:* We showed before that "Most High God" in the original Hebrew is the name El-Elyon, and God himself shows us what that means for us: He possesses everything, because he created everything. The questions for us are not, *"how expensive is it?"* or, *"how big is the debt?"* The questions we should be asking is, *"How much money does God have?"* and *"How many resources does God have?"* or *"How much power does God have?"*

God's <u>resources</u> are abundant! God <u>possesses</u> everything because He <u>created</u> everything!

Psalm 24:1 NIV The earth is the Lord's, and everything in it, the world, and all who live in it;

Psalm 89:11 NIV The heavens are yours, and yours also the earth; you founded the world and all that is in it.

Haggai 2:8 NIV 'The silver is mine and the gold is mine,' declares the LORD Almighty.

Psalm 50:10 NIV *for every animal of the forest is mine, and the cattle on a thousand hills.*

So, for us, the practical truth that should encourage our faith is: **God has a lot of money!** God is not limited by circumstances, because He has so much money, He has so many resources, He has so much power. We struggle to even comprehend how much God has. Let's look at a human analogy and consider the wealth of a human being: Elon Musk. **Elon Musk made USD $203 billion in 2024.** That much money is hard for us to grasp. *He made $556,163,384 dollars PER DAY! He made $23,173,474 EVERY HOUR! He made $386,224 EVERY MINUTE! He made $6437 PER SECOND!* Do you think Elon Musk gets worried about rent going up $500 a month? *That's less than 1 second's worth! Is he losing sleep over the high housing market? $1000 worth of car repairs? Schooling costs? Medical bills? Absolutely not: He has more than enough!* Imagine if you knew Elon personally, or if you were related to him and he said, *"If you ever need money, I'll help you."* Would it make sense then, for you to be losing sleep over high prices and bills? How foolish to say, **"I sure hope Elon can afford it!"**

But if you are born again, you are a child of the <u>King</u>! *John 1:12 NIV Yet to all who received him, to those who believed in his name, he gave the right to become children of God.* You are God's child, not just God's follower. A child has access to the resources of their Father. So, *why should you worry and stress about money when you have access to your Heavenly Father who has lots of money?*

God Gives Abundance

Faith is not only based on God's character, but also His track record. Track record is a term that comes from horse racing. If you want to bet on a horse, you check its track record: How did they perform on a certain track? How did they perform in certain conditions (heat, cold, rain, or dry)? How did they perform against other horses? Knowing a horse's track record can give confidence of future performance.

The Bible gives God's track record of giving and supplying the needs of His people: **God gives abundantly!** Look at some examples of God's abundant giving and abundant supply. *Genesis 13:2 Abram was very rich in livestock, in silver, and in gold.* It doesn't say, "*Abraham barely survived financially from paycheck to paycheck.*" It says very rich! *Genesis 26:12-13 NLT* *12When Isaac planted his crops that year, he harvested a hundred times more grain than he planted, for the Lord blessed him. 13He became a very rich man, and his wealth continued to grow.* It doesn't say, "*Isaac did okay until the weather turned bad, then he really struggled like everyone else.*" It says, "*The Lord blessed him. He became a very rich man and his wealth continued to grow.*"

Please note: In telling you about Abram and Isaac becoming "very rich," I am not saying <u>every</u> Christian will become very rich. I am not a TV preacher who promises that you will be a millionaire if you send in money. (Neither my hair, nor my teeth are good enough to be a TV preacher!) I tell you these examples only to inspire your faith to believe in God's abundance.

Exodus 12:35-36 *35Now the children of Israel had done according to the word of Moses, and they had asked from the Egyptians articles of silver, articles of gold, and clothing. 36And the Lord had given the people favor in the sight of the Egyptians, so that they granted them what they requested. Thus they plundered the Egyptians.* It doesn't say, "*they left with only the clothes on their back.*" It says that the Egyptians wanted to bless them, and they left Egypt with all the wealth the Egyptians had.

Luke 5:5-7 *5But Simon answered and said to Him, "Master, we have toiled all night and caught nothing; nevertheless at Your word I will let down the net." 6And when they had done this, they caught a great number of fish, and their net was breaking.* ⁷*So they signaled to their partners in the other boat to come and help them. And they came and filled both the boats, so that they began to sink.* It doesn't say, *"Jesus helped them catch a couple of fish."* It says they caught so many fish their boats began to sink." **More than enough!**

Matthew 14:19-21 NCV ¹⁹*Then he told the people to sit down on the grass. Jesus took the five loaves and two fish, looked up toward heaven, and blessed them. Then, breaking the loaves into pieces, he gave the bread to the disciples, who distributed it to the people.* ²⁰*They all ate as much as they wanted, and afterward, the disciples picked up twelve baskets of leftovers.* ²¹*About 5,000 men were fed that day, in addition to all the women and children!* It doesn't say, *"Jesus gave them just enough for each one to have a small bite of fish and a few crumbs of bread."* It says everyone ate as much as they wanted, and afterwards there were twelve baskets of bread left over. More than enough!

The Bible shows us the principle of God's fairness or impartiality: ***God doesn't play favorites! Acts 10:34 NIV*** *Then Peter began to speak: "I now realize how true it is that God does not show favoritism.* **God doesn't play favorites:** If He did it for Jews, He will do it for Gentiles! If God provided for someone in the Bible, He will provide for you! If He provided for someone you read about in this book, He will do it for you! That is the point God recording all the miracle stories in the Bible: ***If God did it for them, He can do it for you!***

Faith For Abundance

If God is the God of abundance, if God has lots of money, if God gives abundantly, if God is impartial, *how should we act in relation to those truths?*

Provision key #1: We should trust in God. Trust speaks of an attitude of trust and confidence. ***Matthew 6:31-32*** *31"Therefore do not worry, saying, 'What shall we eat?' or 'What shall we drink?' or 'What shall we wear?' 32For after all these things the Gentiles seek. For your heavenly Father knows that you need all these things.*

If our Heavenly Father knows what we need, He has all power and He loves us: Then whatever comes, whatever we face, we can have confidence that our Heavenly Father will supply; ***abundantly!***

Provision key #2: We should focus on God. Whatever you focus on is what you will believe. If you focus on the problem, the difficulties, the obstacles, then you will believe in a lack of supply and disaster.

Matthew 14:30 NCV *But when Peter saw the wind and the waves, he became afraid and began to sink. He shouted, "Lord, save me!"*
Our focus should be on God, His word, and His promises.

Psalm 123:1-2 NIV *1I lift up my eyes to you, to you whose throne is in heaven. 2As the eyes of slaves look to the hand of their master, as the eyes of a maid look to the hand of her mistress, so our eyes look to the Lord our God, till he shows us his mercy.*

In the past, whenever I have been facing a financial need, I have gone to the Bible and found promises and stories of God's provision. I have written them down, prayed over them, studied them out, and spent time thinking about them. This helps me to be able to believe.

Provision key #3: We should believe and expect abundant provision. Ultimately, faith is based on God's love for us. ***Luke 12:32*** *"Do not fear, little flock, for it is your Father's good pleasure to give you the kingdom.* If God enjoys giving to us, we should believe and <u>expect</u> Him to provide abundantly.

George Mueller ran an orphanage in Bristol, England, in the 1800s. He never sent out appeals for money to fund the orphanage;

he simply prayed and believed God for miracle supply. One morning, the housemother of the orphanage came to him and said, "The children are dressed and ready for school. But there is no food for them to eat." George simply asked her to take the 300 children into the dining room and have them sit at the tables. He thanked God for the food and waited. George knew God would provide food for the children as he always did. Within minutes, a baker knocked on the door. He said, "Mr. Mueller, last night I could not sleep. Somehow, I knew that you would need bread this morning. So, I got up and baked three batches for you. I will bring it in." Soon, there was another knock at the door. It was the milkman. His cart had broken down in front of the orphanage. The milk would spoil by the time the wheel was fixed. He asked George if he could use some free milk. George smiled as the milkman brought in ten large cans of milk. It was just enough for the 300 thirsty children.

Provision key #4: We should ask our Heavenly Father for abundant provision: *Matthew 7:7-8* *7"Ask, and it will be given to you; seek, and you will find; knock, and it will be opened to you. 8For everyone who asks receives, and he who seeks finds, and to him who knocks it will be opened.* What do you need God to provide? Then ask him for it! I believe you should ask God specifically for what you need.

Some years ago, I preached on the verse above about asking God for what you need. Shortly after, I received this testimony: *Dear Pastor Greg, I wanted to tell you of the miracle God did to supply our need. My car broke down and was going to cost a lot of money to fix, so I scrapped it and bought an old Petrol VW Passat that looked a bit battered and old. I wasn't happy driving it to church & picking up converts, but I thought, "praise God I have a car," and I had prayed for "ANY" blessing. But I wasn't happy, because: 1. A Petrol/gas engine kills my money and 2. The car was so ugly. But Pastor Greg preached and said be specific with God in prayer. So, I said, "God, I want you to make a way for me to have a better-looking diesel Passat to save money." Today, a family who live a few streets away from us knocked on our door and said God had called them to be missionaries to India, and they said God told them to give their car to me for FREE OF CHARGE. It was a 2007 DIESEL PASSAT! My wife cried, because I had told her about my prayer beforehand. I offered them money, but they said no; God told them it's supposed to be free. They don't even know me, they have never been to our church. They go to a church of 600 people and they knew I was living nearby. They told us that God said for them to give it specifically to me. WOW! is all I can say. God is faithful!*

God Spoke to the Owner - *Mike and Liza Major*

I want to share a powerful testimony of what God has done in the process of securing our new church building. For three years, I had been making calls and looking for a building. One day, I contacted an owner about a property he wanted to lease, but told him I was interested in buying it. That call led to us meeting in person, and over several meetings we began discussing the possibilities. He owned a 5,000-square-foot building in a prime corner location with over 100,000 cars passing by every day.

During this time, I was fasting, praying, and seeking counsel from other pastors in our fellowship. At our very last meeting, I told him, *"You need to do owner financing."* To my surprise, he was willing. In fact, he told me that when he first met me, he called his best friend and said, *"Frank, God told me to build this man a Pentecostal church."* Not only did he agree to owner financing, but he is also doing the complete build-out at no cost to us. He even allowed us to use our whole first year of payments as the down payment toward the building.

Before any of this happened, our church had completed a 30-day fast. We also gave a large offering at our conference, as well as a large offering in the Prescott conference. I truly believe that from that 30-day fast and those sacrificial offerings, God released a supernatural building for our church. God is faithful, and this is just the beginning of what He's going to do!

God Prepared Housing in Advance - *Adam and Jennifer Porter*

When we moved to San Jose, California, we needed a place to live. We searched everywhere, but every house we looked at fell through for one reason or another. After 2 weeks of closed doors, Jennifer and I began to contend in prayer, asking God to open a door for a home.

One afternoon, I was driving through neighborhoods when I turned into a beautiful cul-de-sac, and a stunning house caught my eye. It was a quiet street, a great neighborhood, and a park was across the street, exactly what we needed. The front door was open, so I stepped inside and found the entire place under renovation. Fresh paint, new floors, workers everywhere. I asked one of the men, *"Is this house for rent?"* He said, *"Yes. We're remodeling it for whoever moves in. Go ahead and fill out an application. A lot of people already have."* He pointed to a stack of applications sitting on a table.

I grabbed a form, filled it out, and placed it on top of the pile. I asked if I could walk through the house, and he agreed. After looking around, I came back downstairs to find the man staring at my application with a shocked expression. He looked up at me and asked,

"You're a pastor?" I replied, *"Yes."* He swallowed hard and said, *"Hold on. I need to make a phone call."* A few minutes later, he came back, shook my hand, and said, *"Congratulations. The house is yours."* I was stunned. *"What do you mean? You haven't even checked my references."* He said, *"Six months ago, we moved out of this house because my mother had a dream. In the dream, God told her that a pastor and his family were supposed to move into this home, and that we needed to renovate it and get it ready. Honestly, we thought she was crazy, but she's a strong Catholic, and she was so insistent that we did it anyway. And now you walked through the door. We can't believe this is actually happening!"* Right there in the middle of that half-finished living room, God had gone ahead of us. He had prepared a house, stirred a family, spoken through a dream, and orchestrated every detail - long before we ever arrived in San Jose.

The Daniel Blessing - *Trevor Kopp*

I gave my life to God when I was 19. I had felt His calling on my life, and I wanted everything He had for me. I wanted to get married and have children. I wanted an apartment, a car, and a stable job. But I was in my sophomore year of college, and to get experience in my field of study, I had left a job making $12 an hour and working almost 50 hours a week for a part-time job at my university's IT helpdesk. I was making $8 an hour, only working 20 hours a week, and still living at home with my parents. That's a hard salary anywhere, but in New Jersey, with that income, it's impossible to afford a car payment, let alone an apartment and a wedding.

I began to pray that God would open a door for me to find a full-time job: One that would allow me to keep serving in the ministries I was involved in at church and also set me up to establish my life. I knew that God's blessings would open doors for destiny, not pull me away from it. So, I made a promise to God that I wouldn't entertain any position that would cause me to miss church or remove me from my ministries.

Around that time, my pastor preached a sermon out of Daniel chapter 1. He encouraged the church to pray over our work and contend for God to bless us as He blessed Daniel. After that service, every day that I drove to work, I would pray, *"God, make me ten times better than my coworkers."* On the least income I had ever made in my life, I was paying my tithes, giving offerings, and giving to world evangelism, and I prayed with confidence that God was going to honor my giving and my obedience.

God honored my prayers. One day, my boss pulled me aside and asked when I was graduating. I told him I had another two years left, and he apologized. He had been authorized to open another position in the department and wanted me to apply for it, but it required a degree, and he couldn't wait that long. As I turned to leave his office, I was upset, and I remember feeling God press on my heart: This was my blessing, and no one was going to take it from me. So, I walked back into my boss's office and told him I didn't care what the requirements were or who applied. I was going to fight for that position, and I would be the best candidate he interviewed. He laughed, shook his head, and said, *"OK. I'll send you some things to study for the interview."*

I was the youngest applicant by far. Even people my age who applied had two or three more years of experience than I did. Some were men with families and a dozen years in the field. I later learned I was the only candidate they chose to interview without a degree. In fact, at one point, my boss was told directly not to interview anyone without one. But none of that mattered, because I had God's promises ahead of me. One of my high school teachers happened to be the wife of the university's president, and I had listed her as a reference on my application. Even though she said she wasn't allowed to show partiality in situations like that, she privately stepped in. She asked my boss to give me the interview as a personal favor to her, just for the experience.

Every day I prayed, *"God, make me ten times better."* The interview came and went, and although I initially felt confident, I started hearing whispers that I wasn't qualified and they couldn't consider me for the position. I kept praying. A week later, my boss called me into his office, and I'll never forget what he said: *"The job is yours. I interviewed more than a dozen people, and there was no comparison. You were easily ten times better than everyone else."* When those words came out of his mouth, my jaw must have hit the floor. God had answered my prayer and confirmed His handiwork through the very words of my boss!

Later, the university tried to tell me I couldn't be hired because of my degree. Still, no matter what situations arose or what authorities tried to stop my hiring, God intervened. That job paid for the rest of my degree and allowed me to build up enough savings to buy a car and put a deposit on an apartment.

A year later, my parents moved out of state. I would have had no place to live, but because of God's miracle provision, I had everything I needed to move out and establish my life, just in time. He had brought me to church, and when I needed it most, He provided everything I needed to stay rooted in that church.

Blessing Comes by Planting Seed - *Geoffrey Gersten*

As an artist, I am represented by a dealer who has a gallery in San Francisco. During the early part of the year, San Francisco is very cold and rainy. I depend heavily on tourist activity to make sales. So, during this slow period, none of my paintings had sold in over 30 days. On Saturday, March 31st, 2012, I spoke with my dealer by phone. He said, *"It's so cold and dead here; no one is here. If we can just get through this month and make it to May, we'll be fine."*

April 1st 2012, the call for offerings and pledge renewals was made at the end of Sunday morning service. My monthly pledge amount had been the same for a year and a half. During the offering call, God spoke to me very clearly a new amount for a monthly pledge, which was close to double my current offering. I knew I could afford the increased amount; the struggle was giving it up!

As I wrote the number on the pledge slip, I felt God touch me, like I was suddenly filled with the Holy Ghost. That was at noon. At 2:30 pm, my phone rang. My dealer says, *"Congratulations, I just sold eight of your paintings! A couple walked in here and bought an entire wall of your artwork."* Naturally, I was rejoicing.

Monday afternoon, I received another call. A couple from London came in and bought another painting that had a high price. They said they both work at the University of Oxford, and they are taking the painting to hang it there! If I showed up at the steps of that historical university, security would escort me out, but my painting is hanging there!

On Saturday, the gallery owner was saying, *"It's dead, there's no one here."* By Monday afternoon, he exclaimed to me, *"You're the new star of San Francisco!"*

Finally, the following Sunday, I stopped at the bank on the way to Sunday morning service. I took out my new pledge amount, and since I had some extra cash available, I added 30%. During the five-minute drive from the ATM to the church parking lot, early on Sunday morning, I got an email from a local client. They said they want to move forward with purchasing a new painting at a very high price!

All this change in one week because I simply sacrificed more. Being an artist is what I love and all that I want to be professionally. Through giving to world evangelism and God's great blessing, He has made my dream possible.

Miracle Help - *Diego and Kelly Galvan*

In 2011, we had just taken over the church in Casa Grande, Arizona. We were facing more than $218,000 worth of debt; our house in Las Vegas, Nevada, was about to go into foreclosure, worth $170,000; we had a previous hospital bill of $13,000 unpaid, and Kelly had a life-threatening tumor that needed surgery to remove. That surgery was going to cost more than $35,000. In the first week of 2012, we decided to give our first check as a first-fruits offering, believing God would bless that year. We attended the January Bible Conference in Prescott, and on Thursday night, we pledged $500 to world evangelism because God challenged us to give.

Driving home from the Conference, a woman we still have never met to this day who had been trying to help us short-sale the house called us, telling us that she was able to short-sell the house that Friday and that they were sending a check for $1,000. So we were able to give our pledge to Prescott and have extra. That year, God supernaturally helped us with all of our Debt: We found a program that paid for Kelly's surgery in full, the hospital in Las Vegas forgave our previous debt, and we were able to evade foreclosure one day before the bank would've taken our house away. Eight years to the month we gave, God supernaturally blessed us with a house here in Prescott Valley, and a key factor why we were able to have the bank even consider approving the loan was the fact that we did not foreclose our house eight years ago. We are grateful for God's supernatural provision!

God Provided a Building - *Carlos and Carmen Morales*

The church in Norfolk, Virginia had outgrown their rented building due to the wonderful growth God had been giving them. Pastor Carlos Morales was asking and believing God to give them a building. In 2010 he placed an ad in the paper asking if anyone was willing to donate land or a building to their church. He received no replies.

In 2011 he found what seemed to be the perfect building: An empty bowling Alley. He located the owner's information and submitted an offer for $2 million, but got no reply. In 2013 the owner of that building showed up at their rented church building. He looked around, and Carlos was able to explain to him their church, our fellowship and vision.

He asked Carlos to come to his office for a meeting. Instead of selling the building to the church, he proposed <u>donating</u> the building to the church for free as a tax write-off. He asked whether that would be acceptable to Pastor Morales. The answer obviously (and instantly) was, *"YES!"* He then told Carlos he knew the building would require a lot of remodeling to make it ready to be a church, so he also donated $100,000 to help with the attorney fees and construction costs.

On Easter morning 2015, they held their first service in their beautiful 40,000 Square foot facility that can accommodate 1000 people!

GOD PROVIDED A BUILDING

Chapter 11: A Covenant of Honor

We have learned in our home that God's blessing on the nine-tenths, when we tithe, helps it to go farther than ten-tenths, without God's blessing.
Billy Graham

Tithing is an open door to wealth.
Lailah Gifty Akita

William Colgate, renowned soap maker, committed early in life to tithe all his earnings, making faithful giving a guiding principle of his career. As his company grew, he increased his giving to 20%, 30%, and eventually 50%. Colgate credited his success to honoring God first. His principle: *"Pay God His portion first, and the rest will always stretch."*

We have learned that God is the source of all prosperity. If we need God's help to prosper, it's essential to see that we must begin by honoring God.

A Covenant Relationship

We make a mistake if we think prosperity is simply a formula: Some people believe all they need to do is say a certain prayer and make an offering, and millions of dollars will automatically come to us in return, sort of like a holy slot machine.

But, in truth, prosperity is connected to a relationship with God. This is like any relationship: *How do you feel about God? How do you make God feel?* Human relationships suffer when we don't show love or respect. In marriage, wives can complain, *"You don't want me-you want a maid, a cook, and a lover; I feel used."* Husbands can complain, *"I am just a paycheck to you."* Perhaps you've had people in your life who you never hear from until they want something from you or need money. Their treatment of you leaves you feeling offended.

But we are in a relationship with God, and in some ways God is the same: when we treat Him as having little or no value, He doesn't want to help us. **Malachi 1:14 NIV** *"Cursed is the cheat who has an acceptable male in his flock and vows to give it, but then sacrifices a blemished animal to the Lord. For I am king," says the Lord Almighty, "and my name is to be feared among the nations.*

In this verse, God is expressing His complaint to the people with whom He has a relationship (the Jewish people). He says when you give something to me, you give defective things, or things you didn't want anyway. That is offensive because your gift is not in line with who I am (a great King), and it shows that you don't really value Me.

Relationship Revelation

A relationship with God begins with revelation. It starts by God revealing Himself and showing us who He is. **Genesis 28:13** *And behold, the Lord stood above it and said: "I am the Lord God of Abraham your father and the God of Isaac; the land on which you lie I will give to you and your descendants.* In this verse, God reveals who He is to Jacob: The God of his ancestors, and the covenant God who makes great promises to His people.

When God reveals Himself to us, our part is to <u>respond</u> to the revelation of who God is. We must do something! **Genesis 28:18-19 NIV** ¹⁸*Early the next morning Jacob took the stone he had placed under his head and set it up as a pillar and poured oil on top of it.* ¹⁹*He called that place Bethel (House of God).* In this verse, Jacob responds to the revelation of who God is with **a covenant**, which means *"promise, or a vow." **Genesis 28:20-21*** *20Then Jacob made a vow, saying, "If God will be with me, and keep me in this way that I am going, and give me bread to eat and clothing to put on, 21so that I come back to my father's house in peace, then the Lord shall be my God.* When it says *"Jacob made a vow,"* it means he made a **covenant**: in ancient times, two people could enter into a covenant. It was very serious: You would kill an animal, cut it in half, and walk between the two pieces as you made your vow. You were each saying, *"I will do my part, and you will do your part."* Making a covenant while walking between the pieces of a dead animal showed these were not light words based on a sudden, random urge, but that you were taking your covenant relationship seriously.

Jacob's covenant was a covenant of <u>honor</u>: Honor means respect, value, and worth. Jacob was saying, *"I recognize God's great value and worth."* Jacob's obligations in this covenant relationship had several aspects:

I will honor God with my life: Honor literally means, *"To place high, to carry weight, or to show value."* So, Jacob was telling God, *"You are valuable to me and worthy of respect."*

I will obey God with my decisions: Genesis 28 begins with Jacob honoring God in relationships: *I won't marry an unbeliever, because You don't approve of doing that.* Jacob chose to obey God by placing God's will before his own wants and needs. **You cannot prosper if you will not obey God!**

I will put God first in my life: *Above everything else, and before everything else.* **Matthew 6:33 NIV** *But seek first his kingdom and his righteousness, and all these things will be given to you as well.*

The Sign of Covenant

Jacob made a vow to honor God, but notice that he did something to demonstrate his heart's decision. ***Genesis 28:22 NIV*** *...this stone that I have set up as a pillar will be God's house, and of all that you give me I will give you a tenth."* When God revealed to Jacob who He is, Jacob's response was: *I will give you 10% of everything you give me! The word tithing = tenthing, or 10%.* Jacob said to God he would give Him 10%, but God Himself puts <u>His</u> approval on the principle of tithing: ***Malachi 3:10*** *Bring all the tithes into the storehouse...* Some Christians have the wrong idea about tithing. They view it simply as a church funding program: *It's a way to pay the bills.* Tithing does help pay the bills, but paying church bills is the <u>least</u> important factor in tithing!

Tithing is honoring God! It is recognizing who God is, in His greatness and worth. ***Proverbs 3:9 NCV*** *Honor the Lord with your wealth and the firstfruits from all your crops.* This scripture speaks of the firstfruits, which is another word for the tithe, and it says when you tithe, you are honoring God: *That is the true purpose of tithing!*

- **Tithing is a visible way of demonstrating that you recognize God's great worth.**
- **Tithing is a visible way of demonstrating that you recognize God's ownership of your money and possessions:** From the beginning of time, God has always had a reserved portion built into having a relationship with God. In the garden, God told Adam, *"You can eat of any tree, except one tree."* Why? God did not explain why. It was a reserved tree; God was saying, *"it is mine."* It was a visible way to show God that you agree that He is God, and you are not. We know that Adam and Eve ate from that tree because

of the idea *"you can be as gods."* Anyone who doesn't tithe shows God they believe that they are God, and He is not. Anyone who tithes shows God they recognize God is God, and they are not. This is why those who do not tithe do not do well spiritually, because they are rejecting who God is!

- **Tithing is trusting God:** It is the visible method of showing that you trust God. You are saying, "I'll do better on 90% of my income with God's blessing than if I keep 100% without God's blessing."

Malachi 3:10 NIV Bring the whole tithe into the storehouse, that there may be food in my house. Test me in this," says the Lord Almighty, "and see if I will not throw open the floodgates of heaven and pour out so much blessing that you will not have room enough for it.

Elements of Covenant Giving

Look at the elements of covenant giving:

Covenant giving involves a set amount: We have a wrong idea if we believe that the amount we give to God is up to the individual. Many Christians say, *"As long as I give something to God, then that's ok."* The modern anti-tithing idea is called Grace-Giving. The idea is that because we are now under grace, you can give whatever you feel like giving. But somehow, those who have experienced God's abundant grace end up giving less than those who were under the law. Charles Wesley said, *"**If we give less under grace than they did under the law, it is a disgrace.**"* But God is very clear about how much we should start with in a covenant relationship: The amount is up to <u>Him</u> – not us!

Malachi 3:10 NIV Bring the whole tithe into the storehouse. God says the <u>whole</u> tithe, which is 10%. Not <u>part</u> of the tithe, which is less than 10%. If <u>we</u> set the amount, then we are God (which defeats the point of tithing).

Covenant giving involves a set place: Through many years of pastoring, I've had people tell me, *"I tithe here and there: I give to charity, to family, and to neighbors."* Other Christians send their tithe to TV preachers or online ministries. But if you send your tithe anywhere you choose, that would make <u>you</u> God! God tells us where we are to tithe: **Malachi 3:10 NLT** *Bring all the tithes <u>into the storehouse</u>* ...The "storehouse" is speaking of the treasury rooms built along each side of the temple. The temple was the place where God's people could meet with God. So, God instructs them to bring their tithe *<u>to the place where they met with God</u>!* Our modern equivalent is the church. Your local church is where you are fed and helped. Your local church is where you can meet with God in prayer meetings, worship, sermons, and altar calls. Your local church is where you can get counsel and direction for your life. Your local church is where you can get married and have funerals performed for your family. It is the Pastors and people from your local church who will visit and pray for you and your family in the hospital. Next time you're in the hospital, call your favorite TV preacher and ask him to visit you and pray. See how well that works out.

Covenant giving involves a set time: Another mistake Christians can make is thinking, *"I will tithe <u>whenever I get around to it.</u>"* But a key command concerning tithing is the principle of **firstfruits**. *Exodus 23:19 The first of the firstfruits of your land you shalt bring into the house of the LORD your God.* In ancient Bible times, those involved in farming or agriculture were to bring the first of the firstfruits. That meant the very first portion (and we know the portion is 10%) they were to bring to God and offer it to Him. God doesn't just want the ten percent of your income – <u>eventually</u>; He wants it <u>first</u>! This is a Bible principle we see: God speaks of His rights and claims on the firstborn and firstfruits. When we tithe first, it is a real and visible way of showing God that you put Him first!*1 Corinthians 16:2 On the first day of the week let each one of you lay something aside, storing up as he may prosper, that there be no collections when I come.* This scripture teaches that they were to give on "the first day of the week," or Sunday! For us, the principle would be, "as soon as you get paid," or "the first time you go to church after you get paid."

Dishonoring God

If you are reading or listening to this book, it is because in some way you want or need your finances to prosper. If so, you must understand that **you cannot prosper if you don't tithe!** If you're not in a covenant relationship with God, which is demonstrated by tithing, you are dishonoring God. *God does not bless those who dishonor Him! Malachi 3:8-9 NIV* *8"Will a man rob God? Yet you rob me. "But you ask, 'How do we rob you?' "In tithes and offerings. 9You are under a curse—the whole nation of you—because you are robbing me.*

This verse explains that the Jewish people of that time were experiencing financial reversals in their farming and agriculture (which was their income). God says that is a direct result of them dishonoring Him by not tithing! If you had someone in your life that consistently told you, *"I think you're dumb, ugly and I don't really like being around you,"* and then they ask if you will lend them money, would you agree? No, because they are dishonoring you! So, why should it be any different with God? Through the years, I've had a number of people tell me that at some point they stopped tithing, then had various financial catastrophes happen to them. In some instances, the cost of the financial catastrophes was equal to the tithe they should have paid: *To the cent!* That's not a coincidence; it's a message from God.

The Blessings of Covenant

The amazing thing about God is His willingness to bless us for our obedience. This is amazing: Why should God bless us for obeying Him? If He blesses us for paying the tithe (which belongs to Him), He is rewarding us for not stealing! Do we do that in our lives? Do we pay burglars a bonus for not breaking into our house? Do we give thieves a reward for not stealing from us? But, amazingly, that's what God does! God is very definite in His willingness to bless our obedience in the tithe. *Malachi 3:10 Bring all the tithes into the storehouse, That there may be food in My house, And try Me now in this," Says the LORD of hosts, "If I will not open for you the windows of heaven And pour out for you such blessing That there will not be room enough to receive it.*

Why would God bless our obedience when we are simply doing what is right? Because we are in a relationship! When we tithe, God sees that we love Him, honor Him and trust Him! God also blesses us when we tithe because His honor and reputation are at stake. In **Malachi 1:14,** God declares that *"I am a great King..."* Imagine if we say to others that God is a great King in character and power, but He does nothing to help us. That is unacceptable to God! His name is at stake. God's promise is that if His people will honor and obey Him in the tithe, He will *"open the windows of heaven." Malachi 3:10 Bring all the tithes into the storehouse, That there may be food in My house, And try Me now in this," Says the LORD of hosts, "If I will not open for you the windows of heaven..."* Three dimensions of blessing are seen if there are open windows in heaven:

Open windows in heaven bring a positive supernatural dimension of the favor of God. This is speaking of a supernatural dimension of answered prayer. You can bring your needs to God in prayer and ask for His supernatural help. When you pray and you are tithing, you are in favor with God because you honor Him for who He is! *Deuteronomy 14:29 ...that the LORD your God may bless you in all the work of your hand which you do.* The context of Deuteronomy 14 is written to people involved in farming. If God blesses all the work of their hands, they would be fruitful: Crops would grow well. For modern Christians, we can apply this in the area of fruitfulness, or winning souls for God. God will bless our work of witnessing to unbelievers, or our outreaches. Something more will be added to our labor and the words we speak, which will cause our words to be effective.

Open windows in heaven bring a supernatural dimension that overcomes demonic assaults. *Malachi 3:11 And I will rebuke the devourer for your sakes, So that he will not destroy the fruit of your ground, Nor shall the vine fail to bear fruit for you in the field," Says the Lord of hosts;*

Farming or agricultural people sometimes would struggle with natural factors that either blocked or destroyed their crops: Drought or insect infestations. God says He will "rebuke the devourer," which means He will prevent those things from eating up their crops. This is what happens to people today. The enemy of our souls attacks our finances to make us miserable, consume our energies, and prevent us from investing in God's work. But when we tithe, God says He will help us to overcome demonic assaults that would hurt our finances. In Genesis 28 Jacob promised to tithe, then we see how the blessings of his covenant of honor with God worked out in his life. Laban kept trying to cheat him by changing his wages, but God got involved. *Genesis 31:7-9 ⁷yet your father has cheated me by changing my wages ten* times. *However, God has not allowed him to harm me. ⁸If he said, 'The speckled ones will be your wages,' then all the flocks gave birth to speckled young; and if he said, 'The streaked ones will be your wages,' then all the flocks bore streaked young. ⁹So God has taken away your father's livestock and has given them to me.* The cheating didn't work because God overcame those strategies against Jacob's finances.

Open windows in heaven brings a positive supernatural dimension of financial blessing. *Malachi 3:10 Bring all the tithes into the storehouse, That there may be food in My house, And try Me now in this," Says the LORD of hosts, "If I will not open for you the windows of heaven And pour out for you such blessing That there will not be room enough to receive it.* We will look at this dimension of blessing in later chapters but blessing that is poured out *"that there will not be room enough to receive it"* is speaking of the overall promise of *"more than enough!"* God does not want His children to live with *"less than enough,"* or *"barely enough."* He wants His people, and His churches to have *"more than enough!"*

The Purpose of Blessing

If we want God to prosper us, we must make sure that we understand the true purpose of prosperity. The mistake of many so-called "Prosperity Preachers" is the wrong emphasis on the purpose of prosperity. It is often presented as simply, *"God wants you to live the good life"* or, *"God wants you to live like a King's kid."* The emphasis is often selfish: *"If God prospers you, you can drive a nice car, live in a nice house, have nice jewelry, go on nice vacations..."* God doesn't have a problem with you being blessed and enjoying nice things. I know some people say it is wrong to have more than you need, and that you should give it all away to poor people, but that doesn't line up with the record of

Abraham, Isaac, and Job, who God specifically tells us were very rich.

The ultimate purpose of prosperity is to further the purposes of God! From the beginning of God's relationship with Abraham, God promises that He will bless him. We can see later that 'blessing' included his finances. But at the same time God promises to bless Abraham, he tells him the purpose of the blessing: *Genesis 12:2-3 2I will make you a great nation; I will bless you And make your name great; And you shall be a blessing. 3I will bless those who bless you, And I will curse him who curses you; And in you all the families of the earth shall be blessed."* Ultimately, the purpose of God blessing Abraham was to fulfil God's purposes:

- **God wanted to establish a great nation** (The nation of Israel).
- **God wanted Abraham to bless other people.**
- **God wanted Abraham to bless all the families (ethnic groups) of the earth.**

Financial blessing is included in God's purposes. The financial blessing will enable the blessing to be brought to all the people of the earth. I believe the ultimate purpose of God is the evangelization of the lost. I cannot speak for other churches or fellowships of churches: I can only tell you what our church (The Potter's House in Prescott, Arizona) and our Fellowship of churches (Christian Fellowship Ministries) do with the money God's people give. If the ultimate purpose of God is that lost sinners come to know Him, then the highest purpose for our money is to fund evangelism. In our church (and fellowship) we use the money that God's people give to fund evangelism in four main ways:

Our tithes and offerings fund local outreach: We have concerts, plays, healing crusades, and many other forms of outreach to draw sinners so we can preach the Gospel to them.

These require money to be able to do this, whether that is printing, renting venues, equipment, food, or whatever enables these local outreaches.

Our tithes and offerings fund outreaches out of town: We have churches in other cities that we send teams of people in vans to help them evangelize. We send bands and drama teams to do outreaches in different cities. These also require money to be able to purchase, maintain and fuel the vans that carry these bands, drama teams or outreach (impact) teams. It requires money to purchase the equipment necessary to put these out-of-town outreaches on.

Our tithes and offerings fund church planting: Our vision is called pioneering. This means we send couples to other cities to start brand new churches. We don't just tell them to be blessed and let them go; we fund these church-planting ventures. Money is required to get the couples there, to get them housing, equipment, buildings, outreaches and anything they need to get the new church going.

Our tithes and offerings fund world evangelism: From the beginning of God's covenant relationship with Abraham, God commands him to be a blessing to "all the families of the earth." For New Testament believers, God commands us to *"Go into all the world and preach the gospel to every creature,"* (**Mark 16:15**) and, *"Make disciples of all the nations."* (**Matthew 28:19**). We believe our calling to fulfill God's worldwide purpose is to send missionary couples to plant churches in every nation of the world. This is by far the most expensive thing we do as a church, or as a Fellowship. We don't follow the pattern of many Christian organizations, which is to allow couples to go overseas as missionaries only if they raise their own money! This is a common pattern that mission organizations follow: The missionary couple go around to various churches and ask for donations before they can go. They must return home for extended periods of time every few years to repeat the fundraising. In our church and Fellowship, we don't do this. If we are sending the couple to another nation, we also fund their mission with the giving of God's people. We believe that is the ultimate purpose of why God blesses us in the first place.

Philippians 4:15-17 *15Now you Philippians know also that in the beginning of the gospel, when I departed from Macedonia, no church shared with me concerning giving and receiving but you only. 16For even in Thessalonica you sent aid once and again for my necessities. 17Not that I seek the gift, but I seek the fruit that abounds to your account.* Paul was pastoring in the city of Philippi, Macedonia. He wanted to go to another nation, and he says that when he went, the people in the church in Philippi contributed their money to enable him to establish the church in Thessalonica. He says their finances enabled *"fruit to abound to their account,"* referring to the people that were saved as Paul preached the Gospel there. That is the ultimate purpose of the blessing of God in prosperity.

If we honor God with the covenant of tithing and if we use the blessing God gives us for His purposes, God will return further prosperity. He has no problem with meeting our needs, and no problem with us enjoying His blessings: if we always remember the reason He blesses us!

A rich English merchant was requested by Queen Elizabeth to take up certain affairs of hers. He said, "Your Majesty, I am willing enough, but if I do your bidding, my business will be ruined." The Queen replied, "Sir, you attend to my business, and I will attend to yours."

This is true when considering the issue of prosperity. If we always make sure we honor God and take care of His purposes, He will release His blessing in prosperity in our lives and churches.

It All Started With Yes - *Raja and Chandu Kumar Gudipalli*

I completed my Bachelor's degree in 2007 and started searching for a Job in Bangalore, India (573 km from my hometown). One of my relatives lent me $70 each month to survive and to get a job in Bangalore. He did this for four months. In four months, I had applied everywhere and was rejected by 44 companies. I was utterly discouraged and did not know what to do. I felt like I had lost hope and began thinking I might not get a job.

One day, I knelt down in the bathroom where I was living with five of my friends in one single room and prayed to God, *"If you help me to get a job, I will give my entire first month's salary."* The next week, I got a job. . I had lost 33 pounds due to stress and worry. (I was 92 pounds when I got my job). I had thought I might never get a job.

I came to the Potter's House Bangalore in September 2007 and gave my entire month's salary. I told my relative that I will pay the $280 I borrowed from him in the next month. Then we got hit by the global financial crisis in 2008-09. Every company was laying off thousands of employees because of the recession. At that time, I was in a financial crisis and on the verge of losing my job. At that time, we had a revival with Pastor Daryl Elliot. He asked, *"Is there anyone looking for a financial miracle in your life?"* I came forward, he prayed and gave me a word, then asked me, *"If God will bless you, will you be faithful in your tithes?* I said *"Yes."*

That single decision changed my life. I didn't lose my job, but there were no raises. I was faithful to tithe. After one year, my manager said that, in recognition of your hard work, we want to give you a bonus equal to half your yearly salary. After six months, they raised my pay by 56%. I was thankful to God for provisions and started tithing 11%. After one year, they promoted me to the next level and increased my salary by 20%. Then I started tithing 12%. After 6 months, a consultancy firm approached me and asked me to take a 5-day training session, and they paid me 2 months' salary for it. Then, I went to Canada to work for three months. For three months' work, they paid me the equivalent of four years' salary. I then started tithing 13%.

I attended one of the India Bible Conferences, and in that conference, there was a call for World Evangelism. I thought of one big amount to give. While I was praying, I felt God stir my heart and increase it fourfold, which was a huge amount. After that, I felt in my heart and started tithing 20%. Nothing happened for 1-1/2 years, but I faithfully tithed 20%. After 1-1/2 years, I was promoted to the next level and received a 25% pay increase.

One month later, I got a call from Amazon and got a job. They gave me a 60% raise from my current pay. I married Chandu, and we faithfully tithed 20%. After 6 months, I moved to Seattle, and my pay was increased by 500%. After 6 months, my wife also got a Job at Amazon. God doubled our wages!

I never asked my manager to increase my pay. I know only <u>God</u> will increase. A few years back, I had nothing in my life, and today God has given me so much. Everything changed after I said a simple *"Yes."*

How Do I Begin? *Loic and Kimberly Didier*
Port Louis, Mauritius

My fiancé and I had some financial goals we wanted to achieve but could not achieve them. One service Pastor Josh Walsh spoke about tithing, and I went up after and asked him how we could tithe with no money & no job?

But as soon as we did, the miracles began. I had just qualified as an electrician, and shortly after, I received a call from a contractor who offered me a steady stream of work. I haven't been out of work ever since. In fact, I was so blessed that I was able to buy two tickets from Mauritius to the Sydney Conference, which was such a blessing.

During the Sydney Conference, we did not have a lot of money, but God spoke to us to give what we had, and when Pastor Rob Walsh took the world evangelism offering on Thursday night, we gave a very large amount for us. Since that offering, God has powerfully blessed us financially.

1. People began to say to us, *"God spoke to us,"* and then gave us money...in fact, we have been given 10x's more than we gave in the offering. Even after the conference, we're still receiving money from family, friends, and even people we don't know.

2. My fiancé was a trainee at an architecture company, and she received an email saying they were giving her a full-time job at well above the award wage in Mauritius.

3. Finally, my dad blessed me with a Ford Ranger Ute for my business.

Rebuking the Devourer - *Tony and Nette Tinio*
Davao City, Philippines

My name is Tony Tinio. My wife and I had a flourishing bakery business in Davao City, Philippines. In spite of our being so busy, we faithfully served the Lord and supported the work of God. Every Sunday we closed our 4 bakery outlets and required all workers (almost 50 people) to attend church services. God honored us by prospering us not only financially but more so in spiritual things.

It was in 1993 when God confirmed to us **Malachi 3:11** *"And I will rebuke the devourer."* One morning about 2:00 am, I was awakened by a phone call. The caller informed me that our bakery was on fire. My first reaction was to pray, and I declared, "GOD GIVES, GOD TAKES AWAY." I told my wife about the fire and suggested she stay home. I drove to the place and saw that the firefighters could not contain the fire. The building which we rented had a lodging house on the second floor. On the ground floor were several businesses, including our bakery. Everything was engulfed by flames. Amazingly, I had peace in my heart while watching the burning building. I stayed for awhile, then went home. I reported to my wife that our bakery was gone.

When morning came, I took my wife and daughter to the site. We saw firefighters bringing out dead bodies of people who had been trapped in the burned lodging house. There were 9 people dead. We later learned from the police report that the fire started at the mezzanine level of the building; the same level the bakery was on.

Two days later, we were allowed to inspect the burned bakery. To our amazement and joy, the fire had not damaged the bakery! Although, there was water everywhere, everything inside the bakery was spared from the heat of the fire. Plastic wares didn't melt, and glasses and mirrors did not break. In fact, the contents of the refrigerator were still cold. We opened a bottle of cola; it was still ice cold! It seemed that God surrounded the place and saved the bakery. People passing by would take a look and say it was a miracle! You could still see the burn marks on the buildings on either side of the bakery.

We got the approval of the City Engineer's Office to demolish the upper portion of the burned building and then renovated the place. A month after the fire, the bakery was back to business. Glory to God! The miracle did not stop there. The insurance of the company paid us enough money to cover the cost of renovation. As an additional blessing, when we reopened the bakery (which is located next to a college with thousands of students), many students and all kinds of people wanted to buy bread from "The Miracle Bakery" that God didn't let burn, so God actually blessed us with extra money as a result of the fire! Truly our God is a Savior, Deliverer and Provider!

Faithfulness Rewarded - *James and Liz Wilson*

I've been paying tithes all my life - since I was a young boy. Sometimes my faith in tithing is tested. It was our anniversary while we were attending the conference, so my mom gave us $100. It was not a huge amount, but we were at conference. I was pioneering a church and working a job. It crossed my mind to hold on to all of it. I reasoned, "It was a gift!" But I paid tithes, and then, just to poke the devil in the eye, we put the rest towards world evangelism. Tuesday of the **very next week after the conference**, my boss called me in and gave me a $4,000 pay raise! Thank you, Father!

Then, as it sometimes is with pioneering, the money was tight. It was the 31st of the month, but because of conference expenses, etc. I didn't have any money. Our rent was $1200.00 exactly. I went to prayer that morning, and when I walked in, I found an envelope shoved under the door addressed to my wife and me. Inside was $1200! It always, always pays to give your tithes. Don't be stingy! No matter how long you've been doing it, God will still surprise you over and over.

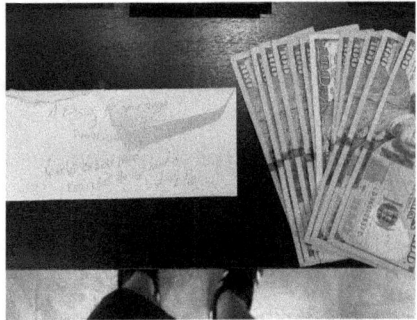

Obedience Changed My Marriage - *Carol Zammit*

My husband retired from the army in 1998. He took several jobs driving trucks, but soon decided he would prefer an office job. Over about 1-1/2 years, he applied for perhaps 100 jobs, many of which he was well qualified for, but nothing would open for him. He even did a course at college to improve his prospects, but to no avail.

My husband had been in and out of the church as a perpetual backslider, but was now making good decisions and starting to do well. However, the issue of money had not been dealt with.

The night before Pastor Mark Aulson called people to pledge money, He had preached a sermon, and in it, he said wives often hear from God better than their husbands. When the pledge was taken, my husband wrote down a figure that was certainly a stretch for him, but easily attainable. I wrote down a figure five times higher! With last night's sermon ringing in his ears, he decided to put my figure in as our pledge. It took several months to save the money to pay the pledge, and another few weeks for my husband to summon the faith to honor it.

Almost immediately, everything changed on the job horizon. My husband is now in an office job far above his qualifications that pays $10,000 more per year than he was earning driving trucks. The company is putting him through university (all expenses paid) with the prospect of earning $10,000 more per year within five years.

This has been an excellent landmark for my husband. He has become a faithful tither and has broken the backsliding habit.

Tithing Brings Deliverance- *Brandon and Elizabeth Kwesiga*

When I was pioneering our first church in England, I met a young Muslim man during Ramadan. He started attending our services, and, unknown to me at the time, he was drowning in debt of about £36,000. He never mentioned a word to me about it. After about 6 months in church, he asked me to meet his mother. He was in his late twenties, so the request felt odd, but I went, hoping she might come to church as well. When I arrived, she was not home yet. As soon as she buzzed into the building, he broke down. The real reason he invited me was for me to help him tell his mother that he had gambled away her entire life savings. She had spent years earning money as a cleaner after coming to the UK from Eritrea. Because she could not read or write, he handled her banking.

She also had a friend in their community who had remortgaged her home and was planning to give her that money so she could buy her council flat through a government scheme. But he had lost everything. When she walked through the door, she hugged me and thanked me. She kept saying how much God had changed her son, his behavior, his focus, his whole life. Then came the moment we had to tell her the truth. She almost collapsed. Right there, I had a moment of faith. I prayed for her and told her plainly that God is able, and what He was doing in her son was real and supernatural. She asked me to go with her son to speak to the woman who had remortgaged her house to explain they could not buy the flat. We walked downstairs, and I encouraged Solomon the whole way, telling him I believed God was going to step in. Just as we got into the car, his mother called us back up. She said someone had just called for Solomon. We waited. The phone rang again. It was a wealthy woman whose house his mother had been cleaning for years. She was in America at the time. At the exact moment we had prayed, she felt compelled to give Solomon money. She transferred about £38,000. The funds cleared in three days.

But that was not the real miracle. Within his first month in church, Solomon felt convicted to start tithing, and he did, faithfully. When he started putting God first with his money, the gambling addiction broke instantly. That was the miracle.

Today, Solomon is married, has two children, is a leader in our church, and we are preparing to launch him into ministry next April at the South London conference.

Chapter 12: Seeds of Prosperity

Money is like a seed, plant it wisely and it will grow into a tree of wealth. But neglect it, and it will wither away.

Unknown

'Suddenly' miracles are made of quiet moments of faithfulness.
Andrena Sawyer

James L. Kraft, moved to the U.S. in the early 1900s and began selling cheese door-to-door with only $65 after his first business collapsed. By 1909 his venture had grown into J. L. Kraft & Bros. Co., and in 1916 he revolutionized the industry by patenting a cheese-pasteurizing process that enabled nationwide shipping. Beyond business, Kraft was a devoted Christian who gave generously throughout his life, directing much of his wealth to churches, missions, and religious education. He said, *"The only investment I ever made which has paid consistently increasing dividends is the money I have given to the Lord."*

Once we understand the principle of a covenant of honor through tithing, and see that the purpose of prosperity is ultimately to further God's purposes, we are ready to see what triggers miracle prosperity: The principle of planting seed.

The Seed Principle

As creator of the universe, God has set the laws of life: How things work in life and how they will work best. A foundational principle for all of life is **the seed principle.** *Genesis 8:22 "While the earth remains, Seedtime and harvest, Cold and heat, Winter and summer, And day and night Shall not cease."*

Everything in life begins with a seed, and everything in the Kingdom of God begins with a seed. Trees began as seeds. Crops began as seeds. But we need to understand that seeds only grow by being planted! Years ago, I got interested in developing a vegetable garden. I built a raised-bed garden. I filled it with soil and fertilizer. Then I went and bought packets of seeds that I intended to plant. But at the time I should have planted those seeds, I was out of the country for several weeks. Then, when I returned, I was extremely busy and became sidetracked. Those seed packets sat on a shelf in my garage for the entire season and never grew a thing, *because seeds only grow if we plant them!*

When considering financial prosperity, this principle is also absolutely true. The Bible refers to our money as seed, but just as in nature, the seed of money will only grow if we plant it! There are several laws of the harvest in the kingdom of God that we need to understand if we want to prosper.

Seed principle #1: You will only reap <u>what</u> you plant! *Galatians 6:7 NCV Do not be fooled: You cannot cheat God. People harvest <u>only</u> what they plant.* This scripture teaches us that you will not get money or get more money only by asking God for money! Prayer works! God wants us to pray! I believe in prayer! But prayer alone will <u>not</u> bring financial prosperity. In God's kingdom: *If you need money, you must plant seeds of money!* Planting seeds of money is called <u>giving</u>: *Releasing what belongs to you. 2 Corinthians 9:7 NCV Each of you should give as you have decided in your heart to give. You should not be sad when you give, and you should not give because you feel forced to give. God loves the person who gives happily.*

Tithing is not <u>giving</u>, because the first ten percent of our income belongs to God, not us! Imagine if I loaned you $100, then you say to me, *"I'm feeling generous, so I'm going to give you $100."* If you return what I lent you; it isn't generosity or a gift, because it was mine to begin with.

Malachi 3:8 NIV "Will a man rob God? Yet you rob me. "But you ask, 'How do we rob you?' "In tithes **and offerings**. The tithe is 10% of our income: The amount is up to God, not us. We show God that we agree it belongs to Him by paying our tithe, or 10% of our income. You don't <u>give</u> the tithe, you <u>pay</u> it.

Offerings are anything we choose to give over and above the tithe: *The amount is up to us! 2 Corinthians 9:7 NCV Each of you should give **as you have decided in your heart to give**. You should not be sad when you give, and you should not give because you feel forced to give. God loves the person who gives happily.* Every Christian should build into their budget or money planning regular giving of **offerings**. In the Old Testament, God's people tithed, but there were also regular offerings built into having a relationship with God. <u>Anything</u> above the tithe is called an offering. My wife and I practice this in our own finances. We tithe, and each week when we tithe, we give regular offerings, plus we participate in the outreach pledge we use to fund outreach, church planting, and world evangelism. To clarify, both our regular offerings and our outreach pledges are offerings. We just chose to separate them into two different categories of regular offerings. As **2 Corinthians 9:7** says, you can give *'as you have decided in your heart to give.'* The classic old saying concerning the difference between tithing and giving:

Tithing is a debt I owe; Giving is a seed I sow.

Principles of Multiplication

Seed principle #2: Only what is given away is multiplied. *Luke 6:38 NIV Give, and it will be given to you. A good measure, pressed down, shaken together and running over, will be poured into your lap. For with the measure you use, it will be measured to you."* The context is giving in relationships, but the principle applies to money: **Your <u>receiving</u> is connected to your giving!**

John 6:9, 11 NLT ⁹ *"There's a young boy here with five barley loaves and two fish. But what good is that with this huge crowd?* ¹¹*Then Jesus took the loaves, gave thanks to God, and distributed them to the people. Afterward he did the same with the fish. And they all ate as much as they wanted.* Andrew found only one boy who was willing to give, but logic tells us that in a crowd of many thousands of people, there must have been others who did have some food to eat. But the miracle of multiplication only came on what was <u>given</u>! Anyone else who had food but failed to give it to Jesus – *their food was not multiplied!*

Seed principle #3: You only reap <u>after</u> you sow, not before. *Mark 4:26-29 NIV* ²⁶He also said, "This is what the kingdom of God is like. A man scatters seed on the ground. ²⁷Night and day, whether he sleeps or gets up, the seed sprouts and grows, though he does not know how. ²⁸All by itself the soil produces grain—first the stalk, then the head, then the full kernel in the head. ²⁹As soon as the grain is ripe, he puts the sickle to it, because the harvest has come." This story is very helpful to correct some wrong tendencies in some Christians. There are people who intend to be generous <u>after</u> God gives them a lot of money. When we were missionaries in Johannesburg, South Africa, a man came to church one day to see me. He told me how much he appreciated what I was doing in the community. He said someone was giving him 500,000 Rand. That was a huge amount of money for someone who had been living in poverty. He asked me, *"What do I need all that money for?"* He said, *"When I get it, I'm going to give half of that money to your church!"* I started to get excited, because we were in the middle of building project. But then I thought, *"Who would be giving him so much money?"* So, I asked him, *"Who is giving you that much money?"* His eyes lit up, and he asked me, *"Have you heard of the Reader's Digest Sweepstakes?"* He had gotten a letter in the mail from The Reader's Digest

Magazine, saying, *"You <u>may</u> already be a winner!"* He was willing to be generous with money he <u>didn't</u> have. But he never gave any money that he <u>did</u> have! That kind of heart will never enter into prosperity because it goes against God's instructions in His word for our money. ***2 Corinthians 8:12*** *For if there is first a willing mind, it is accepted <u>according to what one has</u>, and not according to what he does not have.*

Seed principle #4: You will reap <u>more</u> than you sow. The amazing thing about seeds is that when you plant a seed, you don't just get one seed back: *The seed multiplies!* You get many, many seeds back for what you have given away by planting.

In ancient Egypt, they would bury people and place wheat seeds in their mummified hands. They believed the dead person would need the seeds in the afterlife. 3,000 years later, an ancient Egyptian mummy was found in a tomb in Egypt with wheat seeds in its hand; the number of seeds was exactly the same as when it was placed there! The seeds never grew, because they were never planted! One man calculated that if those seeds had been planted back when the man died, and continuously replanted year after year, they would now produce a significant percentage of the world's wheat needed for bread.

The Bible gives us the promise of miraculous multiplication that comes from giving. ***Luke 6:38 NIV*** *Give, and it will be given to you. A good measure, pressed down, shaken together and running over, will be poured into your lap. For with the measure you use, it will be measured to you."* This refers to ancient times when you purchased some kind of grain. The seller would pour into the container, filling it to the top. But if you press it down, you could fit some more in. Then, if you shake the container, removing air pockets, still more could be put in. But God ensures that it is not just barely enough to fill the container, but that there is so much it runs over, spilling into your lap.

But the key to this multiplied abundance is that first we must give out! Are you experiencing the "more than enough" of blessing? Are you seeing the overflowing multiplication in your life? This is the possibility for those who get a revelation of giving.

1 Kings 17:15-16 NIV *15She went away and did as Elijah had told her. So there was food every day for Elijah and for the woman and her family. 16For the jar of flour was not used up and the jug of oil did not run dry, in keeping with the word of the Lord spoken by Elijah.* The widow of Zarephath believed and obeyed God by giving of what she had to God first. It is after she gave out that God did a multiplying miracle: Each day, she went to the jar of flour and the jug of oil to make bread for herself, her son, and Elijah, and each day what was in the jar and the jug multiplied supernaturally. She experienced a continual supply for over 3 years. This is what God wants to do for those who obey him in giving: A continual supply of resources, instead of a one-time blessing that quickly runs out. Are you experiencing the continual blessing of God's multiplying supply? This is what God can do for his obedient children.

Types of Seed Offerings

If we want to experience God's miraculous prosperity in our lives, and if we grasp that multiplication only comes on seed that is sown, we must factor into our thinking and our money planning the sowing of seed through giving offerings. There are numbers of categories of offerings where we need to develop faith and obedience:

Regular giving: We need to plan to give regular offerings or pledges. (I have to explain what a pledge is for those who are not a part of our church or Fellowship. In our church, we put the needs of evangelistic outreach, church planting of new churches, and world evangelism before the local congregation. We invite everyone to make a pledge offering, which is simply writing down the offering we will give in the next six months to fund these Gospel endeavors. The pledge is anonymous and simply helps the Pastors to know what we can plan to do for God). The amount of an offering that you give above your tithe is entirely up to you and your revelation, and faith level. But, I believe Biblically, according to **Malachi 3:8**, that every Christian needs to participate in giving offerings. This is planned giving, not a random or emotional urge. My wife and I give a regular amount of offerings each week, because we plan to do so.

Special giving: There may be times we give that are not planned, but in response to God speaking to us. This unplanned giving may be in response to a need, or God giving us a special instruction. In **John 6,** it tells of the feeding of the multitudes, and the miracle that was triggered when Andrew spoke to a boy who was willing to give his lunch so Jesus could use it. His mother probably packed his lunch for his own use, not to feed anyone else. But in some way, God spoke to this boy through Andrew, and he was willing to give his lunch for Jesus to use.

The Bible gives other examples of special giving: The widow of Zarephath giving her last bit of flour and oil to Elijah, the owner of the donkey's colt in *Luke 19:34 And they said, "The Lord has need of him."* In a church setting, God often speaks to people in conferences and rallies, or special offerings, such as building funds or mission trips. The amount is up to us, but I believe that if you are in tune with God's Spirit, He may at times speak a specific amount for us to give. You will find personal testimonies throughout this book of people who felt God speak a certain amount to give. God may also speak to us to give to a particular person to help them (more about that in the next chapter).

Special giving is a <u>test</u>: God will speak to us to give in special offerings outside of our regular giving. He does this very deliberately and specifically at times. The purpose of Him challenging us to give is to see whether we can be trusted with blessings. *1 Kings 17:13 NIV Elijah said to her, "Don't be afraid. Go home and do as you have said. But first make a small cake of bread for me from what you have and bring it to me, and then make something for yourself and your son.*

The elements of special giving are: *Do you have enough vision to see what your giving can do? Do you love God enough to obey? Can you believe that He can do a miracle if you obey Him in giving?* **It's a test!**

Please understand that whenever God speaks to you to give specially, it's because He wants to do a miracle for you! God is <u>not</u> trying to take away all your money so you never get ahead. He speaks for us to give because He already is planning on releasing a miracle of abundance for you. ***The miracle is in the giving!***

Setting The Limits

Seed principle # 5: <u>You</u> set the limit of your miracle multiplication. *Luke 6:38 NIV Give, and it will be given to you. A good measure, pressed down, shaken together and running over, will be poured into your lap. <u>For with the measure you use</u>, it will be measured to you."* There are people who give technically (they give something over and above their tithe), but they give as little as possible. They play it safe, because they are selfish, they lack revelation of what giving can accomplish, or they lack faith to trust God. But Jesus says whatever measure you are giving out with, that is the measure that comes back to you! *2 Corinthians 9:6 NIV Remember this: Whoever sows sparingly will also reap sparingly, and whoever sows generously will also reap generously.*

You set the limits of your reaping! When you have a revelation of giving and trust in God's love, power, and faithfulness, you give generously! But this scripture tells us that generous giving <u>out</u> releases generous receiving <u>in</u>. *2 Kings 4:3-7 NIV* ³*Elisha said, "Go around and ask all your neighbors for empty jars. Don't ask for just a few. ⁴Then go inside and shut the door behind you and your sons. Pour oil into all the jars, and as each is filled, put it to one side." ⁵She left him and afterward shut the door behind her and her sons. They brought the jars to her and she kept pouring. ⁶When all the jars were full, she said to her son, "Bring me another one." But he replied, "There is not a jar left." Then the oil stopped flowing. ⁷She went and told the man of God, and he said, "Go, sell the oil and pay your debts. You and your sons can live on what is left."* Here is a true story of a woman in financial need. The man of God gives the practical instruction of how God will meet her need – pouring the oil out. But he gives her a challenge in asking her neighbors for empty jars: *Don't ask for just a few.* Get as many jars as you possibly can. When she began to pour out, the oil kept pouring miraculously to fill as many jars as <u>she</u> collected! If she gathered more, she could have had more! In some ways, you set the limits of your miracle multiplication.

I pray that God will give you a revelation of the power of giving, and your faith will rise so you will obey God in giving. If you do not currently give offerings, start now. If you have God speak to you about special giving, please obey Him, **because the miracle of multiplication is in the giving!** *Genesis 26:12* Then *Isaac sowed in that land, and reaped in the same year a hundredfold; and the LORD blessed him.*

God Provides a House - *Joe Campbell*

We were pioneering a new church in Phoenix, Arizona. We lived in an apartment, and we had a revival meeting at church. The visiting speaker gave Connie a word. He said, *"God's going to give you a house,"* and I thought, *"Yeah, right."* But my wife Connie took it seriously. She began to look for a house. She got a realtor, and she was dragging me around looking at houses. But we had no money. We were pioneering, we had no savings, we were driving an old car, but Connie was looking for a house to buy.

Finally, she saw a house, and she told me, *"Honey, I believe this is it. I believe this is the one God wants us to have."* We had signed an offer to buy the house, and it was getting close to the deadline. The realtor had probably seen the car we drove, maybe even driven by the little church building, so she said, *"You know, you're going to have to put some earnest money down."* I said, *"Yes, I'm aware of that,"* and I sort of ignored her. Then, a week later, she asked me again, *"Have you got your funds prepared to purchase this house?"* I said, *"Yes."* She was pressing me, so I told her, *"My Father is wealthy."* But she was getting wise. We've been talking to her, quoting scriptures. She asked, *"Who is your father? Where does he live?"* I said, *"Heaven."* She gave me a look, like, *"Oh no, there goes the sale!"*

But a few days before closing, there was a knock on our door, and a man was standing there. I looked behind him, and he had an old, beat-up Jeep. He told me, *"God spoke to me to give you this,"* and he gave me an envelope. I turned and gave it to Connie. It was filled with $100 bills and there was around $2,000 - exactly what we needed for closing. And we bought that house, praise God! We stayed there about a year later we went to pioneer in Illinois. We sold the house and made about $15,000 profit.

We were in a church service in Sparta, Illinois. We were sitting by Terry and Leigh Ann Haynes, with me next to Terry and Connie on the other side of Leigh Ann. We had made money from the sale of our house, and we were thinking about buying a home in Illinois. But during the offering, God began to deal with me to give it all. I didn't want to, so I kind of looked at Connie, *"Is God speaking to you?"* She nodded her head yes. I held up two fingers (for $2000), and she raised her thumb up - meaning higher. Eventually, we gave it all, and she threw in her wedding rings as well. Nobody told her to. Someone else later bought them and returned them to her. But we gave it all. Then, when we went to Marion, Illinois, to pioneer a new church, we opened a checking account. One day we got a bank statement, and there was a lot of money in our account. I showed it to Connie, and she said, *"Honey, that's not ours. You'd better go down to the bank and sort it out."* I said, *"Well, it's in our account."* But I went down to the bank, and when I walked in and went up to the teller, she said, *"Mr. Campbell, we've been expecting you. The bank manager wants to speak to you."* I went in to speak to him, and he said, *"An anonymous person, they don't want you to know who they are, came in and put that money in your account."* We had put $15,000 in the offering. There was now $20,000 in our account. Praise God! We used the money to buy a house.

People ask me, *"Why, when you take offerings, am I so compelled to give?"* I thought about it, then I realized when you obey God in giving, stories of miracle provision in the Bible aren't just Bible stories of God providing for Peter or Paul – it's your story! And that adds completely another dimension to faith. Something more is added to your planning, praying, and fasting, witnessing, giving, pioneering a church; a miracle dimension of faith that activates the blessing of God.

Hearing, Obeying and Receiving - *Brent and Sharni Underwood*

During the Perth Bible Conference, two of the conference offerings spoke to me personally. The first was Pastor Nigel Brown's. I'd preached a revival recently and been given a love offering, so we decided to give from that. The second was Pastor Greg Mitchell's offering. He spoke about asking God what He wants you to give, which my wife and I hadn't really done in a while. I wanted to hear from God, but it was only once the basket had passed me that the amount of $1200 came to mind. I wrote it down and put it in my briefcase, unsure of what to do. Thursday night, I felt God prompt me to put it in, as well as a world evangelism pledge from our Church (I intended to take an offering when I got back to our Church on Sunday). When I told my wife what God told me to do, she looked at me and said, *"Where are we going to get that?"* I was a bit taken aback. I said, *"From the love offering."* She reminded me I'd already pledged from that! Somehow, it had slipped my mind! At that moment, I was slightly panicked, but I turned to her and said, *"God told me to give this amount; He knows what we have and what we need."* We would pull it from any savings we had and trust God.

The next Sunday, during Bible Hour, we were watching a Memorial Stones Series video when an usher told me that a visitor insisted on seeing me. I went to talk to the man and asked him how I could help. He asked me to pray for him, then pulled out a wallet stuffed with cash to give me. I pushed the wallet away and told him that I didn't need money to pray for him, which I then did. Afterwards, he handed the wallet to me and told me he'd been saving the money for a while to give to the Church. When I told him he should stay and put it in the offering himself, he said he had to go and asked me if I could do it for him, then ran out the door! I gave the wallet to the ushers and continued the service.

When I got home, I pulled the wallet out and realized it was stuffed full of $50 notes! 189 of them in fact! $9450! I was blown away. I'd never had anyone give that much in an offering before! It was an answer to prayer, as I had been praying for a financial breakthrough so we could save up some money as we aimed to launch our first baby church. Not only that, but when I pulled the World Evangelism pledge in my Church, we had more come in than I had pledged on their behalf, which had never happened before either!

But that isn't all. The Monday after the conference, my wife decided to check the status of a Family Tax Benefit we had applied for in November last year. We hadn't heard anything from them since our application had been lodged, but when Sharni checked online, she saw that it had been approved, and we received $11,000 on Tuesday after the conference!

Our Miracle Baby - *Phil and Annie Ouma*

We had been trying to start a family for over 2 years. It took a major emotional toll on us, but it was especially affecting my wife. Every month, she would look forward to taking a pregnancy test only to be disappointed again. It broke my heart to see my wife in tears every month, as we faced yet another disappointment. We spent money on specialists and fertility clinics, and yet again Annie would return a negative pregnancy test.

On the Monday of the 2022 Perth Bible Conference, I approached Pastor Greg Mitchell to pray for us as we wanted God to work a miracle for us. That night, he called out other couples struggling with barrenness, and you prayed for all of us. After that, we continued to believe in God but were still unsuccessful in conceiving a child.

In the 2023 Perth Bible Conference, we pledged a significant amount in the offering (the largest we had ever given). On the back of the pledge card, we wrote some of the things we were believing God for, and, by an act of faith, we pledged them. After the conference, I was wrestling with the amount and thought it was just my emotions getting the best of me. I finally told her that I hadn't yet given what we had pledged. She said, *"Phil, hurry up and just pay it,"* so finally I did. Two days later, she did a pregnancy test, and it came back positive! Our miracle child Dakoda Grace Ouma, was born in 2023. We trace it back to our giving in a conference offering. *Who would have thought that obeying God in a conference offering would trigger our own personal miracle?*

Thank you, Pastor Greg, for challenging us to believe God. I pray our testimony challenges other people's faith, to believe Him for supernatural miracles in their own lives.

OUR MIRACLE BABY

Growing Family, Growing Blessings - *Nate and Ashley Rush*

My wife and I had always been faithful with our finances. But as our family continued to grow (six children), the financial pressures grew right along with it. At the time, I was working for a large corporate company. The company was very strict with its rules and firmly adhered to the annual evaluation with a minimal-raise mindset.

I had accepted a position that should have eventually put us on a strong salary track, but everything was moving painfully slowly. We prayed, we fasted, and we asked God specifically for increase. But for a while, nothing seemed to move.

During the Kingdom Prosperity Sunday School, both Ashley and I felt stirred and challenged to give a faith offering for a pay increase. We prayed very specifically for a $ 25,000-per-year raise. It didn't happen overnight. But within about a month, God stepped in and did what only He can do. Through a few turns of events, the company ended up giving me a raise of $28,000 per year, three thousand more than what we had believed! Then, at the end of that same year, I received a $13,000 bonus on top of that!

We are fully convinced this breakthrough was directly connected to that step of faith; the challenge we responded to and the faith offering we gave. God didn't just meet our need, He exceeded it.

Inspired to Believe and Obey - *Sergio and Andrea Martinez*

We attended the 2025 San Antonio Bible Conference. On Monday night, the Holy Spirit spoke to me to give $1000. I am a full-time pastor, and the problem was that we only had $2,200 in the church account. It made no sense to me. I didn't respond that night. On Wednesday night, Pastor Roman Gutierrez pulled the offering. In it, he spoke about praying for a man who was a drug addict and living on the streets. The man got radically saved, and later his father gave Pastor Roman a bag containing $10,000. When I heard that, the Holy Spirit quickened me again to give the $1000. So, before I lost the inspiration, I quickly wrote a check for $1000. I told God that is what I need, what pastor Roman said, $10,000.

That Sunday morning at my church, someone gave a check for $10,000! I'm so glad I listened to the Holy Spirit's voice. Thank you, Pastor Roman, for your testimony, because it inspired me to obey God.

God is faithful! I took a picture of the check to always remind me to obey the Holy Spirit.

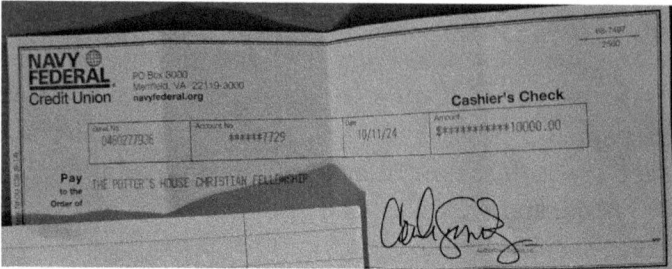

INSPIRED TO BELIEVE AND OBEY

God Provides it All - *Rangi and Danique Pou*

We have a Pastor in Napier, New Zealand, named Rangi Pou. One time, he asked me, *"We need a building, and I want to go full-time. Which one should be the greater priority that I should go for first?"* I told him, *"I believe God can do both. Why don't you believe Him and ask?"* Rangi had been praying for a church building. The one they were meeting in was far too small. He went to a Bible Conference, and during the offering, he was challenged to give. He and his wife intended to give money personally, but they thought of their spare vehicle at home. They decided to sell it and give the money. He told God, *"We need a building, and we want to go full time."*

Six weeks later, he saw a building that had been damaged by vandalism. He tried to call the manager, but Rangi was told that he was at the building cleaning up the damage. Rangi went to the building and asked him if he wanted help. The man (Gerry Sullivan; Director of the Napier Building Society) said yes. Rangi quickly had some guys from the church hurry over to the building and work to help clean it up. As they worked, the men from the church were telling Gerry their testimonies. Some of them used to be gang members, drug dealers, and criminals, but now they are saved and transformed.

After they finished cleaning up the damage, Rangi told Gerry they needed a church building. Gerry called Rangi two days later and asked him to meet at the building. He said, *"I've spoken to the trust, and told them the stories of what God has been doing in the lives of your people."* He handed Rangi the keys, and said, *"You can have the building for free, for as long as you like."* It is a 6000 square foot building, plus it has two full basketball courts. The church put some money into fixing the building up, then the trust paid them $15,000 to cover the costs! So not only did they get the building for free, but the renovations were paid for! Because they weren't paying rent, Rangi was able to go full-time as Pastor immediately. Also, because they weren't having to pay rent, they were able to plant their first church! All three blessings came after he heard the voice of God and gave in obedience.

GOD PROVIDES IT ALL

Chapter 13: A Generous Life

For it is in giving that we receive.
St. Francis of Assisi

Give what you have. To someone,
it may be better than you dare to think.
Henry Wadsworth Longfellow

Curtis Dixon was on his way to pawn his wedding ring so he could pay his electric bill. On the way to the pawn shop, a blind man asked for help getting up. Curtis helped him get to his feet, then the blind man asked him for some money. Curtis told him he would give him some money as soon as he pawned his ring. But what he didn't know was that the man wasn't blind at all: He was social-media influencer Zach Dereniowski, who films people while he asks for help and money. If they respond to him with generosity, he gives them money. When Curtis came back to give the money to the man he thought was blind, Zach gave him USD $5000. The pawn shop added another USD $2500. Then Dereniowski posted the story on his feed and people began to donate. They wound up buying Curtis a car, then ultimately Dereniowski gave him another USD $100,000! **Curtis Dixon's life was changed by generosity!**

If you want to prosper financially, you need to know that God blesses those who are generous to other people in need.

The Purpose of Blessing

We must understand the purpose of money: *Why does God gives us money and prosperity?* **God does not give us money just for** us! *Genesis 12:2 I will make you a great nation; I will bless you And make your name great; And <u>you shall be a blessing</u>.* The principle of blessing built into a relationship with God is that we are to be a blessing to others. The reason God blesses us is so we can bless others. We are blessed to be a blessing. We already said in chapter 11 that the purpose of prosperity is to further the purposes of God. The primary way we do that is by financially participating in God's purposes in a local church. *Ephesians 1:22-23 22And He put all things under His feet, and gave Him to be head over all things to the church, 23which is His body, the fullness of Him who fills all in all.* These verses tell us that everything God does on earth comes through the church. So, suppose God gives us money to further His purposes, and the main expression of His purposes is the church. In that case, the starting point of us being a blessing must be in a local church.

God expects us to bless other people with what He has blessed us with

'Being a blessing' is not limited to tithing and giving in our local church. God also gives us money to bless other people. *2 Corinthians 9:10-11 NIV 10Now he who supplies seed to the sower and bread for food will also supply and increase your store of seed and will enlarge the harvest of your righteousness. 11You will be made rich in every way so that you can be generous on every occasion, and through us your generosity will result in thanksgiving to God.*

This is a part of Christian Stewardship: *I manage money for God and for His purposes.* So, I must include God's plan to help and bless others as part of my money planning.

Romans 12:13 NIV Share with God's people who are in need. Practice hospitality.

Hebrews 13:16 NLT And don't forget to do good and to share with those in need. These are the sacrifices that please God.

2 Corinthians 9:7-9 ⁷So let each one give as he purposes in his heart, not grudgingly or of necessity; for God loves a cheerful giver. ⁸And God is able to make all grace abound toward you, that you, always having all sufficiency in all things, may have an abundance for every good work. ⁹As it is written: "He has dispersed abroad, He has given to the poor; His righteousness endures forever."

These verses speak of sharing, hospitality, doing good, and good works. All of these must involve the material realm: *Not just nice thoughts and prayers!* **James 2:15-17 NIV** *¹⁵Suppose a brother or sister is without clothes and daily food. ¹⁶If one of you says to him, "Go, I wish you well; keep warm and well fed," but does nothing about his physical needs, what good is it? ¹⁷In the same way, faith by itself, if it is not accompanied by action, is dead.* What are we to give to others? Money, food, housing, vehicles, opportunities - <u>anything</u> that will help and bless someone else!

Biblical Examples of Generosity

We find stories of generosity and sharing throughout the Bible:
- *In **1 Kings 18** Obadiah hid and fed one hundred prophets to protect them from Ahab.*
- *In **Ruth 2** Boaz generously provided food for Ruth & Naomi.*
- *In **2 Samuel 17** Barzillai provided for the king when he was on the run from Absalom.* ***2 Samuel 17:28-29 NCV*** *²⁸They brought beds, bowls, clay pots, wheat, barley, flour, roasted grain, beans, small peas, ²⁹honey, milk curds, sheep, and cheese made from cows' milk for David and his people. They said, "The people are hungry and tired and thirsty in the desert."*

Jesus told a parable of compassion to illustrate what true followers of God are to be like. The example of compassion is a man who shares his finances to help someone in need.

Luke 10:33-35 NCV *33Then a Samaritan traveling down the road came to where the hurt man was. When he saw the man, he felt very sorry for him. 34The Samaritan went to him, poured olive oil and wine on his wounds, and bandaged them. Then he put the hurt man on his own donkey and took him to an inn where he cared for him. 35The next day, the Samaritan brought out two coins, gave them to the innkeeper, and said, 'Take care of this man. If you spend more money on him, I will pay it back to you when I come again.' "*

The Book of Acts tells of what happens when the Holy Spirit is at work in people's hearts: He produces generosity in action.

Acts 2:44-45 NCV *44All the believers were together and shared everything. 45They would sell their land and the things they owned and then divide the money and give it to anyone who needed it.*

A Life of Blessing

In order to be generous, we need to develop eyes of generosity.

We should be looking for people in need: *We should try to be aware of what people are going through and what they need.*

Luke 10:33 NCV *Then a Samaritan traveling down the road came to where the hurt man was. When he saw the man, he felt very sorry for him.* If you are alert, you will see that people are struggling financially in some way. You may hear that there is a current need in their life.

We should be praying for God to guide us to those in need: God may speak to you about people you know, but you may not know exactly what their need is. Sometimes you will be prompted by the Holy Spirit to do something specific to help them. The specific thing may be to give them money, bring them food or groceries, give them a vehicle, or anything else the Spirit leads us to do for them. So many times in our church, I have had people tell me that someone came up to them and said, *"I felt God tell me to give this to you,"* Then they say to me, *"It was exactly what I needed!"* There may be people in life you come into contact with that God would want you to give money, or some other gift to.

My parents were incredibly generous. Only God knows how many cars they gave away through the years. At times, they helped people with bills. They gave cash, checks and many other things to help others. One time they bought a small house for someone in need. My wife and I have followed in their footsteps. We give to help others in many ways.

Guidelines for Giving

I have been asked on occasion whether we should give to every homeless person or to someone on the street holding a sign asking for money. Here are some practical guidelines that may be helpful.

Giving guideline #1: Don't help people sin. Anyone who is addicted to drugs or alcohol will likely be asking every person they know or come into contact with for money so they can feed their addiction. If you are giving money a person with an addiction, they are likely going to use it to sin. By giving them money, you are helping them sin. You are participating in sin with them. But there is a balance to this: It's not necessary to have people fill out a questionnaire; *If I give you money, will you be using it for any of these ungodly behaviors?* You don't need to get them to sign an agreement only to use the money for godly purposes. Sometimes life is very complicated: Children suffer for their parents' sins. An addict may have spent the food money on their addiction, but the children still need to eat! Sometimes we need to have a life of prayer so we can make wise choices in the moment. At other times, we may have time to pray about it and weigh up whether we feel it is wise to give.

Giving guideline #2: God's people should have priority. I have been asked, *"Is it wrong to give to unsaved people, or strangers you don't know?"* Some Christians use **Acts 2:44-45** that I quoted before as proof that real Christians need to give all their money away to the poor; A sort of Christian Socialism. Some perspective on those verses: it was a unique case where thousands of people had made a pilgrimage journey from other places in Israel, and even other countries, to come to Jerusalem. When the Holy Spirit was poured out, and thousands of people were suddenly converted, many of them were from out of town or out of the country. They wanted to be in Jerusalem to be part of the church but did not have the money to stay. The pooled generosity enabled those people to be established in the faith. It is not meant to be a universal command for every Christian.

One factor to consider when thinking of giving money to strangers to help alleviate their Poverty: You will need to recognize the futility of giving money to unsaved people. Unsaved people in poverty may be in poverty because of sin, bad decisions, and curses of poverty on their lives. It doesn't mean it's wrong to give to unsaved people, but you need to recognize that you will not be successful in lifting them out of poverty with your gift. In the United States, President Lyndon Johnson declared war on poverty in 1964. Since then, more than **$22 trillion US dollars** has been spent on welfare, but the poverty rates are about the same as during the Johnson Administration.

But having said that, I believe we need to make room in our hearts for helping anyone! *Galatians 6:10 NIV Therefore, as we have opportunity, <u>let us do good to all people</u>, especially to those who belong to the family of believers.*

I know of people who pray that God will let them meet people in need. When they do, they give money to them as a means of witnessing to them. Sometimes, we might be wasting our money by doing so, but we are actually doing it for God! I think that God is pleased by our hearts and will bless us, regardless of the practical results of our giving.

Biblically, the priority of our giving to other people should be believers first: *According to the Bible, they are your true spiritual family!* Let's look at the same verse we read before, with a different emphasis: **Galatians 6:10 NIV** *Therefore, as we have opportunity, let us do good to all people, especially to those who belong to the family of believers.* Believers in your local church are the ones you labor together with to accomplish God's will. Hopefully, they are less likely use the financial blessings you give them to sin.

The Reward of Blessing Others

There are great rewards that come from our giving to other people.

Reward #1: You get to be someone's answer to prayer. People in financial need often pray to God for financial help. They may be praying for money, a vehicle, or housing. Sometimes the answer to their prayer actually has a name: **YOUR NAME!** Have you ever been someone's answer to prayer? It is exciting when you give to meet someone's need, and they tell you, *"This is exactly what I was praying for."*

Reward #2: You can cause other people to praise God. 2 Corinthians 9:11 NIV *You will be made rich in every way so that you can be generous on every occasion, and through us your generosity will result in thanksgiving to God.* God is the one who gives us money to share, and God is the one who moves on our hearts to give to others. So, it's only right that the people we bless give thanks to the one who is responsible for it all!

Reward #3: You will experience the joy of giving. Sometimes what is in our hearts can keep us from experiencing the joy of giving. Years ago, before I became a Pastor, I was teaching a new believer's class. The lesson that day was on giving, I quoted *2 Corinthians 9:7 "God loves a cheerful giver."* A new convert lady asked me, *"Is it OK to give, if you're not very happy about it?"* There was honesty! Sadly, many Christians have never broken through their own selfishness, greed, and fear enough to enter into the joy that comes from giving. But you were made to give! If you obey God and learn to make progress in giving, you will feel the joy that giving brings. There is joy when you realize what a difference you have been able to make by helping someone through giving. Sometimes you will see the joy on their face as their need is met, at times see tears of joy, and receive words of thanks. *2 Corinthians 9:7 NCV Each of you should give as you have decided in your heart to give. You should not be sad when you give, and you should not give because you feel forced to give. God loves the person who gives happily.*

Reward #4: Giving to those in need is remembered by God: Even though you may be giving to <u>people</u> to help them, you must understand that ultimately you are giving to <u>God</u>. *Acts 10:3-4 ³About the ninth hour of the day he saw clearly in a vision an angel of God coming in and saying to him, "Cornelius!" ⁴And when he observed him, he was afraid, and said, "What is it, lord?" So he said to him, "Your prayers and your alms have come up for a memorial before God.* God sent an angel to a giver! The story of Cornelius shows us three important things about giving:

God sees and keeps records of giving. Cornelius had been giving to help poor people for some time, not realizing that God saw everything he ever gave. Never think that your giving has been wasted or forgotten.

God showed up for a giver. An angel came down to Cornelius' house, partly because he was a giver. Isn't that what every Christian wants: For God to come out of heaven and enter into their situation, to help them?

God connects our giving to our prayers. When you have a need and pray about it, God doesn't just look at your prayers: He looks at your giving to other people. *Proverbs 19:17 NIV He who is kind to the poor lends to the Lord, and he will reward him for what he has done.* You are planting seeds of prosperity when you give to other people. Generosity triggers a miracle dimension in your finances! Think of some of the miracle provision stories in the Bible: *Many of them involved giving to other people!* The widow of Zarephath gave to Elijah, and that triggered supernatural supply. A boy gave his lunch to help feed others, and it triggered a miracle of food multiplication.

Remember what we said previously in the book? God doesn't play favorites! If God released miracle supply for them as they gave to others, that is what will happen for you as well. *Proverbs 11:24-25   24There is one who scatters, yet increases more; And there is one who withholds more than is right, But it leads to poverty. 25The generous soul will be made rich, And he who waters will also be watered himself. Proverbs 22:9 NIV A generous man will himself be blessed, for he shares his food with the poor.*

Blessings for World Evangelism - *Adam and Taya Dragoon*
As a former missionary, I have witnessed firsthand the blessings God has in store for those who step out in faith into the arena of World Evangelism and Missions.

Coming home from the mission field, we inherited a wonderful church facing somewhat difficult financial circumstances. The rent payment was six months behind, and the church struggled to pay its own expenses. Many times, we wondered whether God would supply for even the basic needs as we stepped out in faith for nearly every revival and church event. Thankfully, God was faithful to cover us without getting any further into debt. Over the course of a year and a half, we were able to catch up on rent payments and become more stable with day-to-day expenses. But it was a struggle for us to step out in faith for more than just the everyday expenses with the church bringing in between $5000-$6000 each month.

One thing we did do was to establish a new tradition in our church: World Evangelism Sunday. On the last Sunday of each month, we had at least one message focused on world evangelism. We called missionaries in the field to get live reports of international churches. We asked for pledges to support the Chandler church in its missionary efforts. Little by little, we saw our hearts being molded into the very heart of God toward overseas evangelism.

God challenged us to do something impossible: go on an overseas mission trip with the church. That was extremely difficult at the time, based on the finances. We announced the trip one year in advance to begin raising funds for plane tickets and travel expenses. The church was excited to give for this, and we quickly raised enough funds for my wife and me to buy tickets for the trip - nearly $2000. It was set aside, earmarked for our trip. Then I went to the conference.

On Thursday night of the conference in 2011, having already given healthy offerings in the days prior and wiped out our general funds account, God dealt with me to give the money we had saved for our trip. So we did! Without any assurances that we could raise these funds again, we trusted God to supply for our overseas trip. Well, God DID supply, and we WERE able to go on our trip without incurring any debt, by the mercy of God. It was a powerful trip during which we felt God's presence in a tangible way, and over 40 souls prayed for salvation. And though we didn't see major financial miracles, God did supply our daily needs as we faithfully did what we needed to do. I prayed for God to give us the resources to do more. We fasted, believing God for breakthroughs.

Fast forward to the summer of 2012. On one of our monthly World Evangelism Sundays, we showed the World Evangelism video from the Tucson conference. After the video, I challenged the church once again to give towards world evangelism. That night, someone put in a $5,000 check in the offering. We rejoiced to be able to send that in to Chandler to support all the work that God is doing.

The next day, I received a phone call from the person who had given that money. They said that they had a few things that they'd like to donate to the church. They said that God had clearly spoken to them to release a few things into our hands. While this person wished to remain anonymous, I can tell you that their donations totaled over $290,000!

This radically changed the dynamics of our church. I was exceedingly joyful to write the largest tithe check of my life. At the August conference, we were able to give a World Evangelism Offering that was 10 times more than the previous year's gift. We were able to move into a new building that is more than twice the size of our former one.

Meanwhile, even amid this incredibly miraculous gift, our church has been changing. We have been seeing couples get saved and locked in. New converts abound, and our church's regular giving has jumped to nearly $12,000 per month! More than enough to supply for next year's mission trip!

I have been absolutely amazed to see how God radically blesses those who have a heart for World Evangelism and are willing to risk to support it. Truly, you can never out-give God! I pray that this testimony will encourage every struggling person and pastor to give sacrificially and to raise miraculous money for the Kingdom of God. To Him be all the praise and glory.

Greater Investment, Greater Blessing - *Robert and Imelda Diaz*

My wife and I have been buying, selling, and leasing properties for several years now as a second business. In 2024, I agreed to part ways with a property so that we could accomplish some personal goals with the proceeds. We finalized the sale of this particular property in December of 2024. We immediately gave our tithe, then put the money away as we worked out the details of these goals.

But God had other plans. As the new year rolled around, we really felt God challenging us to give all the money from the sale of that property to world evangelism. This was challenging for a few reasons: First, we had been planning our financial goals for months, and we felt as if we were going backward. Second, it would be the largest offering we had ever given in our lives.

We finally decided to be obedient. As we did so, we felt at peace because of how much God has blessed our finances. We never thought that this decision would be linked to anything else, as it turned out to be. For years, we had owned a larger property that had appreciated significantly, and I had received many offers and contracts on this particular property, but nothing had ever materialized. We had actually spent thousands of dollars on attorney fees entertaining these offers.

And then the unexpected happened. Four months after we gave the offering, I was presented with a contract, but this time, it was completely different. It wasn't another disappointment or stalled negotiation. It was a real deal. We had placed some very specific conditions on the sale, and all the boxes were checked off. This new contract was worth over ten times the value of the offering, plus additional income opportunity!

Forced to Seek God for Provision - *Danny and Jessica Hernandez*

The greatest financial miracle I have witnessed in my life so far took place in my second year of pastoring the church in Horizon City, Texas. We were in a small town outside of El Paso. Due to an influx of families from Fort Bliss, our city was growing rapidly. This was good in some ways, and bad in others. Our lease was coming to an end in the building we had spent the last 6 years in. The Landlord would not budge on our rent or CAM fees (Common Area Maintenance - a fee included on top of rent that is used to cover maintenance costs for a building). In total, our small church was paying about $ 3,500 a month for 2,500 square feet! I would joke that we were paying Florida prices, but without the beach!

Every building owner I spoke to told me they could not lower their monthly rent due to the city's rapid growth. On top of this, we had accrued a debt of over $8,000 because we had agreed to come under a payment plan until the church could afford to become current on rent. We were stuck. If we left and got a new building, it would be bad. If we stayed in that same building, it would be bad. I had done everything I knew to do to break this financial blockade. I preached on money. We outreached more. My wife and I gave more, and yet nothing seemed to be happening.

At my wits' end, I did what I dreaded, I met with my pastor and asked for Help. I thought Pastor Paul Stephens would write me a check that day and make it all go away. He didn't. He challenged me to believe God for finances and also informed me that the support we had been receiving would be scaled back in a few months. I was stunned. Looking back, I know exactly what he was doing. I had nowhere else to turn. I had done everything in my power to get my church out of this problem. What was left? The hardest thing I've ever done - fast. I personally initiated a fast that had no end date. I was going to have a solution, or I was going to starve. Nothing happened on the third day of that fast.

On the fourth day, our landlord called. I answered reluctantly, but what I heard shocked me. When I heard it, I literally leaped for joy in my living room. The landlord informed me that he had sold the property and would forgive our debt in full! We went from being in debt over our heads to having the next month's rent and some left over. I don't think the decision I made in the beginning should be a template for every pastor, but I do believe the key was fasting; fasting that makes you utterly dependent on God. Through all of this, God showed me how much He loves His church and how He has our backs.

Hearing God, Receiving Blessing - *Peter Peravali*

At the Perth, West Australia Bible Conference on Monday night, Pastor Rob Walsh was taking the offering and started by saying, *"God will put a specific amount on your heart for tonight's offering!"* I was careful to hear from God an amount, and you reminded us, the greater the investment, the greater the return. At that very moment, God told me to give $4000, which I was not happy about. I thought, *"It's only Monday night, what will I give the rest of the week? I need that money for my house settlement next month. I'm not sure I heard from God."* So, as a good Christian, I brushed it off & gave $100, not $4000.

Later, Pastor Greg Mitchell preached and said that some of you didn't give what God told you to give because of fear. I knew straight away that it was me, but I brushed it off again. That night, I couldn't sleep, so I said to God, *"OK, I'll do it."* So I transferred the $4000 at

2:48 am Tuesday morning. That morning, I was not happy about it, and I came and told you that your offering hurt me. I was not smart and didn't understand the future blessing.

Then, just before my house settlement in April, out of the blue, my dad, who lives overseas, called and told me he was giving me $20,000. Then God blessed me with a reduced price on my house. I put $16K into the offset account and even flew to the Prescott conference later that year. God truly blessed me beyond measure. I am so glad I gave what God told me to give at the Conference.

Personal and Church Provision - *Dax and Rose Veazey*

My wife and I were pioneering our first church in Beenleigh, Queensland, Australia, in 2017. We moved into our first building, and the deposit cost us everything; we were left with $19.00 in the bank. We were so broke as a church that we couldn't afford chairs and other church needs. As a family, we were also broke financially. We couldn't afford to buy Christmas presents for our kids or even a hamburger from a fast-food restaurant. We prayed for a miracle, and that Sunday we received an invitation to lunch from a man we had never met before. He gave us a check for $10,000 on one condition: Half was to be used for us, and half for the church. That Christmas, we bought toys for the kids, were able to eat, and also purchased chairs, fittings, and carpet for the new church.

Later, we took a step of faith and moved into a building five times the size of the first. Again, when we moved in, we had zero money left. That Sunday, more than $60,000 came in the offering. We renovated the church and equipped it with lighting and a sound system. It is still running today.

More Than Double - *Roman and Nora Gutierrez*

On December 17, 2023, Evangelist Andy Anderson took an offering for World Evangelism in the McAllen, Texas Church (for the McAllen church). We (Roman and Nora Gutierrez) felt stirred to pledge $50,000 from our own funds to the offering. Shortly after we gave that pledge, we received a miracle check from an insurance company for $108,000 out of the blue.

Chapter 14: Sanctified Saving

Gain all you can, save all you can, give all you can.
John Wesley

Regularly saving money is a skill and a system.
Not doing enough can lead to a massive loss of opportunity.
David Angway

Someone told me their story: For many years, we lived paycheck to paycheck. We barely managed to pay the bills. This was a stressful way to live. I thought about money all the time. My stress would spill over into my marriage and family. I would lose sleep worrying about money. A big problem of living paycheck to paycheck is that unexpected emergencies would happen: I would get sick, miss work, or something would break and need to be repaired. Each time that happened, I was forced to either borrow money from people or put things on credit cards. Consequently, I was getting deeper into debt. I finally began to cry out for God to help me. I broke the curse of poverty off my life, and began to budget (and stick to the budget). Over time, I was able to pay off all our debts. That was a great day! I call it freedom day! But then I moved beyond that and began to save. I had never had savings in my life. Having savings has been life-changing. I no longer live with constant stress. If unexpected things happen, I can meet the need without stress or drama in my life. I can respond to opportunities to give to various offerings. I have even been able to help others with their financial needs. I will never go back to living financially the way I used to. I thank God for His blessing!

Prosperity is not having just enough money to pay your bills. If you want to prosper, **you need to have money set aside in savings.**

Misunderstanding Savings

There are some wrong ideas about savings that can hurt your prosperity.

Wrong idea #1: Having money in savings is unspiritual. There are Christians who believe that God does not want us to have savings at all. Usually, this is based on misunderstanding and misapplying scripture. This is the scripture usually quoted: *Matthew 6:19-20 NIV* ¹⁹*"Do not store up for yourselves treasures on earth, where moth and rust destroy, and where thieves break in and steal.* ²⁰*But store up for yourselves treasures in heaven, where moth and rust do not destroy, and where thieves do not break in and steal.* If this scripture actually meant *"do not have any savings,"* then let's use some logic: **How much savings would be unacceptable?** Would it be having any extra money? Would ten dollars extra be acceptable? Would one hundred dollars be acceptable, but one thousand dollars be bad?

The problem is that anti-savings Christians misunderstand these verses. Jesus was warning of the dangerous effect money can have on our hearts and our relationship with God. This passage is dealing with what we put our <u>trust</u> in. If your trust in life is in your savings, you will be tempted to make decisions in life based on the effect each decision will have on your savings: *Instead of God's will, the needs of people, and faith.* Our trust cannot be not in our savings; our trust must be in God!

Then Jesus winds up with the real danger of money poses to our hearts: *Money demands service!* If you allow a spirit of greed to lay hold of your heart, money will demand service: Money will start to determine all the choices in life, becoming your master. You will choose what's best for money, not God!

Matthew 6:24 *"No one can serve two masters. Either he will hate the one and love the other, or he will be devoted to the one and despise the other. You cannot serve both God and Money.* **But this is a choice!** Jesus is warning us of these dangers so we will make right choices and not allow money to be what we place our trust in, or what determines the choices of our lives.

The idea that God doesn't want His people to have any savings is illogical, because of the people in the Bible whom God holds up as examples for us: Abraham, David, and Job. The Bible shows us that they had a lot of money left over (which is what savings are). So logically, savings in themselves cannot be unspiritual or bad.

Wrong idea #2: Having money in savings is a lack of faith: Some believe you should have no savings at all and simply trust God to supply your needs. If God specifically tells you to have nothing and trust God to supply your needs, that's fine: But in my experience, that is very rare! Usually, those who believe you should not have any savings will quote this verse: ***Luke 9:3 NIV*** *He told them: "Take nothing for the journey—no staff, no bag, no bread, no money, no extra tunic.* They will take this one-time preaching ministry instruction given to the twelve apostles and apply it to <u>all</u> believers. This is bad doctrine: We should never take one verse, or one instance in the Bible, and make an entire doctrine that applies to all believers. In **Luke 9:3**, Jesus is sending the disciples to preach in surrounding villages. This was both to spread the Gospel of the Kingdom, and to train them for future ministry. So, we need to see why Jesus told them to *"take nothing for your journey."*

This preaching tour was a short-term ministry opportunity: It was not meant to be a permanent lifestyle.

Jesus was impressing on them the need for <u>priority</u> in doing the will of God: Many disciples say they are willing to do God's will, but say they must get their finances set up first: *"I need to make a lot of money to set myself up for the future. I need to establish multiple income streams, so I don't have to struggle financially while pastoring. I need to make enough money first, so my retirement is secure.* Jesus knows the human heart, so He insisted they make the will of God in ministry a <u>priority</u> (ministry first!): He wanted them to trust <u>God</u> for the supply of their needs and their financial future.

Finally, Jesus was showing them the priority of preaching ministry: *Men of God should make their living from preaching!* A working Pastor may be acceptable at first to get a church off the ground, but every Pastor needs to aim at being a full-time Pastor, whose main income comes from preaching the Gospel.

Although I recognize there have been men of faith in the past who "lived by faith," such as George Mueller, in my personal experience, *often those who "live by faith" are actually lazy <u>takers</u> who don't want to work jobs; but they have no problem asking for money!*

Wrong idea #3: Having money in savings would be displeasing to God: Those who believe this way sometimes are motivated by a guilt mentality. They think, *"You could do more for God if you gave all your money away."* They may tell others, *"There are people who don't have enough money, so how can you have more than you need to pay your bills? That is being selfish and greedy."*

Some Christians feel guilty if they have any money at all. They put everything in the offering, not because God told them to do so, but simply because they feel guilty at having any money. That is a very unhealthy view of God. My Father, Wayman Mitchell (founder of our Fellowship of churches), was very wise: He guided people with Godly financial wisdom through the years. On several occasions, people would come to him and say they were going to sell their house and give all the money to the church, and he would tell them not to! He recognized that people with rejection issues, unresolved guilt, or excitable emotions tend to be imbalanced in their decisions concerning money.

On other occasions, people would tell him they had received large inheritances and didn't know what to do with the money: Should they give it all to the church? Apart from tithing, he would advise them not to spend it or give it away, but to put it in savings or into a safe financial investment so they wouldn't be emotionally manipulated into giving it all away. That would give them time to pray and hear from God. He knew some people feel guilty if they have any money saved. They think they should give it all to God every time they have any money. They might say, *"But Jesus told the Rich Young Ruler to sell everything you have and give it to the poor."* But that was said <u>one</u> time! Jesus sees the heart, and knew money was his god, so he is challenging him to reorder his entire approach to life and follow Jesus.

In giving offerings, my Father used to teach that we should participate in offerings (give something). The key is listening for the voice of God, not the voice of guilt. I have known of people who have <u>genuinely</u> heard from God, and he told them to give all their savings. I have no problem if God truly tells you to do that. Still, I am showing you it is not an automatic assumption that you must give everything away, simply because you have extra.

Living without savings doesn't make sense: If, for any reason, you are living without having any savings, you need to see that this is not a healthy way to live, both <u>practically</u> and <u>spiritually</u>.

Living without savings creates stress and crisis: Look at some American statistics concerning savings. (I am giving American statistics because I live in America).

- Nearly 29% of Americans have no savings <u>at all</u>!
- 54% of Americans have less than a three-month cushion of savings.

If you have no savings, if you miss work for one or two weeks for any reason; ***Your life will be in crisis!*** Sadly, this is true of many Christians, who are serving the God who owns everything.

Living without savings creates stress! From the time you wake up, to the time you go to sleep (if you can sleep), there is the constant pressure of finances: *How am I going to pay the bills? How are we going to eat?*

A further problem of living with financial stress from having no savings is that you will push your stress onto other people: They either must live with your unhappiness caused by stress, or feel the pressure of needing to help you, because you have no savings.

Those who live without savings do not prosper over time:
I have been a pastor for 40 years, in three different nations. This has allowed me to see how living without savings works out in people's lives – and in churches!

- People who live without savings never seem to enter into the blessing of prosperity.
- Pastors who live without savings – their churches never prosper.

The reason why this is true is that **living without savings is ignoring the wisdom of savings found in God's word.** Please understand my heart: If you have no savings currently, I am not writing this to make you feel bad. I am writing this to help you! I believe God has a better plan for your life and your church.

Principles of Multiplication

The Bible speaks of the wisdom of savings. *By definition, "savings" refers to the portion of your income that you **do not***

spend, *but instead set aside for future use.* Saving is <u>anticipating</u> future needs and putting something aside to meet those needs. **Proverbs 6:6-8 NCV** *6Go watch the ants, you lazy person. Watch what they do and be wise. 7Ants have no commander, no leader or ruler, 8but they store up food in the summer and gather their supplies at harvest.* God gives us examples of wisdom from nature. The ant knows that winter is coming (a time of no food), so it saves up food in summer! It would be sad if an ant is wiser than we are. **2 Chronicles 31:11-12 NIV** *11Hezekiah gave orders to prepare storerooms in the temple of the Lord, and this was done. 12Then they faithfully brought in the contributions, tithes and dedicated gifts.* The temple is the place where we meet with God. Notice the temple had storerooms – where they saved up the offerings. This shows us an essential Biblical and financial principle: **Savings are Holy!**

Having savings is important to God: *Genesis 41:35-36 NCV* *35They should gather all the food that is produced during the good years that are coming, and under the king's authority they should store the grain in the cities and guard it. 36That food should be saved to use during the seven years of hunger that will come on the land of Egypt. Then the people in Egypt will not die during the seven years of hunger."* Joseph was known for having wisdom, because the spirit of God was in him. These verses show a practical application of Godly wisdom: *He <u>saved</u> for future needs!* That is the logic of having savings: There will always be future needs!

There are five kinds of needs that all require savings:
- **Known future expenses:** If you use common sense, you know some future expenses that will be coming. If you have a car, tires wear out, and vehicles require maintenance. If you have children, they will need

shoes and clothing as they grow. You can't be surprised that tires wear out, or teenagers need new shoes!

- **Unknown future expenses:** Life also has unexpected expenses. Things break sometimes. People get sick. You can't see the future, but we logically know these are possibilities. Many wise people have said, *"A budget without savings is a budget waiting to blow up!"*
- **Wants:** There are always things we would like to have. You may want to have a nicer car, or one with more room. You may want to be able to take a vacation or a holiday. These require money.
- **The future:** Most people can't work forever! You definitely will not live forever. If so, then you need to answer some basic questions: *How will you survive financially when you can no longer work? How will your family survive after you pass away?*
- **The ability to give:** Throughout life, there will be opportunities, or promptings from God to give. Sometimes it may be an opportunity to give to God's purposes: Church-planting, world evangelism or a new church building. Or, you may see someone else with a financial need, and you would like to help them.

The answer for all of these is savings: *Money that you do not spend, but instead set aside for future needs.*

Proverbs 21:20 TLB The wise man saves for the future, but the foolish man spends whatever he gets. You can only save for the future if you don't spend it all. A consumerist mentality that spends everything keeps many people from having the savings needed to prosper. Pastor Joe Campbell says, *"Savings gives you dominion over a consumer mentality."* I believe every person, and every church, should be putting money aside in savings each week or each month. Christian financial advisers have a saying: *"Pay God. Then pay yourself. Then pay everyone else."* "Paying yourself" means setting aside money instead of spending it. **Proverbs 21:5** *The plans of the diligent lead surely to plenty, But those of everyone who is hasty, surely to poverty.*

When you put a portion of your paycheck in savings, you're "spending" money to build your future and achieve your goals. **Proverbs 13:11 NCV** *Money that comes easily disappears quickly, but money that is gathered little by little will grow.*

When you save money by putting it away, that means you can't use it right now: *But it builds up for a good future!*

There are five kinds of savings:

- **Saving for emergencies:** Emergencies are unknown expenses that arise. The bare minimum should be to save enough money to cover one month of expenses. (for some people that will be absolutely life-changing!) Saving enough money to cover three months of expenses is a standard amount recommended by financial advisers. Aiming to save enough money to cover one year's worth of expenses would be fantastic!
- **Saving for known future expenses**: Such as vehicle maintenance, clothing, school expenses, etc.
- **Saving for your wants:** Things you want to buy or want to do. Purchases, vacations, etc.
- **Saving for the future:** *Putting aside money for retirement, or when you can no longer work, and setting aside money for your family's needs after you pass away.*
- **Saving for giving:** *We need money to respond to opportunities to give to the Kingdom of God and also to be able to help other people financially.*

The Blessing of Savings

The Bible teaches us that saving brings blessings to our lives!

If you have savings, you can live with peace rather than stress: Joseph knew that seven years of famine was coming. But by the time the famine arrived, he had done all he could to be ready for it by saving enough grain to survive the famine. Having peace is a natural result of saving; it is not meant to be an obsession! You don't have to be so obsessed that you are afraid to spend a single cent. That is imbalanced and unhealthy. Our ultimate security should be in God – not our savings!

God supernaturally blesses savings: *Genesis 41:38-40 NCV 38And the king asked them, "Can we find a better man than Joseph to take this job? God's spirit is truly in him!" 39So the king said to Joseph, "God has shown you all this. There is no one as wise and understanding as you are, so 40I will put you in charge of my palace. All the people will obey your orders, and only I will be greater than you."*
Joseph having the wisdom to save, brought incredible blessings:

- The nation of Egypt was saved.
- God was glorified through Joseph's wisdom to save.
- The purposes of God in preserving the nation of Israel were accomplished.
- Joseph's brothers were touched spiritually through Joseph's wisdom in saving. Saving does more than make you able to pay bills!
- Joseph's future was connected to his wisdom in saving!

All of these factors can be at work in your life if you understand God's wisdom in saving. *Proverbs 3:9-10 NCV 9Honor the Lord with your wealth and the firstfruits from all your crops. 10Then your barns will be full, and your wine barrels will overflow with new wine.*

Money is Supernatural - *Heath and Renee Flitcroft*

When I was a disciple in Prescott, I had money set aside to buy a guitar, but God challenged me to give it. I obeyed and gave it all. After conference, Pastor Greg Mitchell took me out to breakfast and asked if I had any questions. Because I just gave an offering that was on my mind the most. He told me, **"Money is supernatural!"** I had no idea that that was going to be one of the most valuable pieces of wisdom for me moving forward.

During the July 2020 Prescott Bible Conference, Pastor Greg Mitchell pulled an offering for a new nation (Laos). I had been working side jobs to pay off debt so we could go be missionaries. God spoke to me and said to give my entire month's income in that offering, so I obeyed. The next morning, some money we had been waiting for appeared in our account. Right after the conference, I received an email saying I'd be receiving a payment from my Grandma's life insurance policy! We received 13 times the amount we gave, and we paid off our debt! We even put $19,000 in savings.

At another Prescott Bible Conference, Pastor Joe Campbell preached and called for missionaries to go to India. We had no debt, I had a good job, so I figured it was the right time for us to go overseas. I volunteered, but instead of sending us, Chris and Vicki Wendt were sent to Kolkata. I told God, *"If you won't send me, then send my money."* We gave the largest world evangelism offering we had ever given. As a result of our decisions to obey God with money, we were sent out 6 months later to St. Lucia.

Blessings Out of Our Comfort Zone - *Luke and Nat Smith*

Port Louis, Mauritius

I want to give a praise report from the 2025 Sydney Conference. Usually, my wife and I agree on a figure, and we give it. This year was a little different as we had been saving for a family holiday, and we both knew there were some savings in our bank account.

We still gave each night generously, and we were easily able to give without touching the holiday savings. But by Friday night, we felt like we were still in our safe zone! I asked my wife to put down an amount. She wrote on the offering card our biggest ever one-time offering. After the shock wore off, I agreed, and we gave more in that one offering than we have in a whole week of any conference. Yes, we sacrificed our holiday, but there was joy and excitement in giving to support what God was doing through the Conference.

In the first month after that offering, our business was so blessed that we saved ALL the money we gave in a week of offerings, which had never happened before. The same thing happened the second month! On top of that, we have received 3 times what we gave that week through unexpected blessings. In the last two months, God has given us over $40,000 as a direct result of stepping out of our comfort zone on the Conference offering.

God Provides a Vehicle - *Casey and Monica Mammen*
We were saving money for a new vehicle to facilitate our growing family and had saved $2000. At the January 2010 Bible Conference in Prescott, Pastor Wayman Mitchell took the Thursday night World Evangelism offering, and God stirred us to give that full amount for the newly announced missionary works. We obeyed in faith and gave all $2000. We kept that decision to ourselves and did not tell anyone, not even family. The following week, my Dad called out of the blue and gave us a vehicle for free that exactly met our needs and was worth twice what we paid. We praise God for His miraculous provision and give Him all the glory!

Saving, Giving, Receiving - *Remy and Gereline Opree*
In 2019, at the Bible conference in Zwolle, Holland, we were challenged during an offering by Pastor Greg Mitchell to give. We were saving for the buyer's costs if we found a home. We needed 10,000 Euros. God spoke to our hearts to give1,000 Euros. We obeyed God. We prayed to God, and we said, "*We give in faith and ask that we be able to save 10,000 Euros so we can buy a house.*"

After the conference, we continued to pray, and as Pastor Greg said in his offering, to keep reminding God of our offering and need (watering the seed). Two times in 2019, I received a substantial pay raise. This enabled us to set aside the funds for the buyer's costs. House prices were going up enormously. We had a nice house in mind, but it was too expensive for us. We offered 10,000 Euros below the asking price, and the sellers agreed! In 2020, we were allowed to move into our beautiful, spacious home, one year after we gave! This was our answered prayer! At that time, people all offered way above the asking price, but God did a miracle for us. In the next three years, my pay was increased five times.

In 2022, our Pastor took an offering to buy our own Church building. God told me to give 6,000 Euros. I was shocked by the amount, and when I told Gereline, she was just as shocked. We had built up a buffer again in 2 years, and that would now disappear again. But we decided in faith to obey and trust God again.

In 2023, we were sent to pioneer in Goes. We put our house up for sale and began looking for a house in our new city. We found a nice home. The sellers had a Christian broker, and he was very enthusiastic when we explained why we were looking for a house in Goes. He put in a good word for us, and the buyers agreed to our offer. We had offered the asking price, and again, it was amazing that they agreed since most people offered much more than the asking price.

We have now sold our house, and because we had more than 100,000 Euros in equity, we could buy the house in Goes! And because we are moving on from one owned house to another, we did not have to pay transfer tax, which saves us 6,000 Euros. Exactly the amount we gave for the building in Dordrecht!

We are incredibly grateful to God for everything He has done for us, and He shows us again and again that if you obey Him and believe, He will take care of you.

Chapter 15: Being Blessable

Faith in God will elevate you to next level blessings.
Germany Kent

Giving is always a blessing; Generosity is always life-changing.
Todd Stocker

There was a man in one of our churches in Australia who once told his pastor, *"If I had a lot of money, I wouldn't be here - I'd be travelling the world."* The pastor gently replied, *"Then I'll pray you never get that kind of money. I'd hate to see God's blessing become something that destroys your spiritual wellbeing."*

If your desire is for God to prosper you financially, you need to see that prosperity depends on being **blessable**: Would you <u>qualify</u> for blessings? Could you be <u>trusted</u> with blessings?

Untrustworthy Stewards

Many of Jesus' parables are stories of stewardship: A wealthy owner entrusts what belongs to him to another person to manage on the owner's behalf. *Matthew 25:14 "For the kingdom of heaven is like a man traveling to a far country, who called his own servants and delivered his goods to them.* Stewards are expected to make decisions that are in the <u>owner's</u> best interests! The steward makes practical decisions with the money entrusted to him. But it is possible to make financial decisions that are not in line with the owner's will, and are not in line with his best interests.

The Bible records a number of stories that illustrate bad stewardship. *Luke 16:1 He also said to His disciples: "There was a certain rich man who had a steward, and an accusation was brought to him that this man was wasting his goods.*

Two kinds of bad stewards

We are bad stewards when blessings produce bad things in us: There are people who, as soon as God blesses them, *it damages their salvation!*

Some people desperately need a job. They pray, the pastors pray, the church prays - and God answers! The job is a blessing. Yet as soon as God provides it, they begin missing the very church where they heard about the blessing and received the prayers that brought it.

Some people forget where the blessing came from. *Deuteronomy 8:12-14 NIV* *12Otherwise, when you eat and are satisfied, when you build fine houses and settle down, 13and when your herds and flocks grow large and your silver and gold increase and all you have is multiplied, 14then your heart will become proud and you will forget the Lord your God, who brought you out of Egypt, out of the land of slavery. In pride we can take credit for the blessing*: *We can start to think I did this! I am blessed because I'm so smart. The reason I am blessed is because I worked so hard for it.* But who gave you your intelligence? Who gives you the strength to work hard? I've seen many people who take pride in their strength and work ethic get sick. Then suddenly they realize the blessing wasn't all because of their ability. If blessing causes you to forget where it came from, you are a bad steward.

Some people become unthankful: They fail to appreciate and thank God for the blessings He has given them. *Luke 17:17 NIV Jesus asked, "Were not all ten cleansed? Where are the other nine?* If you fail to be thankful for what God has blessed you with, you are a bad steward.

We are bad stewards if we fail to use God's money for God's purposes. God gives us money first and foremost to fulfill <u>His</u> purposes!

<u>Some people fail to tithe</u>: They do not honor God with the first 10% of their income. The work of God is not meant to be funded through fundraising appeals or selling things. The practical result of the tithe is that it funds the regular work of God through the church. Statistics show that only 5-12% of American Christians tithe. This is sad, in perhaps the most financially blessed nation in the world. Consequently, many churches struggle to carry out God's will. Years ago, it was popular for people to bumper stickers on their cars showing what they loved. You would read such messages as, *"Honk if you love skiing. Honk if you love surfing..."* I liked one that some Christians put on their bumper: *"Tithe if you love Jesus. Any fool can honk."* **Malachi 3:8** *"Will a man rob God? Yet you have robbed Me! But you say, 'In what way have we robbed You?' In tithes and offerings.* If you fail to tithe, you are a bad steward.

<u>Some people fail to invest in what God loves</u>: God loves the church! The church is His plan, and all that he will accomplish in the church will come through the church. **Ephesians 1:22-23** [22]*And God placed all things under his feet and appointed him to be head over everything for the church,* [23]*which is his body, the fullness of him who fills everything in every way.* Giving offerings is a demonstration of our love. *"Show me where you spend your money, and I'll show you what you love."* Some people say they love God, and they love their church, but they fail to give generously so that the work of God and the mission of the church can be carried out. It's not just programs that suffer; sometimes, it is the great work of God in evangelism, church planting, and world evangelism that are hindered. If you fail to invest in what God loves, you are a bad steward.

Some people fail to be generous to other people: *Genesis 12:2 I will make you a great nation; I will bless you and make your name great; And you shall be a blessing.* God blesses us so that we can be a blessing to other people. We can pass on the blessings given to us to help others in times of need. If you receive God's financial blessings and fail to be generous to other people, you are a bad steward.

God Does Not Bless Bad Stewardship

In any of the parables that illustrate bad stewardship, the steward's relationship with the owner is altered and damaged because of their bad stewardship. Not one time is the owner pleased when he sees bad stewardship, and in every case, what they have is affected negatively.

God does not allow supernatural blessings to come into the hands of some bad stewards. There are people who pray for God to bless them, but the blessing doesn't flow to them. That is not because prosperity isn't Biblical, or because God is unfair. It's possible that God doesn't give some people much money because He knows it would damage them spiritually. *Proverbs 30:7-9 NIV 7"Two things I ask of you, O Lord; do not refuse me before I die: 8Keep falsehood and lies far from me; give me neither poverty nor riches, but give me only my daily bread. 9Otherwise, I may have too much and disown you and say, 'Who is the Lord?' Or I may become poor and steal, and so dishonor the name of my God.* If money will make you backslide or damage your family, perhaps you should stay poor. That isn't fate, as though some people are destined to poverty, it's a choice!

God takes away financial blessings from some bad stewards. *Matthew 25:28-29 28"'Take the talent from him and give it to the one who has the ten talents. 29For everyone who has will be given more, and he will have an abundance. Whoever does not have,* *even what he has will be taken from him.* Ultimately, if you will not honor God, obey God, and do God's will with the finances He blesses you with, God may choose to take it away! Through the years, I have seen several financially blessed people who dishonored God with their blessings and wound up losing them.

The Test of Money

A Bible principle all through the Bible is that God tests His people. *Genesis 22:1 NCV After these things God tested Abraham's faith.* What Abraham did with the blessing (his son Isaac) showed what was in Abraham's heart. The word 'test' in the Bible is an assaying word. In mining, assaying ore through heat or chemicals reveals what the ore or metal is. God allows us to be tested, so what is in our hearts will be revealed.

It is crucial that we understand: **Money is a test!** The issue of money is one of the profound areas of testing in our relationship with God. Many of the stewardship parables: *The owner wanted to know whether the stewards could be trusted! Deuteronomy 8:2 Remember how the Lord your God led you all the way in the desert these forty years, to humble you and to test you in order to know what was in your heart, whether or not you would keep his commands.*

We are being tested right now with whatever amount of money is currently placed in our hands.

Thomas Carlisle said, "Adversity is hard on a man, but for every hundred that can handle adversity, there's only one that can handle prosperity."

- Can God trust you to be grateful for the finances God has given you?

- Can God trust you to glorify Him and not take credit for the blessings God has given you?
- Can God trust you to stay faithful to your relationship with Him as He blesses you?
- Can God trust you to honor Him with the Tithe if He blesses you?
- Can God trust you to obey Him if He speaks to you?
- Can God trust you to bless the His work and purposes through the church by giving offerings?
- Can God trust you to pass along your blessings to help people in need?

Searching For People to Bless

You have a wrong view of God if you feel you have to <u>force</u> God to bless you! The truth is that **God is <u>looking</u> for people He can bless!** *2 Chronicles 16:9 For the eyes of the Lord run to and fro throughout the whole earth, to show Himself strong on behalf of those whose heart is loyal to Him...*
It is in <u>God's</u> best interest to bless people with <u>more</u> finances!

If God can trust us with more finances, the Kingdom and His purposes will be blessed: *We can do more of God's work if we have more resources to do so!*

If God can trust us with more finances, more people in need will be blessed: *We can help more of God's people if we have more resources to do so!*

So, if God is looking for people to bless, **why not be the person God can bless?** The big question when considering prosperity: **Are you blessable?** That means, would you <u>qualify</u> for blessings? Could you be <u>trusted</u> with blessings? *Luke 16:10-12 NIV* ¹⁰*"Whoever can be trusted with very little can also be trusted with much, and whoever is dishonest with very little will also be dishonest with much.* ¹¹*So if you have not been trustworthy in*

handling worldly wealth, who will trust you with true riches?
12And if you have not been trustworthy with someone else's
property, who will give you property of your own?

So what would make us blessable?

We can be blessed if we make a covenant of blessing with God in advance. We can determine and promise God: In advance - I promise to do right with the blessings you give me. *Genesis 28:20-22 20Then Jacob made a vow, saying, "If God will be with me, and keep me in this way that I am going, and give me bread to eat and clothing to put on, 21so that I come back to my father's house in peace, then the Lord shall be my God. 22And this stone which I have set as a pillar shall be God's house, and of all that You give me I will surely give a tenth to You."*

Decide to honor God and be faithful before we have even received the blessing.

Whether or not we can be blessed is determined by our current faithfulness. When you ask God for a blessing, He looks at what you are currently doing with what you have already been given. *Luke 16:10 NIV "Whoever can be trusted with very little can also be trusted with much, and whoever is dishonest with very little will also be dishonest with much.*

In some ways, you shouldn't bother asking God for more if you're not being faithful now! When we lived in Johannesburg, the manager of the local grocery store was caught breaking into the store's safe and stealing company money. Would it make sense for him to then ask the owners for a pay raise? If you're not faithful now, you need to first repent! <u>Then</u> ask God to help you. Fortunately, we serve a gracious and merciful God. Gracious means God gives us what we don't deserve. Merciful means He doesn't give us what we <u>do</u> deserve!

We can be blessed if we demonstrate carefulness when we are blessed: How do we be careful with blessings? By an attitude of worship and gratitude for our blessings. The antidote and answer for an unthankful, forgetful spirit is __remembering.__ *Deuteronomy 8:18 "And you shall remember the Lord your God, for it is He who gives you power to get wealth, that He may establish His covenant which He swore to your fathers, as it is this day.* To remember means "to make a mark so you can recognize something." *It means to **think (about), meditate (upon), pay attention (to) something. Psalm 103:2** Bless the LORD, O my soul, and forget not all his benefits:*

A protective Christian discipline is to deliberately think about and list all the good things God has done for you, and what God has given you. Grateful people have the greatest chance of being able to handle the blessings God gives them.

Being Blessed With More

You can have more than you have right now! I cannot promise that every Christian will become a millionaire, but I can absolutely Biblically tell you that God wants you to have more than you have right now! God is willing to give you more!

Matthew 25:20-21   20"So he who had received five talents came and brought five other talents, saying, 'Lord, you delivered to me five talents; look, I have gained five more talents besides them.' 21His lord said to him, 'Well done, good and faithful servant; you were faithful over a few things, I will make you ruler over many things. Enter into the joy of your lord.'

Luke 16:10 NCV "Whoever can be trusted with very little can also be trusted with much, and whoever is dishonest with very little will also be dishonest with much.

The more God can trust you with – the more God can give to you!

Luke 6:38 *Give, and it will be given to you. A good measure, pressed down, shaken together and running over, will be poured into your lap. **For with the measure you use**, it will be measured to you."*

2 Corinthians 9:6 *NIV Remember this: Whoever sows sparingly will also reap sparingly, and whoever sows generously will also reap generously.*

There have been many Christians that God blessed with incredible resources.

RG LeTourneau was a Christian businessman who believed in tithing. He said God would wake him up at night and give him ideas for earth-moving machinery. The ideas God gave him caused his company to prosper incredibly. He started by tithing: Giving 10% and living on 90%, but God kept blessing him so much that he kept upping the percentage of his giving until he finally was living on 10% and giving 90%.

David Green: He started his first craft shop with a $600 loan. That small craft shop became Hobby Lobby. His personal net worth is currently estimated at USD $15 Billion! (When I first taught this series in 2022, his estimated net worth was USD $6 Billion. It has grown $9 Billion in less than four years!) He and his family give away hundreds of millions of dollars a year to causes that further the Kingdom of God!

Faith, Obedience and Provision - *Anthony and Gina Trujillo*

Our Church has been meeting in storefront building for the last 18 years. I felt God challenging me to begin transitioning from a storefront to a church building. I received a phone call from the property owners of the storefront property where we were currently meeting. They said they would no longer renew our lease because the new owner did not want a church on that commercial property. That meant we would have to go month-to-month at a very high cost due to the economy here in Denver.

At the July 2022 Prescott Bible Conference, Pastor Greg Mitchell spoke by Faith on Monday night about specific breakthroughs that would happen to churches by the end of the week; one was that several pastors would receive Church buildings by the end of the week. God challenged us to give for world evangelism on Thursday night, and we also gave on Friday night in the offering.

The very next day (Saturday) after the conference, I received a phone call from a property owner, a Pastor of a Church, whom I had inquired about leasing the property a year ago. Since COVID-19, his Church had closed. He tried to reopen, but no one has been coming. He said, *"We've been trying to reach you. I received your message and felt I should call you today. I met with our church council, and they agreed to lease the church building to you."*

Not only did we receive an impressive, fully furnished building, but it also came with sound equipment, seating, Sunday school rooms, and an amazing sanctuary area ready to go. The rent is actually $1000 less than what we were paying at the storefront because we don't have to pay utilities. In the last two months since being in the building, we have had visitors, water baptisms, and baby dedications! With this financial breakthrough, we can continue investing even more in world evangelism and revivals, and we're so looking forward to seeing what God is doing here in the Colorado area.

A Lifelong Blessing - *Adrianne Tegegne*
In January 2015, at the Prescott Bible Conference, Pastor Joe Campbell pulled an offering. He talked about being obedient in giving, and he also said we can ask God for certain things when giving. I had been saving up money for a trip to Israel, but I felt stirred to give it away. I gave $5,000 in that offering, and I told God it was for His purposes, but that I would also like a good husband. In July 2015, I met the man who is now my husband. We got married in June 2016 and have been going strong since then. We are currently serving the Prescott church as Concert Directors. We are both so grateful for Pastor Joe and Connie Campbell's ministry and example, and that he pulled that specific offering that night.

Fasting Releases a Blessing - *Jared and Latanya Jake*

My name is Jared Jake. My wife and I currently pastor the church in Cuba, New Mexico. Our church is small, with about 15 people attending. In September 2025, more people began attending. At this time, the building developed plumbing problems. We did not have the money to hire a plumber, so I had to learn how to do plumbing repairs. We had to request financial help from our mother church. My wife and I have been pouring our personal money into the church, which has been hurting us financially. My wife and I were praying one day, and she said, *"I'm not sure if God is speaking to me or if I am just thinking it, but He said that we need to fast for our finances."* Up to this point, we had been praying for miracle finances, but we were still struggling. I told her, *"Let's try it, we haven't done that before."* I thought to myself, *"it's worth a shot, fasting is FREE."* I fasted for one day on Wednesday. I prayed for miracle money. I remember specifically telling God, *"I believe you have more money than we ever could fathom, I know you are good God, a just God, you love us, and I know you will always provide because we are being obedient to your will, please help us!"* We didn't receive money that day, or the remainder of the week. I didn't get upset at God. I continued to believe what I said in prayer.

That Sunday, after the morning service, a man walked in the door. He seemed to be looking for something. I introduced myself, and let him know that service was over. He said, *"My name is Leonard, and it seems like I just missed it."* I told him, *"Yes, but we have service tonight."* Leonard grabbed a tithing envelope and a pen. I thought nothing of it because people will often drop by the church and put a couple of dollars in the plate after service. Leonard then sat down in the back row of the church. He asked, *"If I write a check, who do I make it out to?"* I told him, *"The Cuba Potter's House."* He then asked where the plate was while holding the envelope. My daughter held the giving plate out, and he dropped the envelope into it. I encouraged him to drop by for evening service, and he said, *"I'm just passing through, going to work in Texas, and I always see the church. I won't be here for evening service, but I needed to take care of some business."*

After we left the church, I began to count the offering. When I got to Leonard's envelope, the amount on the outside read, "$5,000!" I ripped open the envelope and saw the check amount: $5,000. I told my wife, and we began praising God, tears of joy running down my face. This was a complete miracle because $5,000 is 2-3 months of income for our church!

I called Leonard and thanked him for giving to our church. I asked him what led him to give, and he said, *"I always pass by your church, and something told me to give. I believe your church helps people dealing with alcoholism. I am in a position to help the church, and that is what I wanted to do."* I thanked him for being obedient to the voice of God, and he said, *"Don't thank me, thank Jesus. Tithing is found throughout the whole Bible; I'm just doing what God told me."*

I pray this testimony will encourage couples or people who are going through financial drought and difficulty. God is working behind the scenes. Continue to believe God for your financial breakthrough!

God Keeps Good Books - *Frank and Nikki Brunner*

When our church in Green Bay, Wisconsin, closed, we decided to move to Prescott, Arizona, to be in the church. To be able to move, we sold our house. The moving costs and lost equity from our house totaled $30,000.

In April 2019, Pastor Greg Mitchell preached a sermon on planting seeds, giving offerings, and connecting it to specific prayer requests. We gave in that offering and specifically prayed about buying a home (we were currently renting), and that God would restore the $30,000 in equity we had lost when we sold our house and moved to Prescott.

In May, our landlord informed us that he had a medical issue and needed to sell our home. So, unless we were able to buy it, we would have to move. We couldn't buy at market price, so we began packing.
Forty-five days later, we still had not found housing, and our landlord contacted us. He said God had spoken to him to sell us our house at a price we could afford, with monthly payments not to exceed our current rent.

Due to the timing of his finances, the tax implications, and the Covid shutdown, it took more than a year to close on the house. However, during that time, he paid to replace all our flooring (which was another specific prayer request we had). When we finally closed on our home in November 2020, he sold us the home at 60% of its value! This instantly gave us equity more than three times what we had lost! (About $100,000). God is so faithful!!

God Knew in Advance - *Peter and Claudia Hounslow*
Pastor Walsh, thank you for your offering challenge on Monday night of the Perth Bible Conference and the miracle that unfolded. I pledged a large sum of money, but it was quite a stretch. I said, *"Lord, you're going to have to help me."*

The very next morning, as I was praying, I noticed one of the Beechboro church workers walking around with an envelope in their hand, looking for someone. Jesus prompted me in my spirit that the envelope was for me, and sure enough it was! Inside was a check for the exact amount I pledged the night before. It had been mailed anonymously <u>the week before</u> to the Beechboro Church P.O. Box, with my name on it, along with a letter of appreciation for our ministry.

This miracle is just the beginning of greater things God has for us. Thank you for being faithful in bringing the word of God and not being ashamed to challenge the hearts of His saints to obey God's commands and promptings.

Long-term Faithfulness is Rewarded - *Josh and Melanie Neal*
The church in Blythe, California, has met in an old building for decades. It is small, and the church has grown; they needed a building. In 2024, Pastor Josh Neal found a large, unused church in town. He thought it would be perfect for their congregation. They began negotiating to purchase it. But then negotiations fell through, partly because they couldn't afford it. After that, Josh said it was frustrating to drive by the building that could have been a blessing, if only they could have afforded it. Josh's wife, Melanie, said, *"If God wants us to have the building, we'll have it."*

In early 2025, an older gentleman visited one of the services. He has homes in multiple locations and was temporarily staying in Blythe while the weather was still cool. (If you've experienced a Blythe summer, you understand why he leaves during those months)! Before the service ended, Josh prayed for him because he was in pain, and from that day forward, he began attending whenever he was in town.

Later, Josh heard that the building they wanted had been sold again, about a year after the original sale. He wondered who had bought it? He found out it was the same gentleman who had been attending from time to time. Josh asked him about it. He told Josh he was on his way to Los Angeles to look at investment properties and that, on the way, he stopped off in Blythe. He wondered if there were any investment properties in Blythe, and the church building was one of the first he saw, so he bought it. He told Josh, *"I don't know why I bought it – I don't need it."* Josh mentioned that they tried to buy the building in 2024. The man said, *"It's yours if you want it."* He offered it to the church rent-free.

The property covers an entire city block! The sanctuary seats 500 people! The building has two kitchens, a fellowship hall, six classrooms, a nursery, and a playground. For perspective, their old church building could fit inside the foyer! They have been given permission to use 3 adjacent plots for parking by making one phone call. The person who bought the building in 2024 bought all new carpet, then decided not to go ahead with using the building. When they heard that the church was getting the building, they called and offered the carpet for free!

Josh says, *"God hasn't just given us space, He's given us momentum. We have had visitors in every service since moving into the new building."* One outreach they did at the new property drew more than 500 visitors.

The man said he intends to give the building to the church. What he didn't know was that long before they ever met him, the Blythe congregation had already laid hands on the building twice, asking God to give it to them.

I (Pastor Greg) asked Josh if there was a particular offering he gave that triggered this miracle. He said, *"Honestly, I can't think of one dramatic offering that released this. But I can say that we have given faithfully, trusted God with our finances, been good stewards and stayed consistent over time."* But that is also part of prosperity: We are to faithfully pray and believe God and consistently obey and invest financially over time. Because obedience builds up, and one day may be the day that God intervenes on our behalf. Like Cornelius in **Acts**

10:4 NIV *The angel answered, "Your prayers and gifts to the poor have come up as a memorial offering before God."*

Josh says: What I can say is that this testimony proves **that God answers prayer in His timing, and His timing is always perfect.** We are so grateful for all He has done and all He is going to do. He is drawing souls in Blythe, California, and we have the privilege of being part of His work.

LONG-TERM FAITHFULNESS IS REWARDED

Chapter 16: Discipleship Provision

The answer to our fears is faith. Real, fear-shrinking faith in the God who loves us and gave himself for us.
Jani Ortlund

Hearing how God is moving in other places encourages and inspires our faith for what God wants to do in our own corner of the world.
Matt Brown

Ray Dalio made money caddying at a golf course as a boy. At age 12, he bought his first shares in the stock market. Those stocks tripled, which birthed an interest in investing. He kept investing throughout his teen years, then got a finance degree in college. His success at investing led him to found a hedge fund called Bridgewater Associates, which is one of the largest and most successful hedge funds. His personal worth is now over $18 billion. His decisions in money set him up for his future.

Anyone who feels God has called them to preach must have faith in God's ability to provide. We are going to examine a story in the book of Luke that is a discipleship training story. Jesus was training His disciples for future ministry, and in this story, He teaches them a powerful lesson: **Disciples need to understand and experience miracle provision!**

Luke 5:4-11   *⁴When He had stopped speaking, He said to Simon, "Launch out into the deep and let down your nets for a catch." ⁵But Simon answered and said to Him, "Master, we have toiled all night and caught nothing; nevertheless at Your word I will let down the net." ⁶And when they had done this, they caught a great number of fish, and their net was breaking. ⁷So they signaled to their partners in the other boat to come and help them. And they*

came and filled both the boats, so that they began to sink. ⁸When
Simon Peter saw it, he fell down at Jesus' knees, saying, "Depart
from me, for I am a sinful man, O Lord!" ⁹For he and all who were
with him were astonished at the catch of fish which they had taken;
¹⁰and so also were James and John, the sons of Zebedee, who were
partners with Simon. And Jesus said to Simon, "Do not be afraid.
From now on you will catch men." ¹¹So when they had brought
their boats to land, they forsook all and followed Him.

Supernatural Ministry

In this story, Jesus was preparing His disciples for future
ministry. In all Jesus' instructions to the disciples, and all the
events that happened, He was putting into them things they
would need to be effective in ministry. Think of all the things
disciples need to help give future ministry effectiveness:

- **Disciples need heart character:** We minister what we are
  on the inside. We need to have a love for God. We
  need integrity. We need to be faithful in all areas.
- **Disciples need Bible knowledge:** They need to understand
  sound doctrine. It would be helpful if they could
  memorize scripture.
- **Disciples need to learn how to preach:** Pastors are called
  to be preachers of the word! We need to understand
  how to mine truth from a passage of scripture, how to
  develop and apply that truth in a logical message, and
  how to declare it effectively.
- **Disciples need people skills:** Pastoring is a people
  business! You need to learn how to be friendly, know
  how to put people at ease, and connect with
  strangers.
- **Disciples need a supernatural dimension:** Pastoring
  requires the supernatural miraculous power of the

Holy Spirit if we are to see people converted, delivered, and transformed. It will help us greatly if we have evidence of a supernatural dimension at work in us before we become a Pastor. This may involve miracle healings and the gifts of the Spirit.

- **Disciples need to be involved in evangelism and have personal fruitfulness in winning souls:** If you want to pioneer a new church someday, how do you think new people (sinners) come? Through evangelism! Disciples need to be able to witness and win souls now. That will give them confidence for the future.

But even if all of those things listed above are at work in your life, you must take into account a very practical factor: *Ministry for God involves money!*

- **You will have personal needs in the ministry:** You will need money for your housing, food, utilities, vehicles and transportation costs, clothing, schooling, and any number of bills.

- **You will have ministry needs:** It costs money to rent or purchase buildings, to buy equipment, to fund outreaches, revivals, special events, children's ministry, and many other things.

- **You will minister to people who need money:** You will get people saved who are struggling with personal debt. They will be bound by curses of poverty. They will have personal financial needs of housing, food, utilities, vehicles and transportation costs, clothing, schooling, and any number of bills – and many of them will be in great debt! You must be able to help them get their own breakthroughs in finances.

Money and the Future

The Bible teaches that your future will be determined by money!

Money is supernatural. Money is not just math. It is not just income and expenses. The Bible teaches us that what happens in your money affects <u>every</u> area of your life!

Money affects your <u>heart</u>: Your attitudes towards money affect what happens in your heart. If you are not right in your heart in the area of money, your heart will not be right with God over time! *Luke 12:34   For where your treasure is, there your heart will be also.*

Money affects your <u>prayers</u>: What you do with money has a direct effect on the prayers you pray and whether they are effective or not. *Acts 10:1-4 NIV [1]At Caesarea there was a man named Cornelius, a centurion in what was known as the Italian Regiment. [2]He and all his family were devout and God-fearing; he gave generously to those in need and prayed to God regularly. [3]One day at about three in the afternoon he had a vision. He distinctly saw an angel of God, who came to him and said, "Cornelius!" [4]Cornelius stared at him in fear. "What is it, Lord?" he asked. The angel answered, "Your prayers and gifts to the poor have come up as a memorial offering before God.* The angel told him that God has seen your giving, and He has heard your prayers. If you are not obeying God in giving it will affect your prayers.

Money affects your <u>fruitfulness</u>: In 2 Kings 4, it tells of a couple who are generous, and because they have vision for what Elisha's ministry is, they invest in it by building a room for him to stay in when he comes through. God moves Elisha to pray for a blessing on the wife, and it is interesting that the blessing God gives is a miracle of fruitfulness: God gives a barren woman a son. *2 Kings 4:15-16 NCV [15]Then Elisha said to Gehazi, "Call her." When he called her, she stood in the doorway. [16]Then Elisha said, "About this time next year, you will hold a son in your arms." The woman said, "No, master, man of God, don't lie to me, your* *servant!"* If you want to be fruitful in ministry, what you do with money is directly connected to fruitfulness.

Money First

In the story we opened with, there's a principle that affects ministry, and that principle is: *Money first!* Jesus taught His disciples a lesson about <u>provision</u> in Chapter 5 before sending them out to <u>minister</u> in Chapter 9. This principle is seen in other men of God in the Bible. Elijah experienced <u>miracles of provision</u> before he saw ministry impact. Before the confrontation with the prophets of Baal and his impact on the nation, he first experienced personal miracles of provision. God had Ravens feed him in the middle of the desert, then for three years arranged a miracle supply of food for himself, a widow woman, and her son.

Why does God want disciples to experience miracle provision before they enter the ministry?

Money involves a supernatural dimension of faith. <u>Faith</u> is directly connected to money: Hebrews Chapter 11 is called the roll-call of faith. It tells us what faith is, then gives practical examples of faith. It's interesting that the first example of faith in the Bible was an <u>offering</u>! *Hebrews 11:4 By faith Abel offered to God a more excellent sacrifice than Cain...*Why would God have the first example of faith be an offering? I believe it is because if you can't believe God for provision in money, you will struggle to believe God in every other area!

- I never see someone greatly fruitful in ministry who is not generous in giving.
- I never see someone who has great miracles who is not generous in giving.

Money involves a supernatural dimension of dominion: *Dominion is the ability to overcome the powers of hell.* That is what ministry for God is all about: *Overcoming demonic powers that fight God's will.*

- How do you overcome demonic blindness so people can get saved? *You overcome demon powers!*
- How can you get people to change? *You overcome demon powers!*
- How do you overcome negative factors that are supernatural in origin? *You overcome demon powers!*

There is a connection between money and dominion: *What you do with money affects dominion!*

1 Samuel 7:10 NCV *While Samuel was burning the offering, the Philistines came near to attack Israel. But the Lord thundered against them with loud thunder. They were so frightened they became confused. So the Israelites defeated the Philistines in battle.* While Samuel was making an offering, God went to work supernaturally to help God's people defeat the enemy. If you can gain dominion in money – you can have dominion in any area of life!

In our Fellowship, we have a Pastor in McAllen, Texas named Roman Gutierrez. Roman was raised in poverty. When he got saved, he obeyed God in giving. He got breakthroughs in money. But Roman also has breakthroughs in fruitfulness: He has seen powerful conversions in his ministry. God has helped him to raise up disciples, plant churches, and send missionaries to other nations. But the order of blessing in his life has been: **Money first!**

Supernatural Discipleship

Our story in Luke Chapter 5 is a discipleship scripture, which means it involved training for future ministry.

Training for future ministry involves miracle provision of money: *For fishermen, fish = money.* Jesus wanted his disciples to develop <u>faith</u> in God's miracle provision. *Luke 5:6 when they had done this, they caught a great number of fish, and their net was breaking.* This provided a reference point they could always use in the future: ***God can supernaturally provide to accomplish His will!*** This lesson was repeated throughout their discipleship.

Two different times thousands were fed: One time, Jesus by a miracle fed 5,000 men, plus women and children, and another time, Jesus by a miracle fed 4,000 men, plus women and children. *John 6:11-13 11And Jesus took the loaves, and when He had given thanks He distributed them to the disciples, and the disciples to those sitting down; and likewise of the fish, as much as they wanted. 12So when they were filled, He said to His disciples, "Gather up the fragments that remain, so that nothing is lost." 13Therefore they gathered them up, and filled twelve baskets with the fragments of the five barley loaves which were left over by those who had eaten.* The lesson from these stories was: ***God can supply whatever you need – no matter how big the need is***

Peter caught a fish: Money was in the fish's mouth to pay their taxes. *Matthew 17:27 NCV 27But we don't want to upset these tax collectors. So go to the lake and fish. After you catch the first fish, open its mouth and you will find a coin. Take that coin and give it to the tax collectors for you and me."* The lessons from this story: ***God can provide for us in miraculous ways! God is not limited to one person, one job, or one method in order to supply our needs!***

A donkey was provided by a miracle so God's will could be done: *Luke 19:30-35 30saying, "Go into the village opposite you, where as you enter you will find a colt tied, on which no one has ever sat. Loose it and bring it here. 31And if anyone asks you, 'Why are you loosing it?' thus you shall say to him, 'Because the Lord has need of it.' " 32So those who were sent went their way and found it just as He had said to them. 33But as they were loosing the colt, the owners of it said to them, "Why are you loosing the colt?" 34And* they said, *"The Lord has need of him."* ³⁵*Then they brought him to Jesus.*

This story is amazing: Find a donkey sitting there and take it. If anyone asks what you are doing, just tell them, *"The Lord has need of it!"* If you try that with a car parked in the street, you may wind up either in jail or dead! The lesson learned from this story: **God can cause strangers to want to help you!** I have heard many stories of people helping to provide for a child of God, and the person said, *"I don't know why I'm doing this..."*

The Passover room and Passover meal was provided: Mark 14:13-16 ¹³*And He sent out two of His disciples and said to them, "Go into the city, and a man will meet you carrying a pitcher of water; follow him.* ¹⁴*Wherever he goes in, say to the master of the house, 'The Teacher says, "Where is the guest room in which I may eat the Passover with My disciples?" '* ¹⁵*Then he will show you a large upper room, furnished and prepared; there make ready for us."* ¹⁶*So His disciples went out, and came into the city, and found it just as He had said to them; and they prepared the Passover.* This was not a pre-arranged event. A man who prepared a Passover room and meal for himself and his family will let us use it! That wasn't in the man's best interest: *If he lets Jesus and the disciples have it, where will he celebrate the Passover meal with his family?*

The lesson learned from this story: *God can cause people to help in ways that are not in their own best interest!* An example would be owners of houses or church buildings lowering the price and renting to God's people for less than they can get from other people: *Why should they do that?* **A miracle! Because God provides!**

The Indispensable Dimension

Faith for provision is indispensable: *You can't minister in the future without this dimension at work in your life!* Whether the provision will be for your needs, the church's needs, or people's needs: *You have to have this at work <u>now</u> so you can have it later!* So, if you are facing financial needs now, the issue is far bigger than the current need or the current problem: **You are determining your future!**

Where in your life right now is there a need for finances?

- Do you need a job? A favorable job with decent hours? A job that pays enough to meet your needs?
- Do you need a car? A car that is reliable? A vehicle that is large enough for your family?
- Do you need housing? Do you need a house large enough for your family? Do you need affordable housing?
- Are you currently in debt? *Debt changes your ability to minister!* If you are in debt, you need a lot more money beyond your current needs. You not only need money to pay for housing, food, utilities, transport, etc., but you also need extra money to repay your debt. Is there a family curse of poverty at work in your life? *Did your parents and grandparents always struggle with money? Does it seem like you can never get ahead?*
- Have you ever gotten a financial breakthrough? Have you ever broken the spirit of poverty off your life financially?
- Have you ever seen God do a miracle of provision for you? Miracle money, miracle housing, miracle jobs, miracle vehicles, etc.?

In this story, Jesus teaches them a lesson about financial provision <u>now</u> – to help them in the future.

Breakthrough miracles are transferable: If you get a miracle breakthrough in one area, you can get it in <u>any</u> area! *1 Samuel 17:36 NIV* [36] *Your servant has killed both the lion and the bear; this uncircumcised Philistine will be like one of them, because he has* *defied the armies of the living God.* David said, God helped me with the lion and helped with the bear; so I know that God will help me fight the giant!

Passing on the Miracle

If you get a breakthrough in money now, it won't just help you. You will be able to pass the miracle along to others! *Luke 5:6-7* *6And when they had done this, they caught a great number of fish, and their net was breaking. 7So they signaled to their partners in the other boat to come and help them. And they came and filled both the boats, so that they began to sink.*

I talked in Chapter two about Tom Payne breaking a curse of poverty off his life. When he broke the curse, he said something changed from that day, but it didn't just help <u>him</u>: *He has been able to inspire others to give generously and get their own breakthroughs – all over the world!*

Supernatural Provision

Our story in Luke 5 tells how can we develop a miracle dimension of financial provision in our lives now.

The principle of ownership: *Luke 5:3 Then He got into one of the boats, which was Simon's, and asked him to put out a little from the land. And He sat down and taught the multitudes from the boat.*

You must settle a basic question: *Who owns your boat?* In other words, who owns the money you have? Jesus was claiming higher ownership: He told Peter what He wanted Peter to do with the boat currently in his possession. We must acknowledge God's ownership over all our finances. The starting point of acknowledging God's ownership is tithing, giving God the first 10% of our income. Tithing is the visible way we demonstrate submission to God's ownership. But this principle applies to all of our finances: God is the owner, and we are stewards of what belongs to Him.

The principle of obedience: *Luke 5:4 When He had stopped speaking, He said to Simon, "Launch out into the deep and let down your nets for a catch."*

God will speak to you about what He wants you to do with the money He has entrusted to us. Whenever He speaks to us and tells us to give, He is testing us – for the future!

- **God may tell us to give money in offerings:** These are profound tests. He may ask you to give at inconvenient times., or ask you to give beyond our comfort level. *But God asks you to give, because He wants to do a miracle for you! Like the widow of Zarephath, who was challenged to give to the Lord first; God didn't ask that because He was trying to take from her, but because He wanted to give to her miraculously!*

- **God may tell us to give money to other people:** God will lay the need of someone else on your heart and prompt you to give to them. If you will obey, God will reward you – including in your future ministry! *Proverbs 19:17 NIV Whoever is kind to the poor lends to the Lord, and he will reward them for what they have done.*

I repeat the old saying my Father said to us so many times: *If God can get money through you, He will get money to you!*

The principle of faith: You must believe that God loves you and will provide for you! *Luke 5:5 But Simon answered and said to Him, "Master, we have toiled all night and caught nothing; nevertheless at Your word I will let down the net."*

How do you get faith? Faith is only based on God's word. If you hear a sermon and get excited, it won't be enough. If you are stirred by this book, it won't be enough. Faith only comes through God's word. **Romans 10:17** *So then faith comes by hearing, and hearing by the word of God.* If you want to develop faith for financial provision, go to God's word and read, study, write down every verse, promise, and story about miracle provision you can find, then pray over it until it becomes <u>yours</u>!

Faith comes from knowing what God is <u>able</u> to do: **Jeremiah 32:17** *'Ah, Lord God! Behold, You have made the heavens and the earth by Your great power and outstretched arm. There is nothing too hard for You.* It doesn't matter how big the need is. It doesn't matter how expensive things are: *If God made the heavens and the earth, He has enough power to meet our needs!*

Faith comes from knowing what God <u>wants</u> to do: *Luke 12:32 "Do not fear, little flock, for it is your Father's good pleasure to give you the kingdom.* You don't have to force God, or talk God into providing: *He <u>wants</u> to help you! He <u>enjoys</u> helping His children!* If you can get a breakthrough in provision now, it will set you up for the rest of your life and the rest of your ministry!

I often joke that my wife Lisa married me for my money: When we got married, I made $97 a week. We didn't have a dryer, so we scrimped and saved up to buy a dryer. We finally got enough money to buy it. Right at that time, one of the Pastors in our church went to preach in India for the first time. He came back and described the need in that nation. Then he took an offering for India, and God spoke to us to give all the money we had saved. We obeyed God, but had no idea how long it would take to save up the money again. Shortly after we gave the money, someone spoke to my wife and said they were moving to a new place with a dryer, so they couldn't take theirs. They asked if we needed one. They gave it to us, and **we learned that God knows what we need, and He can provide for us.**

Another time, God spoke to me to give all our rent money in the offering. This was scary, as we had no other options to be able to pay the rent if we gave it away. I went and spoke to the Pastor. I was hoping he would say, *"Don't be foolish, you can't afford that."* But instead, he said, *"It could be God. You should pray about it and obey whatever God says."* We prayed, and felt we should do it, so we obeyed God and gave all our rent money. Now we were praying desperately for God to supply money for the rent. I was riding home from work and had the radio on. They were talking about a competition they were running that was sponsored by Suzuki motorcycles. They said, if you saw their radio vehicle and were the first one to go up to them and say, *"Little Suzy rides a Suzuki,"* they will give you a moped. Right then, I looked over to the side of the road, and I saw it! I ran up and said the winning phrase, *"Little Suzy rides a Suzuki!"* I won! I went that week to the official ceremony to collect my moped. A man came up and asked me, *"Are you going to use that?"* I said no. He asked, *"Do you want to sell it?"* **"YES!"** We got more than twice as much money as we needed to pay the rent. **I learned that God can provide, even in strange ways!**

Those lessons (and many others) set me up for future ministry. God has blessed me with a dimension of faith that I am able to transmit and help others to believe God in the area of money.

Learning to Trust God - *Ayele and Adrianne Tegegne*
I wanted to share a testimony about how God opened a door through responding to an outreach pledge. On May 7, 2023, Pastor Greg Mitchell issued a challenge to make an outreach pledge. Honestly, that was the first time I had ever heard of an outreach pledge. I was familiar with tithes, offerings, and world evangelism, but not the pledge. That morning, my wife and I responded in faith. We prayed along with Pastor Greg as he prayed for favor in securing good-paying jobs.

At the time, I was working remotely for the U.S. Patent Office. That job was right for that season of our life, but it was demanding. It required long hours, and often pulled me away from my family and potentially from church. Also, remote work became more difficult with a growing family and limited space.

Shortly after responding to the pledge, I came across a civil/mechanical engineering position at the Veterans Affairs Hospital that was on-site, and I applied. A few weeks earlier, I met a man at a birthday party who worked at the VA, and we developed a great relationship. When I got the call for the interview, I reached out to him, and he gave me a strong character reference, which surprised me, since I had known him for less than a month.

After the panel interview, I received the job offer. It allowed me to remain in the federal system and increased my salary by $9,000 annually. Over the next two years, I received two bonuses of $2,000 each, a $5,000 annual raise in the first year, and a $7,000 annual raise in the second year.

Looking back, that job was not just a financial blessing it was key to my discipleship. It allowed me to attend discipleship class after prayer consistently. Eventually, I resigned from that position and came on staff to pursue pastoral ministry. Today, my wife and I are in ministry because we responded to that challenge. God has not only blessed us financially in abundance, but He has also placed us directly into our calling and destiny.

Provision Tied to Obedience - *Sam and Hannah DiPrete*

I wanted to share a testimony of Supernatural Provision that was tied to giving in obedience. My wife and I struggled financially for years. Even after getting out of debt, we were barely surviving paycheck to paycheck while raising two children. Our cars were old and constantly breaking down. We stayed faithful in giving our tithes and offerings, but we always lived with the sense that one setback would throw us back into debt.

In 2023, I became a self-employed subcontractor for the first time. Throughout the year, I set aside $10,000 to pay my taxes and to finally build an emergency fund. In January of 2024, my wife and I were sponsored to attend the Prescott Bible Conference. I came prepared with an amount to give in the offering, but halfway through the week, my wife turned to me and said, *"I think God told me that we need to give the tax money."* I stared at her, then pushed back and said, *"No, that's not wisdom."* Being a godly wife, she simply said, *"Okay,"* and deferred to me.

But that night, I went back to the hotel and couldn't sleep. I wrestled all night and argued with God that I couldn't afford to do it. I needed to be a good steward of the money, and it was needed to pay our taxes. I finally told God, *"If you really want me to give, I don't see a way. You need to speak to me."* The next day, Jonathan Heimberg preached a sermon called *"doubling down."* I felt as though he was preaching right to me. He mentioned that some people had given before and nothing happened, but that the need was to double down. This was my previous experience when giving an offering at a conference. I had felt that God had let me down or that I had not been a good steward when I gave. Pastor Heimberg also gave a testimony about how destiny can be tied to a gift. He had been sent as a missionary to India when he obeyed God in his giving. The sermon strengthened my faith, and despite all my misgivings, I obeyed God and gave the largest amount I had ever given.

We now view that offering as linked to destiny and supernatural provision. My wife and I were launched out of the April 2025 Cape Cod Bible Conference to pioneer a new work in Albany, NY. God has poured financial increase into our lives, including financial gifts, a new vehicle, favor in landing a job in a place that I was unqualified for, working reduced hours to be able to pioneer, building an emergency fund, and on top of it all, I somehow only had to pay $36.00 in taxes. We received far more in value than we gave. I thank God that we chose to obey.

Multiplying My Investment - *Seth and Asha Olmstead*
Here is a testimony how a challenge to God at the age of 22 took $300 and multiplied it into $20,000. It includes the planting of a church that became my first church to pastor 13 years later.

In 2010, I was 22 years old, stationed in Guam in the Navy, with a fixed salary. I was a new convert and zealous for God to do something supernatural financially through me. Wanting to bless the small baby church I belonged to in Agat. I had $300 and I gave it as an offering, I had strings attached to it, "GOD, you need to multiply this in a way that only you can get the credit." A month after this offering, I was drawn as a finalist and won $15,000 towards a brand new car. It took several months for everything to get finalized and I was able to save up enough money to purchase the remaining balance of the cheapest new car on the lot.

With keys in hand to a 2010 Ford Focus, I handed them over to my pastor and gave the car to the Church. The following month was our Guam Annual Bible Conference. My pastor at the time was launched to pioneer Guam's first church in Hawaii (Hilo, Big Island.) We believed this was God's will and the car sold for $10k. This money was then used to help plant this new work into Hawaii.

Fast forward to 2023, I am married with 3 kids pursuing the call the preach. My family and I get launched to take over the work in Hilo. The work where GOD multiplied my $300 into $10k. The $10k that helped plant this work.

God wasn't done, to show how good he truly is, prior to getting announced during the 2023 Guam Bible Conference, a member in the church came up to me and told me that God had told them to give me $10k. God had spoken this to them 6 months earlier, Before he or I even knew I was getting launched. God can take what we think is small and insignificant, multiply it, and use it to impact our lives and those around us any way or time he sees fit.

Obedience Triggers Visa Help - *Peter Saunan*
Bunbury, West Australia

My name is Peter I got saved in the Potter's House in Bunbury. I was in Australia on a working visa which expired on February 4th, 2024; one month before the Beechboro Conference. The Australian Immigration Department informed me my visa had expired and gave me until the end of March 2024 to finalise my business and leave the country.

On the Monday night of Conference, Pastor Rob Walsh challenged us to 'Go Large Like Marge' and God spoke to me to give the money I had set aside to pay for the International English Language Test and my visa. I gave the money and believed God for a miracle.

When I got back to Bunbury after Conference, everything about my life changed. The Australian Immigration Department miraculously changed their mind and gave me a new visa, I passed my Australian language test and I'm now on my way to a Permanent Residency Visa. God is good all the time and I want to say thank you God for Pastor Rob Walsh.

Blessings With Vehicle and Building

Robert and Debra Hernandez

Back in 2000, my family and I were Pastoring in San Angelo, TX. We had been there 5 years and had just stepped into full-time ministry. My wife wanted a van because it could accommodate more people, since we were constantly picking up new converts for the church. We had been praying about it for a couple of weeks, and then we got a call from my mother-in-law about her neighbor who was selling her van for $10,000. We didn't have the money, but we were able to purchase the van with a loan.

Right after that, we were given some money. We gave our tithe and offering and set the rest aside to pay for the tax, title, and license on Monday. I had already scheduled my Pastor to preach at our church on Sunday evening. In the service, I took the offering. I had already set aside an offering from the church finances to give to Pastor Wade Schultz after the service. But just before I went up to take the offering, God spoke to my wife and I to give the money we had set aside for vehicle as a love offering to Pastor Schultz, plus the offering I had already set aside for him. I was floored, and in my heart I argued with God: "This isn't a revival service!" Besides, I had already given the tithe and offering from that money, and I was going to use it to pay for the tax, title, and license! (As if God didn't know).

I genuinely struggled while I was taking the offering and tried smiling, but the moment I dropped the check into the offering plate, the peace of God settled over me! We had a powerful church service, people were saved and filled with the Holy Spirit, and we blessed our Pastor with a large offering in that one service!

Now we had only paid $500 towards the debt of the van, so we still owed $9500. But God got involved. The remainder of our debt was miraculously paid off, and God provided more money for the tax, title, and license! This great blessing was linked to our giving in obedience. It taught me a profound lesson about obedience, trusting God, and about giving sacrificially, especially when it isn't convenient!

In the January conference in Prescott, Pastor Greg Mitchell said God was going to move while we were there at the conference and open doors for a building. He also preached a sermon called "The Hastening." The very next day after Pastor Mitchell said that about the buildings, our landlord called to say he had a larger space for us. God blessed us! We went from a 1250-square-foot building to a 3800-square-foot building at the beginning of April, and we have been experiencing a Hastening in our church. Our attendance, finances, and involvement in prayer meetings have doubled! We are constantly seeing visitors come in, backsliders are beginning to come back and are locking in!

Chapter 17: The Prosperity Strategy

You must gain control over your money, or the lack of it will forever control you.
Dave Ramsey

Financial freedom is available to those who learn about it and work for it.
Robert Kiyosaki

Money is a terrible master but an excellent servant.
P. T. Barnum

Pastor Tom Payne was invited to Australia in 2009 after Pastor Wayman Mitchell rescued the church in Perth following a season of rebellion. During his time in Perth, Tom imparted to people in Australia many of the principles recorded in this book. For many who heard him, these teachings were entirely new and truly revolutionary. They reshaped the financial understanding of pastors and churches across the nation. The resulting release of financial blessing has been remarkable, opening doors for increased church planting, expanded world evangelism, and the upgrading and purchase of church properties. He gave them practical strategies to break the curse of poverty and enter into prosperity.

In this final chapter, we are going to look at **The Prosperity Strategy**: We will summarize what we've learned in all the chapters, then pray for miracles. I will personalize every lesson and every scripture, using the personal pronoun **I**. The reason I chose to do this, is that human nature tends to generalize truth and fail to make it our own. It is my prayer that as you repeat each statement, you will truly make them your own, and God will cause these truths to become supernaturally effective in your life.

The Mind and the Mouth

I reject wrong teachings about money.
I reject the lie that money is evil or that it is spiritual not to have money.

God blessed the Father of the faith with much money!

I reject the lie that it would be rude or presumptuous to ask God for money and material things.

God wants me to ask for His help!

I recognize that poverty is a curse.
I recognize there are generational curses of poverty in my life.

I recognize there are personal curses of poverty affecting me.

Curses due to sins before salvation.

Curses due to disobedience after salvation.

I recognize there are demonic assaults that try to rob me of financial blessings.

But I believe I have been redeemed from every curse!

*Galatians 3:13-14 Christ has redeemed **me** from the curse of the law by becoming a curse for **me**, for it is written: "Cursed is everyone who is hung on a tree." He redeemed **me** in order that the blessing given to Abraham might come to the Gentiles through Christ Jesus, so that by faith **I** might receive the promise of the Spirit.*

I am freed by salvation, by repentance, and by the authority given to me by the blood of Jesus.

I see that wrong mentalities have kept me from prospering.

I reject victim mentalities that take no responsibility for my own financial situation.

I reject entitlement mentalities that expect to be given money.

I reject feelings of guilt about being financially blessed.

I reject allowing fear to dominate my thinking and actions concerning money.

I have allowed fear to blind me to who God is and blame him for my own actions.

I repent of envying other people who have been blessed.

I confess that I have resented what God has given people who are blessed.

I confess that I have attributed the worst motives and actions to people who are blessed.

I confess that I have spoken against blessed people.

I confess that I have taken actions to limit or damage their These are wrong, because You, God, are the one who gives blessings!

I repent of having accepted poverty as being my portion.

I have accepted lack, poverty, and defeat, and these are NOT God's will!

I confess that I have spoken words against prosperity.

I have cursed my finances by speaking unbelief and accepting poverty.

Actions of Disobedience

I have taken actions that have worked against my prosperity.

I have allowed greed, impatience, and pride to push me into debt.

I confess that debt is not God's will: *It is <u>idolatry</u> – and I repent of it.*

As **Colossians 3:5** *says, Therefore **I** put to death...*
covetousness, which is idolatry.

I choose to believe God, and trust God to prosper over time.

I have failed to follow God's wisdom by budgeting and planning our spending.

I have been disobedient in the area of money.

I have failed to tithe.

I have failed to give offerings.

I have failed to obey God when He has told me to give.

I have failed to share with others as God would have me to do.

These decisions have released a curse, and I repent.

My failure to obey God in giving has blocked financial blessings.

I repent and break the curse of disobedience.

I have failed to save to prepare for future needs.

That was unwise and unscriptural.

I commit myself to saving for future needs.

Doubting God

My poverty has been based on unbelief.

I have doubted God's <u>ability</u> to meet my needs.

I have placed more confidence in circumstances, evil people, and demonic spirits than Almighty God.

I have doubted God's love.

I have accused You, God, of not caring about my financial needs.

I have accused You, God, of being biased in blessings: *I have said that you, God, are unfair.*

I have settled for far less than my Heavenly Father intends for me to have.

> That is a reflection of my unbelief and my lack of confidence in God.

I have robbed myself and my family through my unbelief.
I have robbed the work of God through my unbelief.
I have robbed other people in need of the blessings God intended for me.

The Strategy of Abundance

I repent: *I change my mind, therefore I change my actions.*
I repent of wrong thinking. I repent of wrong words.
I repent of wrong actions.

I break the curse of poverty off my life!

*As **Galatians 3:13-14** says, Christ has redeemed **me** from the curse of the law by becoming a curse for **me**, for it is written: "Cursed is everyone who is hung on a tree." He redeemed **me** in order that the blessing given to Abraham might come to the Gentiles through Christ Jesus, so that by faith **I** might receive the promise of the Spirit.*

> *I am freed by salvation, by repentance, and by the authority given to me by the blood of Jesus.*

I choose to believe and trust God!

It is God's will that I prosper!
God wants to bless me financially.
I trust God as my source of supply.
I ask my Heavenly Father in faith for abundant provision.

*I believe **Luke 12:32** therefore, **I** will not fear...it is **my** Father's good pleasure to give **me** the kingdom.*

I make a covenant with God – in advance.

I will not allow finances and blessings to become a god in my life.

I will put God first!

I will obey God in the area of money and finances.

I will ALWAYS honor God with my tithes.

I will give offerings of gratitude and faith.

I will invest in the work of God in evangelism, church planting, and world evangelism.

I will obey God when He tells me to give.

I will pass on my blessing to other people in need.

I will gain financial breakthroughs now – that will help me in future ministry

I will contend for supernatural breakthroughs in provision

Chapter 18: Further Testimonies of Financial Provision

A Miracle House - *Joe and Ivana Acuña*

My wife and I are Pastoring in New Jersey, where rent is extremely high. As our family began to grow, renting a home to match our family's size was impossible, so we decided we needed to try to save for a house. That is not so easy, as NJ has the hardest housing market in America. For every available house, you have hundreds of people you're competing with. But we decided we need to save up and trust God. Then we went to the West Las Vegas Conference. On Friday night, both my wife and I felt God tell us to double our personal offering. We both looked at each other and said, *"Double?"* Keep in mind this is an offering we saved up all year to give special for this conference, but we trusted God and gave. That was in April.

We got back to Jersey, and 2 months later, we talked about what we needed to buy a house again. I knew we were more than $20,000 short of what we needed for a down payment, so we started saving again. We prayed and trusted that God would help us. But God had other plans. On a whim, I called a realtor to confirm how much we would need for a down payment and was talked into going to see some houses. We did this for two days. Then we saw a house and fell in love.

Out of curiosity, I asked how much they wanted, and the people said they would take the next offer that came in. Behind the scenes, the owners were already living in their new house. They kept having fall-throughs with buyers, so six months later, they're tired of paying taxes and bills on a home they don't live in and wanted to get rid of it. They were frustrated that they couldn't move this house in one of the most competitive markets in the United States.

So when we came in, they literally said, *"We don't care about profit, or competing offers, we are not doing that anymore, we're going to take the next offer that comes in."* So we prayed, and offered them half of what they originally wanted. It was all we could afford. Everything lined up perfectly so that we were the next offer. They accepted it, and we closed in August, four months after the Las Vegas Conference!

Our agent was in disbelief that we paid half the asking price for our house. It makes no sense to people in the world how we got this blessing, but I tell everyone that God provided; He got us a house to match our finances. And since we closed, we have had nonstop fellowships at the house. It has strengthened the church and helped disciples to build relationships with new converts and visitors. We serve a God who can stretch our dollar to fit any need we have.

God Honors Faithfulness - *Quitman and Lorraine Walker*
In 1992, I was stationed with the US Air Force in the United Kingdom. I got saved in 1988 and had positioned myself to stay overseas in the military, at my base, with no scheduled rotation orders. Due to changes in government and the military drawdown, I received orders to leave the UK.

We were heavily involved in our church in Bury St. Edmunds and did not want to leave. I had 3.5 years left on my current enlistment, but the military was adamant about shipping us out. I began to pray. I put in for an early discharge and was told it would be impossible, due to having received a reenlistment bonus and the military having paid for my college. We prayed, and the commander signed my discharge papers. They let me out.

The military would not pay for my getting out, so housing and staying in the UK would be on us, but I knew God had called me to stay. I got out on a Thursday and, by Monday, had found a job as a food service attendant on the Base. It paid $8.91 an hour, down from my old Sergeant's pay in the military.

I showed up to work the first week and got a call from the Civilian Personnel office to come and see them. Because I had not received any government assistance in getting out of the military overseas, the Civilian Personnel Office considered my discharge a hardship discharge. That qualified me to receive what was called the Living Quarters Allowance. My pay went from $8.91 an hour to $21.00 an hour in one day. That paid for all our housing and utilities so we could remain in the UK!

God continued to bless us as the years progressed. I became a Level 3 Test Engineer for The Boeing Company. We pioneered a church here in Jacksonville, eventually going full-time. The church is 150-170 right now, and we have launched four churches out. I attribute all that God has blessed us with to that decision to trust Him with our lives all those years ago. He can and will take care of His people if we seek Him first!

Provision Comes Right on Time - *Tim and Faith Scott*
After years of Pastoring, my wife, Faith, and I began full-time ministry on April 1st, 2025. But the story behind it is amazing. Pastoring in New Jersey is expensive. Everything in New Jersey is expensive. In 2023, we spoke with our Pastor, Paul Campo, about going full-time. The Church's finances were almost there, so we thought we would just step out in faith and trust God. At 60 years old, we desperately wanted to go full-time.

Then, in November of 2023, we found out that Labcorp (the company I worked for) had decided to close our site, and everyone was getting laid off. As I worked in the Archives, our team was the last to go, so the final closing date was March 31st, 2025. It took almost 18 months to close the site. The amazing thing is that New Jersey law requires that any company that closes in that way MUST give its employees severance pay. Pastor Campo told us to ride out the 18 months, then take the severance and go full-time. In the interim, the Church's finances began to increase to support us full-time. As of September, we were also able to pull our Social Security.

So, after all these years of faithfully serving God, and always giving from our personal finances as well as the church finances, the scales have tipped, and God orchestrated us to be able to go full-time with a severance package from our employer.

God is faithful, and now we are having a revival, and the church is excited to have a full-time Pastor. We've been exceeding 40 in our church attendance, and folks in our church have been able to purchase homes, which is no small thing in New Jersey.

Provision Wherever We Are - *Jack and Jan Miller*

My wife and I were pastoring the Potter's House in Winslow, Arizona, my hometown, and the church where I got saved. It was the first time I was a full-time pastor. We had a few churches out & I was able to preach in the U.S. and overseas.

In 2000, God said, *"By the end of the year, you are going to leave."* I replied out loud, *"No!"* Feeling God's displeasure, I said, *"God you're going to have to help me, and You need to speak to my wife."*

We had been approved to buy our first house. We signed the papers and just needed to turn them in, and the house was ours. But in prayer on Monday night of the Prescott Conference, my wife came to me. She said, *"Let's not buy the house. Let's be available for God."* So I told her what God had spoken to me. That week I organized a trip to preach in South Africa a few months later.

That December, God told me to go to the area of Durban, South Africa. We were announced to go there as missionaries in January 2001. Owning a home didn't seem like it would happen. But God told me, *"You will never have to worry about where you will live."* After 12 years in Africa & a short time in Lake Havasu City, pastor Greg asked us to take the church in Palmdale, California.

God has miraculously blessed the church's finances and ours as well. In 2019, we were again about to buy our first home. The day they were going to sign the papers the owner fell down the stairs and died. But her daughter let us move in anyway, and we were to buy the house. It is a beautiful home that can host dozens of people for fellowship. Because we obeyed God, He blessed our sacrifice.

Hearing More and Receiving More - *Steve and Cora Annichiarico*

During an offering taken in a Gallup Conference in 2015, God spoke to me to give $8000. I leaned over and told my wife, *"I think God wants me to give $8000.00."* She said, *"I think it's $10,000."* We decided to give $10,000 that night. That Saturday, while we were driving home from the conference, I received an email saying I would get $24,000 in back pay. In not even 24 hours, God almost tripled what I gave.

Obedience Affects the Church - *Leighton Ainsworth*
Bexleyheath, London, UK

We were moved by God to give our largest offering at the October 2012 UK conference. It was a huge sacrifice and an act of faith, but we knew we had heard from God. Not long after giving into the Bible conference, a young lady who had only attended a few times came to church and gave £1,000. Shortly after giving this amount, she visited again several months later and gave £7,000. This wasn't the only miracle that was connected to our conference offering. A church member gave £1,000 in faith after being told their contract had been terminated! Within one week, they were offered a new contract earning £100,000 a year. As a result of our giving into the bible conference, we saw £9,000 come in.

Obedience and Provision - *Brad and Shannon Ault*

The following is a brief description of the many ways God has blessed my wife and me financially lately. In October, we made our World Evangelism Pledge at an amount that we could currently afford, but it would be a stretch. The real test would come when my wife Shannon quit working, but we wanted to place our trust in God, since he had already blessed us in so many ways before. There has been a steady flow of money since Shannon quit work in December, shortly after we had a baby! We have received many random checks in the mail over the last few months totaling over $4,000, which has been more than enough to cover the amount we lost when she quit working.

The college I attended told me I owed them over $2,000. After months of this, they called me one day to say that the debt had been cancelled. The lady told me she doesn't know how it happened, but the debt has been cleared, and we owe them nothing. I know what happened: God intervened.

For over a year, I have been looking for a promotion at work, but most of the promotions available would have required me to miss a church service. Finally, a position became available in another department, and I applied. I was promoted over 16 applicants, and many of them were already in that department. My new salary is a $2.00-per-hour raise, and my schedule is perfect, so I won't have to miss church. Now I am doing something in my job that I have been wanting to do for a very long time.

I attribute all these blessings to God's faithfulness to us as a result of our consistent faithfulness to him in tithes, offerings, and pledges.

Staying Faithful and Unexpected Blessings - *Mike and Valerie Gomez*
In 2013, the Lord was dealing with me about returning to the ministry of an evangelist again. I told my pastor what God was dealing with me about, and he said we would announce it in six months.

In mid-March, I applied for a job in Northern California. My application was rejected because I failed to meet the minimum requirements. However, two days later, I received another email stating that I was a top candidate. I requested a phone interview because I couldn't break free on such short notice. Then, the following week, I received a phone call stating that I was their top candidate and they wanted a personal interview. I began thinking maybe it's an open door to pioneer a new church in the area. I mentioned this to my pastor, and he gave me the green light to investigate it. I called some of the Pastors in the area. I decided I would spy out the land and do the interview. At the interview I could tell that they liked me. On Sunday morning during prayer, I very clearly heard that "still small voice" from God, saying, *"What are you doing here?"* I knew immediately that the Lord was telling me, *"I didn't call you to pioneer up here. I called you to be an Evangelist."* The next day, while driving home, I heard that voice again, *"What are you doing here?"* The issue was settled there and then. That Monday, I received a call from the employer offering me the job. Having already made up my mind to do God's will, I decided to make some demands to make it easy for them to turn me down. I told them I wouldn't accept the offer for anything less than 30 dollars an hour, and they said, "No problem." I then said I would need some time off for two Bible conferences and a youth boot camp, in June, July and August. They said no problem and even offered some of the time off with pay. I then told them that I wouldn't move my family just for a promotion, that there had to be something more (thinking to myself surely, they'll deny my ridiculous request). But to my surprise, they said no problem, and they were planning to groom me for the superintendent position, which is a six-figure salary. My plan had failed, so I then told them that I respectfully appreciated the offer but had to turn it down. They said, *"Can we ask why?"* I told them that God had called me to be an evangelist. They were infuriated to say the least.

Then in 2020, when Covid hit, all my revival meetings were cancelled. With no meetings, things were getting a tight financially. We were dipping into our savings. But out of nowhere, I received a random check from a workman's compensation claim adjuster for $14,000.00. I called their number and asked about the check. I asked if there was some mistake, and the representative said, *"No, Mr. Gomez, it's not a mistake, you can cash the check."* My wife and I were shouting the victory! She then said, *"There's more."* I thought for a moment there was some sort of catch. She then explained that they conducted an audit of their own on a work injury I had nearly 15 years prior, stating that they had rated it wrong and that the damage was much worse. So, she said, *"We owe you this."* She then said, *"We actually owe you more money, and we will be sending you $500 every two weeks until we pay off our debt to you."* I eventually received $22,000 in total. Praise God!

I then remembered that about six years prior, I had turned down a six-figure job to do His will. During a tough time, God took care of us! He truly has proven Himself faithful to us time and time again.

References

Chapter 1
Jim Bakker was one of the early televangelists...
From the book "I Was Wrong" by Jim Bakker Published by Thomas Nelson, Nashville, TN, 1996

David Platt... announced their plans to cut 600-800 missionaries...
https://www.christianitytoday.com/2015/08/southern-baptists-will-cut-800-missionaries-imb-david-platt/

Chapter 3
MC Hammer (Stanley Burrell), was one of the most famous music artists...
https://www.yahoo.com/entertainment/music/articles/mc-hammer-net-worth-blew-202331699.html

Ruby Payne: A key difference between generational and situational poverty is attitude...
From the book "A Framework for Understanding Poverty" by Ruby Payne. Published by aha! Process, Inc. 2005

Chapter 5
Anglicare Australia...
https://www.abc.net.au/news/2023-09-12/anglicare-poverty-premium-low-income-australians-cost-of-living/102843886

Ruby Payne states in her book...
From the book "A Framework for Understanding Poverty" by Ruby Payne. Published by aha! Process, Inc. 2005

Chapter 6
In a tragic incident in Gujarat, India...
https://timesofindia.indiatimes.com/city/surat/couple-24-year-old-son-die-in-suicide-

The Federal Reserve Bank of Philadelphia...
https://www.fa-mag.com/news/even-high-earners-worry-about-making-ends-meet--fed-poll-finds-78599.html

In a 2014 study paper for the National Library of Medicine titled: "The High Price of Debt...
https://pmc.ncbi.nlm.nih.gov/articles/PMC3718010/

Chapter 7
A man who was over USD $70,000 in debt…
https://medium.com/@kingdomwealthministries50/my-journey-from-debt-to-divine-abundance-42d06c24422c

Chapter 8
One woman tells the impact that establishing a budget together had on her marriage…
https://www.ramseysolutions.com/budgeting/budgeter-success-stories-with-everydollar?
srsltid=AfmBOooFATXMdoCmA_kbRTTj1Z1tbmvlsgcAQJ_m2VrC2Em3xxX3vPgk

Chapter 10
A waitress at a restaurant in West Virginia received a life-changing tip…
https://www.livenowfox.com/news/west-virginia-waitress-big-tip

Chapter 13
Curtis Dixon was on his way to pawn his wedding ring…
https://www.fox2detroit.com/news/mdmotivator-detroit-man-pawn-shop-cash-influencer

Chapter 16
Ray Dalio made money caddying at a golf course…
https://www.cnbc.com/2019/05/01/billionaire-ray-dalio-bought-his-first-stock-at-age-12.html

Acknowledgements

I want to thank all those who encouraged me to turn the "Kingdom Prosperity" teaching series into a book. As I travel extensively preaching, many people have asked, "When's the next book coming out?"

Many thanks to Daryl Elliot. He proofread each chapter and added valuable suggestions. Your help is invaluable to me.

Once again, many thanks to Steven Ciaccio for your technical help in so many ways. Artwork, photo corrections, audio recording, book editing, and setup. We are so proud of the man of God you have become. You are an incredible blessing to Lisa and me, the Prescott Church, and our wider fellowship.

Thanks to Jesse Morales and Matt Sanderlin for their collective effort in proofreading and catching typos.

Thanks again to Manuel Delgado, my hard-working Spanish translator. As always, you are using your gifts to bless the Spanish-speaking world. Thanks for proofreading and catching mistakes and typos as you translated the book.

Thanks to the men in other nations who helped review the Spanish translation for Manuel. They are university graduates and draw on their experience with the language, helping keep the "Spanish" neutral and readable to all Spanish-speaking nations. Fabian Godano: Argentina. Heriberto Lapizco: España. Joyme Cuan González & Ann Yelayne Peña: Cuba.

Thanks to Jonathan Heimberg for his help in proofreading and technical help.

Thanks to Devon Ryals for helping with the recording.

Acknowledgements Continued

Thanks to all those who shared their testimonies with me in writing. God will use your stories to help others believe for their own miracles.

Above all, I give thanks to God. Lisa and I are in awe of all Your goodness to us. Salvation is still the greatest gift you have given us, and it never grows old. You have blessed us so much so that we can be a blessing to others. May this book bring glory to Your Name. I pray You will use it to cause the Gospel of Jesus Christ to be preached around the world; that is the ultimate purpose of prosperity.

I pray that God has stirred your faith to believe for breakthroughs in your own finances. As God helps you, I would love to hear your testimony. Perhaps it can be used to inspire others to believe. Send your testimony to:
kingdomprosperitytestimonies@worldcfm.com

About the Author

Greg Mitchell was saved in Prescott, Arizona as a teenager. He met and married his wife Lisa in Perth, West Australia. He was discipled, trained for Pastoral ministry, and sent out of The Potter's House in Perth to pioneer their first church in Launceston, Tasmania, Australia. He Pastored in Melbourne, Victoria, Australia, on three different occasions (2 different churches - Footscray and Dandenong). Greg and Lisa responded to the call of God as missionaries to Johannesburg, South Africa, where God helped them to establish a thriving congregation in the suburb of Eldorado Park. Greg is now Senior Pastor of The Potter's House in Prescott, Arizona. He is the Leader of Christian Fellowship Ministries, International, a church-planting movement with over 4200 churches worldwide (The Potter's House, The Door, Victory Chapel). CFM has churches in 147 nations. Since 1986, Greg has preached the revelation of God's love and His power to save, heal and deliver: Body, Soul and Spirit. He is also the author of the books Healing Power and Uprooting Rejection.

www.ingramcontent.com/pod-product-compliance
Lightning Source LLC
Chambersburg PA
CBHW071417090426
42737CB00011B/1488